PENGUIN BOOKS

EDEN

Devdutt Pattanaik writes, illustrates and lectures on the relevance of mythology in modern times. He has, since 1996, written over fifty books and 1000 columns deconstructing the symbols and myths of ancient and modern cultures around the world. His books with Penguin Random House India include *Myth = Mithya: A Handbook of Hindu Mythology*; *The Book of Ram* and the *Devlok* series. Devdutt consults with corporations on leadership and governance, and TV channels on mythological serials. His TV shows include *Business Sutra* on CNBC-TV18 and *Devlok* on Epic TV. He illustrates his own books, as he has these ones.

BY THE SAME AUTHOR

Myth=Mithya: Decoding Hindu Mythology
The Book of Ram
The Pregnant King
Jaya: An Illustrated Retelling of the Mahabharata
Sita: An Illustrated Retelling of the Ramayana
Shikhandi and Other Queer Tales They Don't Tell You
Jaya Colouring Book
Sita Colouring Book
Devlok with Devdutt Pattanaik
Olympus: An Indian Retelling of the Greek Myths
Devlok with Devdutt Pattanaik 2
Devlok with Devdutt Pattanaik 3
Shyam: An Illustrated Retelling of the Bhagavata

EDEN

AN INDIAN EXPLORATION OF JEWISH, CHRISTIAN AND ISLAMIC LORE

DEVDUTT PATTANAIK

Illustrations by the author

PENGUIN BOOKS
An imprint of Penguin Random House

PENGUIN BOOKS

USA | Canada | UK | Ireland | Australia
New Zealand | India | South Africa | China | Singapore

Penguin Books is part of the Penguin Random House group of companies whose addresses can be found at global.penguinrandomhouse.com

Published by Penguin Random House India Pvt. Ltd
4th Floor, Capital Tower 1, MG Road,
Gurugram 122 002, Haryana, India

Penguin Random House India

First published in Penguin Books by Penguin Random House India 2021

10 9 8 7 6 5 4 3

ISBN 9780670095407

Layout and design by Dhaivat Chhaya
Typeset in Garamond by Special Effects Graphics Design Company, Mumbai
Printed at Thomson Press India Ltd, New Delhi

www.penguin.co.in

FSC www.fsc.org MIX Paper from responsible sources FSC® C010615

To my teachers at
Our Lady of Perpetual Succour High School, Chembur, Mumbai,
where I participated in plays based on the Ramayana,
the Mahabharata as well as the Bible.

Contents

INTRODUCTION

Retelling Monotheism

Judaism, Christianity and Islam are the world's most dominant faiths today. They account for nearly 50 per cent of the world's population, and a sixth of India's population. All three faiths originated in the Middle East. Judaism, the faith of Jewish people, is over 4,000 years old; Christianity is 2,000 years old; Islam, the faith of Muslim people, is 1,400 years old. Over time, these faiths have had many divisions and subdivisions as well as different schools of thought. Judaism can be Reform, Orthodox or Conservative; Christianity can be Orthodox, Catholic, Protestant or Mormon; and Islam can be Shia, Sunni or Sufi.

The lore of these three faiths informs us about messengers who convey the will of God, spelt in singular with capitalization, who is the one true god, who created the world, and will judge all humanity at the end of the world, elevating believers to Heaven and casting non-believers to Hell. This lore is commonly identified as Abrahamic lore after the most venerated messenger of God, Abraham, known to Muslims as Ibrahim. Abrahamic lore is also referred to as Semitic lore. Semite refers to Shem, an

ancestor of Abraham. Semitic languages include Middle Eastern languages such as Hebrew, Aramaic and Arabic, through which much of Abrahamic lore has been received.

Each of the three faiths, and their many schools of thoughts, has its own version of Abrahamic lore. They disagree on many details. After creating the world, did God rest on Friday, Saturday or Sunday? What exactly was the Forbidden Fruit? Is Adam the first messenger or is it Abraham? Who is the last messenger? Jewish people say the final messenger is yet to come; the Christians say it was Jesus Christ, who was also the Son of God; Muslims say Prophet Muhammad is the final messenger. Do humans still carry the burden of the Original Sin or has God forgiven humanity? Is Mary the Mother of God? What is Heaven actually like, a place of serenity or pleasure? Who is the representative of God on earth today? How will the world come to an end? Is the Devil an angel or a djinn?

These disagreements often take violent forms, resulting in long protracted wars, lasting centuries. Perhaps *because* they believe in one true god, and reject false gods, there is little patience with subjectivity and alternate retellings. Retelling this lore, as a result, is not easy.

- In Christian art, the sheep is the symbol of obedience, the wolf is the Devil and the goat is the symbol of defiance.
- As Christianity dominated Western civilizations, which dominated the world, global history was mapped using the birth of Jesus Christ as the starting point. The years before him were called BC or Before Christ and the years after his birth were called AD or Anno Domini, which is Latin for 'in the year of the Lord'. Historians have found this system to be inaccurate as the historical Jesus was likely to have been born a few years before AD 1, maybe in 6–4 BC. Also, many people do not appreciate the use of this Christian nomenclature to establish global historical timelines. This is why, today, AD has been replaced by CE (Common Era) and BC by BCE (Before Common Era). The Islamic world prefers to calculate time as Before Hajira (BH) and After Hajira (AH). Hajira refers to the year of the migration of the Prophet from Mecca to Medina (622 BCE), a separation that marks the beginning of Islam as a political force. Many Hindus prefer the calendar being mapped to the era of Vikram (57 BCE) or the era of the Sakas (78 CE).
- The value placed on the definite article 'the' and the capitalization of 'God', are

symbolic of the value placed on the absolute over relative truth. Latin languages spoken by pagan Greeks, or proto-German spoken by Germanic tribes, had no definite article. But it appeared centuries later in English (the), French (*le*, *la*, *les*) and German (*der*, *din*, *das*)—languages spoken by Christians. The definite article is found in Arabic (*al*) and is expressed as a special textual suffix in the Hebrew script. Arabic and Hebrew are Semitic languages originating in the Middle East. Neither Sanskrit, the language of the Hindus, nor Pali, the language of the Buddhists, has definite articles. In other words, Indo-European languages did not originally possess this feature. Over time, the Indian branch continued without it, but the European as well as Iranian branches borrowed the term from Semitic languages. Lithuanian, a conservative Indo-European language from Eastern Europe, does not have the definite article either.

Relevance

Why should there be an Indian retelling of this lore? The primary reason is to draw attention to the structural difference between monotheistic lore on the one hand, and lore based on the doctrine of rebirth that informs Hinduism, Buddhism and Jainism, faiths that originated in India on the other. This difference is the root of many unnecessary misunderstandings that continue to plague the study of non-monotheistic belief systems around the world. This difference is clearly demonstrated by the following folktale.

Once, a Jain monk narrated the epics, the Ramayana and the Mahabharata. But his retelling was different from the retelling of the Hindus. So the local king demanded an explanation. The Jain monk said the world goes through cycles of creation and destruction. In each cycle, the tale recurs, with minor differences. In one cycle, Ram killed Ravana and in another, Lakshman killed Ravana. In one cycle, the Mahabharata war is fought between the Pandavas and the Kauravas, in another, the war is fought between Krishna and Jarasandha. Hindus speak of one cycle, and Jains of the other. The doctrine of rebirth thus enables co-existence of multiple truths. This is not possible

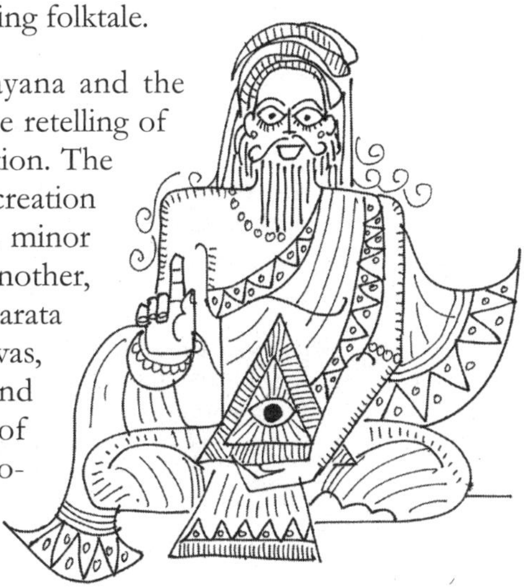

in monotheistic faiths that state you live only once, and you must live that life the right way, or suffer eternal damnation.

This book also draws attention to the monotheistic template that became the benchmark of religion in the nineteenth century, forcing Hindus to reframe their complex faith. Reformists consciously distanced themselves from what was called 'idolatory' even though temple worship was the popular expression of Hinduism. Greater emphasis was laid on Hindu philosophy such as the Vedanta, and Hindu mythology was presented as Hindu history. Academics argued that Hinduism institutionalized inequality and oppression through the caste system. Forced to defend their faith relentlessly, exasperated Hindus came to believe that reform and anti-caste movements were essentially covert operations for destroying the foundations of Hinduism. This has led to widespread popularity of an aggressive nineteenth-century political ideology called Hindutva that seeks to defend Hinduism, restore pride in Hinduism, unite all castes to a common political fold and establish India as a nation for Hindus. In the process, it homogenizes Hindu customs and beliefs, and disregards its very essence, its diversity.

This book spotlights how the same lore has different retellings in Judaism, Christianity and Islam. Instead of creating standardization and homogeneity, the obsession with one truth has generated inter-religious rivalry, intra-religious rivalry and rivalry between religion and science, with arguments against evolution and in favour of a flat earth. Science, secularism and postmodern thinking have overpowered religion in many areas, but have not been able to provide the comfort religion does to the meek and the suffering. Religion, to regain ascendancy, pushes back and strives to be 'scientific' but rationalists call out the obvious science-envy of religions. Such trends are found everywhere, and they are tearing the world apart as everyone wants to be right, and finds glory in being intolerant. Listening to diverse lore helps us appreciate the insecurities that are common to all people and bring in some much-needed empathy to heal the wounds of battle.

- Prabhachandra's compilation of biographies of Jain teachers, *Prabhavakacharita*, refers to the tale of conflict between Hindu and Jain retellings of the epics involving the twelfth-century scholar Acharya Hemachandra.

- While the word *mleccha* or impure barbarian was a pejorative term used for new immigrants of a different faith, the indigenous caste (*jati*) framework in India allowed various Jewish, Christian and Muslim groups to thrive so long as they practised endogamy (marriage within community) and respected local boundaries and hierarchies. The immigrants eventually became landowners (Kshatriya), landless labourers (Shudra) or craftsmen and traders (Vaishya). None became Brahmins, though many Abrahamic communities of India claim to have descended from Brahmins.
- The arrival of the Turko-Afghan warlords 800 years ago made Indians defensive about polytheism. This led to the emphasis on the *bheda–abheda* (dual–non-dual) philosophy of Vedanta from the thirteenth century onwards, which sought to see one God in many gods. It also popularized *nirguni bhakti*, or worship of the formless divine, over *saguni bhakti*, worship of the divine in the form of idols.
- The rise of the British Empire about 300 years ago introduced Indians to ideas of liberty, equality and justice. This was at odds with Hindu ideas of karmic bondage, caste and wheel of rebirths, and made the educated class defensive of Hindu customs and beliefs.
- The idea that Muslims destroyed Hindu civilization was invented by the British, who positioned themselves as saviours of Hindu civilization in the eighteenth century. The arrival of the Persianate culture and monotheistic faith 800 years ago was similar to the arrival of Yavanas–Sakas–Pahalavas–Kushans (Greeks–Scythians–Parthians–Yuezhi) 2,000 years ago. Hinduism adapted then, it would adapt again.
- The popularity of science and history has led to mythological narratives being seen as proto-history. In this pseudoscience, biblical events in the Genesis and Exodus are historical events that took place 6,000 years ago, despite the lack of evidence. Similar trends are seen in all religions. In India, people insist that the stories of the Ramayana and Mahabharata are historical events that took place 7,000 and 5,000 years ago respectively. The matter evokes strong emotions and so is used by politicians to gain power.
- Exposure to Abrahamic mythology via trade routes explains why the concept of a future messiah also manifests as Maitreya, the future teacher in Buddhist lore, and Kalki, Vishnu's future avatar in Hindu lore.

Truth

By deliberately referring to Jewish, Christian and Islamic myths as 'lore', the title of this book draws attention to monotheism's unresolvable yearning for Truth, with a capital T.

In the sixteenth century, the University of Cambridge stated that their charter came from King Arthur. Today, we know that is fiction. Or rather a legend, a quasi-historical belief that legitimizes an institution, for Arthur was chosen by God to lead England, and so his charter legitimized Cambridge University. It is certainly not a fact.

It is only in the nineteenth century that evidence-based history emerged as a subject in European universities. This forced the separation of history from the memories of a people. Traditional stories of ancestors told by tribes of Asia, America, Oceania and Australia were deemed myths. However, few dared to show that Christian lore was also such a cultural memory, a combination of parables (fictions with moral endings), legends (fictions meant to legitimize political claims) and myths (fictions that use metaphors to explain the origins of nature and culture). This was because imperial powers such as Spain, Portugal and England, that supported the universities, were legitimized by the Church.

Only in the twentieth century, following the World Wars and the collapse of colonial empires, was religion grouped along with polytheism as mythology. Atheism acquired the privileged position of being more scientific. But this privileged position was short-lived.

In the twenty-first century, post-structural philosophy and postmodern politics showed how power operates through various belief systems—be it atheism, monotheism or polytheism; how language is used by the elite to corner power. Simultaneously, psychology revealed how people need subjective truth to grant their lives meaning and purpose.

It is now clear that myth is somebody's truth, distinct from everyone's truth, i.e., measurable truth (fact) and nobody's truth (fiction). Some myths like rebirth and God are traditional, inherited over generations. Others like the nation and human rights are contemporary and ideological.

Historians, for example, have reliable evidence of a historical Muhammad and a probable historical Jesus, but none for 'Prophet' Muhammad or Jesus 'Christ'. Notions of the 'Chosen One' and 'God' can never be historical; they remain matters of faith. This rattles believers.

Modern-day activists insist that they are more rational than religious folk. However, they too get rattled when reminded that justice and equality are also social constructs, hence myths, and not self-evident truths. Notions of justice and equality are different for different people—invariably somebody's truth, not everybody's truth.

- Traditional knowledge systems value the word of the master or guru. Science does not value people's opinions by themselves. Hence, the sixteenth-century Latin phrase *Nullius in verba* (not on anyone's word), which forms the motto of scientists of the Royal Society. Religions are based on faith. Science is based on doubt. Religions often claim that they are perfect and cannot improve. Science keeps improving over time, with better measuring and analytical tools, and more evidence.
- Indian religions like Buddhism seek to end suffering. Chinese philosophies focus on order and harmony. In other words, the quest for 'the' truth is not a universal one.
- The Jewish claim on Israel is based on the myth of Zion and the Promised Land. The Christian claim on Jerusalem is based on the idea that Christ was crucified and resurrected there. The Islamic claim on Mecca is based on the belief that it is the spot where angels, Adam and Ibrahim prayed to God. From Jerusalem, Muslims believe Muhammad rose to heaven and returned in a single night. Hindutva argues that since these religions have holy lands outside India, the people of Abrahamic faiths cannot be regarded as natives of India, but only as foreigners. Thus, we see the power of the subjective truth of a people in shaping contemporary politics.

- 'Heaven' (Jannat, in Arabic) and 'Hell' (Jahannum), 'angels', 'djinns' and 'demons', are not scientific facts. But they do shape our moral, ethical and legal views of the world. Such is the power of myth.

Emergence

Abrahamic lore has a long history and multiple influences. It emerged in the Middle East, where it challenged the older worldview of many gods. It was clearly influenced by monotheistic ideas of Zarathustra of Persia and Akhenaten of Egypt, who lived 3,500 years ago.

Stories from the Genesis, such as Noah's Ark, have strong roots in Mesopotamian mythology, traced to the Sumerian *Epic of Gilgamesh*, which tells the story of a mortal king's quest for immortality, which leads him to the only man to survive a devastating world-destroying flood unleashed by the gods long ago. The idea of brothers fighting over inheritance, which recurs in Jewish lore, has its roots in the Egyptian myth of the fight between Seth and Osiris over the right to rule. The ritual of circumcision has been traced by historians to ancient Egypt. The jealous tribal god of Judaism who demanded fierce loyalty and punished transgressors became the wise, loving,

universal God after contact with Zoroastrian mythology of Persia during the Babylonian exile of the sixth century BCE, where all negative emotions were attributed to the Devil.

Two thousand years ago, a Jewish rabbi called Jesus reinterpreted the Jewish truth, emphasizing less on law and more on love. His words became known as Christianity as his followers were convinced he was the messiah foretold in Jewish lore, i.e., Christ. Christianity spread from Israel across the Roman Empire around the Mediterranean 1,700 years ago, through trade routes to the Middle East and India nearly 1,000 years ago, and through colonial rule to Africa, Asia and the Americas.

Rejection of the body by Christian ascetics was shaped by Manichaean mythology, which in turn was influenced by Jain practices. Christian missionary activity was strongly influenced by Buddhist monastic orders that took the Buddha's word outside India 2,300 years ago. Popular Christian festivals like Easter have been traced to the festival of the Babylonian goddess Ishtar. The idea of Jesus being resurrected has a resonance in the story of Ishtar's beloved shepherd-god Dumuzi, who dies every winter and is resurrected every spring. The importance of Christmas tree, snow and Santa Claus bearing gifts at Christmas time has its roots in Norse myths and North European traditions that came to North America with immigrants 200 years ago.

In the seventh century, Muhammad declared God spoke to him and gave him the original version of the faith. He insisted that what Jewish and Christian folk believed and followed was outdated, corrupt and false. This gave rise to Islam, which spread rapidly to the West across Asia Minor (Turkey) and Africa, and to the East across Persia, and Central, South and South East Asia. The spread of Islam divided the Mediterranean region into Christian Europe in the north and Muslim Africa in the south, and changed global history forever.

While Christianity and Islam focus on a transcendent God, the common man needed something more immediate and accessible. Hence, across the world, we find stories and shrines of Christian saints and martyrs, Muslim ghazis and pirs, who are venerated and whose intervention is sought for resolving ordinary mundane issues related to marriage, children, health and jobs. Yes, Judgement Day matters, Apocalypse matters, but so do the common needs of daily life.

- Mesopotamia and India had many gods and many kings. Egypt and China had many gods but one king. Persia had one king who represented the one true god, Ahura Mazda. The idea of a single God and/or single king becomes increasingly popular as local city states gradually expand into vast empires, controlling many regions and multiple cultures.
- Religions often shape each other. The Song of Songs in the Hebrew Bible expresses love for God in sexual terms, indicating influence from Mesopotamia, where sacred priestesses indulged in sexual rites to please the gods. Love in Christianity was more paternalistic and puritanical than romantic, revealing the Greek military influence and its contempt for the 'effeminate sensual ways' of Persia and Egypt. Later, the Byzantine Christianity of Eastern Europe was seen as more sensual than the austere Roman Christianity. The idea of the loving God, in romantic terms, appears in India around 500 CE in the devotional songs of the Tamil poets. This manifests in the Islamic world through the works of Rumi in 1200 CE.

Conflation

For an outsider, Judaism, Christianity and Islam seem like branches emerging from the same Abrahamic tree. However, for the insider, it is not so. Adjectives like 'Abrahamic' and 'Judaeo-Christian' became popular only in the latter half of the twentieth century and are accepted rather grudgingly, but not by all.

For centuries, Christians hated the Jewish people and saw them as Christ-killers. This gave rise to anti-Semitism, a systematic and structural hatred of the Jewish people across Europe. But in the 1940s, the Holocaust or the genocide of six million Jewish people in Christian Europe by the Nazis of Germany during the Second World War shocked the Western world. It forced them to confront their anti-Semitic ways and acknowledge the common root of Judaism and Christianity. Only then did the phrase 'Judaeo-

Christian' come into being. Earlier, it was used for Jewish people who were recent converts to Christianity.

A thousand years ago, Christians fought the Crusades against Muslims for the control of Jerusalem. The conflict took a fresh form nearly a thousand years later, when, after the Second World War, colonial powers, all Christian, took control of the Middle East from the Ottoman Emperor, seen by Muslims as the Caliphate of the Islamic world. Israel was handed over to the Jewish people, upsetting the local Muslim population. Then, at the turn of the century, following the Gulf War and the 9/11 terrorist attack that brought down the World Trade Centre in New York, old wounds were reopened. America declared its War on Terror, which was seen as a veiled attack of the Christian nations against the Muslim world, under the garb of secularism and democracy. To heal these wounds, more and more writers started using the adjective 'Abrahamic' to refer to the common roots of Jewish, Christian and Islamic faiths.

Islamophobia, the structural and systemic hatred of Muslims, began with the Crusades, when Christians who saw sex as sin declared Muslims as heretics as they were comfortable with sensuality and even saw Allah's heaven, i.e., Jannat, as a sensual place full of fountains, gardens and beautiful fairies. Islamophobia has re-emerged in Europe and America as Muslim migrants find their faith at odds with the liberal values of the modern world that is based on equality, secularism, regard for a country's constitution over Sharia (Islamic law), and human rights for LGBTQ+ people.

- In India, there are Malayali Christians who claim they converted under the influence of St Thomas nearly 2,000 years ago. There are Goans who converted under the influence of Portuguese Catholic missionaries since the sixteenth century. There are East Indians and Anglo-Indians who converted under the influence of the Anglican Church of England since the seventeenth century. Tribes in North-east India were converted mainly by American Protestant Evangelists such as the Baptists and the Presbyterians. These Christian groups see themselves as distinct from each other, their divisions following old ethnic, linguistic, tribal and caste divisions in India.
- In India, while there was no anti-Semitism, there was little curiosity about Jewish tales. Synagogues were often confused with the Parsi fire temples and

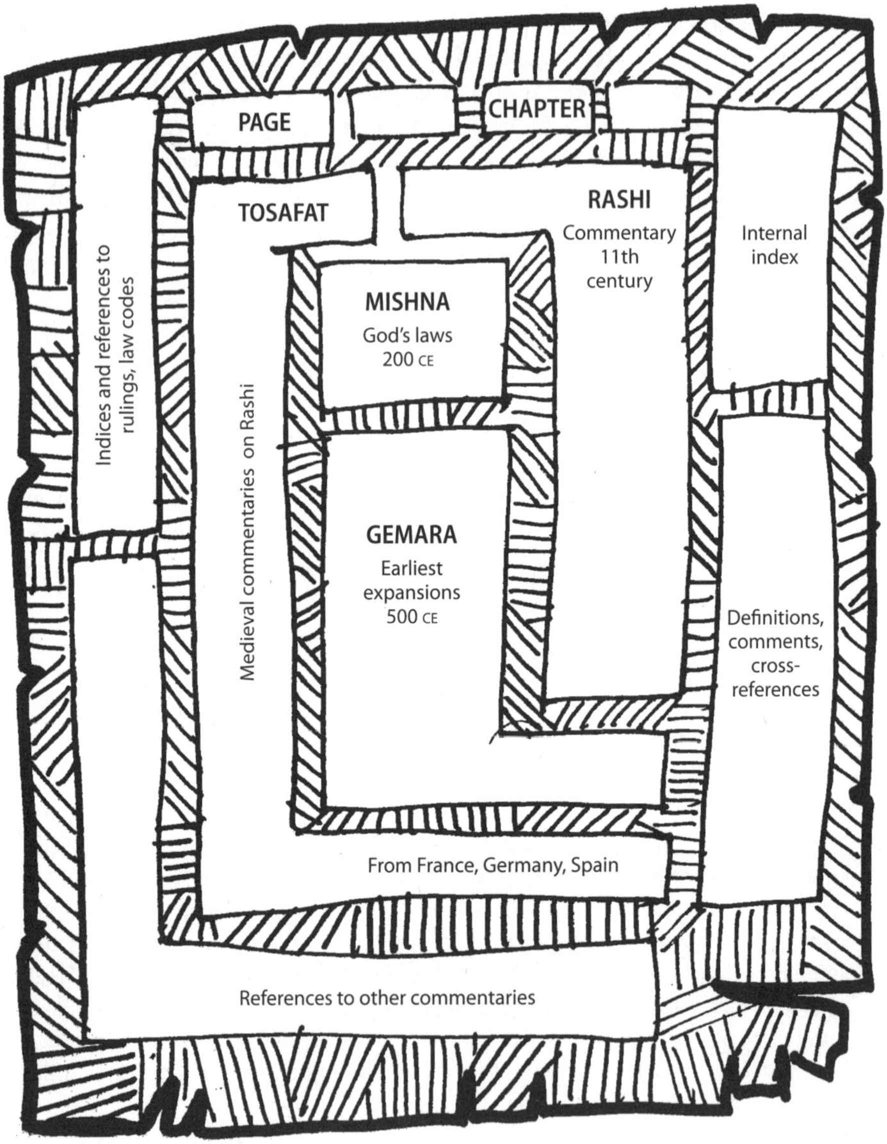

Design of a page of the Talmud showing how conversations between Jewish scholars interpreting God's law have been captured over history and geography.

mosques. In 1958, Sohrab Modi starred in a Bollywood film called *Yahudi*, or 'the Jew', which tells the story of a Jewish man who raises a Roman child and is persecuted by Romans.

- The Muslims of Sindh and Punjab never treated the Muslims of Bengal as equals, resulting in the splitting of Bangladesh from the Islamic Republic of Pakistan. While Islam seeks to be a grand unifying force, it keeps getting split along ethnic and national lines.

Sources

The oldest versions of Abrahamic lore come from Jewish lore, which is over 4,000 years old. Orally transmitted for centuries, the twenty-four books of the Hebrew Bible, known as the *Tanakh*, were compiled roughly 2,500 years ago when the Second Jewish Temple was built with the support of Persians, after the First Temple had been destroyed by the Assyrians. However, what we have today are versions that were codified about 1,800 years ago, a few centuries after the Second Temple was destroyed by Romans. Later literature, also known as Rabbinic literature, contains many retellings. Orthodox Jewish culture, such as the Hasidic Jews, emerged only in the eighteenth century in Eastern Europe.

Christian lore is divided into the Old and New Testaments. The Old Testament is informed by the Hebrew Bible as well as other sources such as the Greek translation (*Septuagint*), the Syriac translation (*Peshitta*) and the Dead Sea Scrolls. The New Testament is based on the writings of the followers of Jesus: Matthew, Mark, Luke and John, written a century after the crucifixion of Jesus. It also includes the letters of St Paul.

Originally, the Bible was written in Hebrew and Aramaic, but by the fifth century it was rendered into Greek and Latin and finally into various European languages by the fifteenth century. It is now being translated into almost every language in the world, owing to the work of Christian missionaries. The most popular and highly influential English version, the King James Bible, is 400 years old.

Different Christian denominations value different retellings of the Old as well as the New Testament. For instance, as compared to the Eastern Orthodox Christians, and the Protestants, the Roman Catholics value different sources and different stories. The Eastern Orthodox Church, which follows the Julian Calendar, celebrates Christmas on 7 January, while the Catholic Church and Protestant denominations, which follow the Gregorian Calendar, celebrate Christmas on 25 December.

The *Book of Mormon* of the Church of the Latter-day Saints has a whole new mythology that was published 200 years ago. It is very popular in the United States and claims to be over 4,000 years old.

Islam is based on the Quran, which contains the message of God as revealed to the Prophet Muhammad. These were codified and standardized about two generations later by the Caliphs, who were the appointed leaders of the Islamic world. It is in old Arabic, and the orthodox resist its translation, insisting that the sound of the language helps in getting a deeper understanding of its contents, much more than its vocabulary and grammar—an approach to sacred scriptures also seen amongst many Vedic Brahmins of India. Value is also placed on the Hadith, which records the life of Prophet Muhammad and his many conversations and practices that continue to shape Muslim life.

Both the Islamic revelation and Islamic traditions contain references to several Jewish and Christian stories, which have since been compiled and retold in various languages such as Arabic (the 1,000-year-old history of prophets and kings, *Tarikh al-Rusul wa al-Muluk*, written by Tafsir al-Tabari; or the 700-year-old *Al-Bidayah Wan-Nihayah*, The Beginning and the End, written by Ibn Kathir; or the 700-year-old *Qaṣas al-Anbiya*, stories of prophets by al-Kisai); Persian (the 600-year-old *Bereshit Nama* and *Musa Nama* as well as the *Ezra Nama* by Shahin Shirazi); even Bengali (the 400-year-old *Nabi-bansa*, Lineage of Prophets, by Syed Sultan); and Tamil (the 300-year-old *Sira-Puranam*, chronicle of the Prophet's life, by Umaru Pulavar). There are also, in India, many religious hagiographies of holy men, pirs, ghazis and sufis that are considered religious folklore locally but are not accepted by the wider orthodox Islamic establishment.

- Abrahamic lore clearly values the textual over the oral. So, it constantly refers to 'People of the Book'. Most cultures around the world transmitted their ideas orally and by use of symbols and rituals. Literacy originated 5,000 years ago in Mesopotamia, which is also the cradle of Abrahamic lore.
- The stone tablets with the law of God inscribed, brought down from Mount Sinai by Moses, were kept in the Ark of the Covenant and placed in the legendary Jewish temple built by David in Jerusalem around 1000 BCE. It is now lost. However, the Christians of Ethiopia believe they still possess it. No one is allowed to access it, so no one is sure.
- The oldest collection of Abrahamic lore comes from parchments known as the Dead Sea Scrolls, which were hidden in caves following the destruction of the second Jewish temple. These relics were discovered in the twentieth century and can be dated to over 2,000 years ago.
- The Quran's first verse clearly states that the law was provided using a pen, privileging the textual over oral traditions. In the story of Moses, God says that the law to be followed by humans is written by his finger.
- There are many books written describing the details of the events in the life of Prophet Muhammad, and these influence the lives of Muslims. However, not all are considered authentic, with different scholars from different schools of thought preferring some narratives over others. It has been observed that the number and details of these accounts increases with the passage of time.

Narration

Presenting Jewish, Christian and Islamic lore in a single book is extremely challenging and not a very common practice in the Western world, which tends to focus on the differences.

Many present the tales as history, rather self-consciously, with excessive deference. Casual narrations, with embellishments, are seen as blasphemous, provoking outrage in some Abrahamic communities. Fear of retribution by

God and God's self-proclaimed representatives is always looming. Orthodox American Jews spell God as G-d as the Third Commandment states, 'Thou shall not take God's name in vain.'

Reverence and distance are deeply attached to Prophet Muhammad, whose name is often written in orthodox circles with the suffix PBUH (peace be upon him), quite unlike how Hindus would address Shiva, Shakti, Ram or Krishna, intimately, often as a friend or a relative, especially within devotional contexts. However, in recent times, new Hindu sects and cults are choosing formality as the preferred way for referring to Hindu deities, rejecting the playful informality of the past. So, at times in fear of rabid politicians, in the Hindi-speaking belt of North India, people expect you to say Ram-ji or Shri Ram, instead of just Ram—as Ram has been addressed for hundreds of years.

Then there is the pressure of political correctness, and cultural sensitivity: Does one use the familiar Old Testament names (Jesus, for example) or the less familiar Arabic names for the same character (Isa)? Since the stories are different in the two traditions, does one treat them as the same character? Should one write words such as god, and prophet, and pronouns for either, with capitalization, or without capitalization?

Which tale is original and which is a variant, which tale is a telling and which is a retelling? The Christian Bible is clear that the Hebrew Bible is the 'Old' Testament. But Islam does not see its stories as variants of the Hebrew Bible or its retellings. It considers all that is mentioned in the Quran, especially, to be facts, and so original tales, and all other renditions are considered as variants. Islam considers Adam to be the first prophet, an idea unknown in Jewish and Christian retellings.

In this book, I have chosen to narrate the stories the way Indian parents tell sacred stories to their children: unselfconsciously, respectfully, but casually, fully aware of my prejudices, and fully accepting that a prejudice-free story does not exist.

I have chosen to use the relatively more familiar Old Testament names—mostly, not always. Also, as names can be complicated and so distracting to unfamiliar ears, simplified spellings have been chosen, and often no name is used to focus more on the idea than the details.

Most importantly, I have included Indo-Christian and Indo-Islamic folklore to familiarize people with narratives that played a very important role in the spread of these religions in South Asia.

- In India, Abrahamic lore is commonly equated with the Old and New Testaments of the Christian Bible, with little or no knowledge of versions found in Jewish and Islamic cultures around the world. This is due to the wide reach of Christian missionary schools, as well as the presence of *Gideon's Bible* in most hotel rooms.
- Among Muslims, storytelling is far more common in Shia communities than in Sunni communities. In Iran, there are plays performed during the month of Muharram based on the tragedy at Karbala, similar to the passion plays on the crucifixion of Christ.
- Creative retellings of Abrahamic lore and the life of Prophet Muhammad are found in Bangladesh along with the hagiographies (*mangal-kavya*) of real and fictional saints known as pirs. This came to be seen with less favour after the elite started educating their children in Europe and the Middle East since the nineteenth century. The children returned with a more global orthodox perspective of Islam based on Arabic education and the idea of Caliphate. They contributed to ideas like puritanical Wahhabism, which has roots in India and which frowns on dargahs or worship at the mausoleum of Muslim saints, especially those who subscribed to Sufi mysticism.

Illustrations

I love illustrating books. But Islamic orthodoxy is against the representation of God, or God's creation. This rule is based less on God's word (the Quran) and more on tradition (Hadith). Painting humans especially is considered sin (*haram*). This belief, however, was not strictly enforced in Persia, where paintings narrating stories of Islamic lore were used for education but not for worship. Then from the 1500s, these images covered the face of the Prophet with a veil.

In the fourteenth century, *Siyer-i Nebi*, a ballad based on the life of the Prophet, was written in Turkish, and in the sixteenth century, the Ottoman ruler Murad

III commissioned a lavish illustrated copy of the work, with the most complete visual portrayal of the life of Prophet Muhammad. Miniature art based on Abrahamic lore was created in the courts of the Mughals, Safavids and Ottomans between the sixteenth and eighteenth centuries. This suggests that the Islamic prohibition against art is more Arabic than Persian in origin, and was clearly an attempt of the religious folk to keep political and popular power in check. In the twenty-first century, with the rise of hard line political orders (Islamism), we increasingly find fatwas (legal opinion) being used against those who specifically seek to create images of the Prophet.

Christians have never shared this belief and have had a long tradition of magnificent biblical art, with grand images of God adorning the walls and ceilings of the Sistine Chapel in the Vatican itself.

In this book, I illustrate all common stories, using the Indian visual metaphor. I have minimally illustrated exclusive Islamic tales respecting popular conventions. To identify holy men and prophets, I have used the nimbus (golden orb) in keeping with conventions of Christian art, and blazing fire in keeping with conventions of Islamic art.

- In 1992, India's state television, Doordarshan, broadcast a Hindi serial based on stories from the Bible called *Bible ki Kahaniya*. It was banned to appease certain Muslim hardliners who believed visualizing the messengers of God was anti-Islamic, and to appease certain Hindu hardliners who saw this as promotion of Christianity and Islam.
- In 2015, a film on the childhood of the Prophet called *Muhammad: the Messenger of God* was produced in Iran. It shows pre-Islamic Arabia through the eyes of the Prophet till the age of thirteen. But many Sunni Arab countries did not appreciate this visualization of the Prophet.

- European caricaturists of the twenty-first century have visualized Prophet Muhammad, especially in response to hard line Islamism, and it has become a contentious issue between those who believe that it is disrespectful of Islamic sentiments and those who believe that Islam does not respect the freedom of expression of non-Muslims. The clash has been violent and remains unresolved.
- Early Buddhist art, created over 2,000 years ago, does not show the image of the Buddha, but chooses symbols like crowns, footprints, trees and thrones, indicating an ancient discomfort with showing someone venerated. Their presence was shown by highlighting their absence.
- Sculptures depicting gods in Hinduism became popular 1,500 years ago. This was done not by denying the human form, but by exaggerating it—depicting many hands, many heads, and replacing the human head with animal heads, or the human body with an animal body.

The capitalized words God and Truth in Abrahamism tend to be qualitative and involve differentiation from false gods and falsehood. In contrast, the non-capitalized god and truth in India are quantitative, a journey of discovery from finite gods (*devata*) to the infinite divine (*bhagavan*), from limited knowledge (*mithya*) to limitless knowledge (*satya*). The two approaches mirror the way the left and right brain function.

The expansion of the mind from the limited to the unlimited, from the finite to the infinite, happens when our mind accommodates all truths, be it Judaic, Christian or Islamic, Hindu, Buddhist or Jain, secular or religious, scientific or mythic. One way to achieve this is by discouraging competitive argument (*vi-vaad*) and encouraging collaborative conversation (*sam-vaad*). So read this book keeping in mind

Within infinite myths lies an eternal truth
Who sees it all?
Varuna has but a thousand eyes
Indra, a hundred
You and I, only two!

Aligning Abrahamic Lore to Modern History

	Abrahamic Lore	Historical events in Middle East and Mediterranean	Historical Events in Indian Subcontinent (South Asia)
10000 BCE		End of the Ice Age; construction of temple of Gobekli Tepe in south-eastern Turkey, around which the agricultural revolution began	Petroglyphic (rock art); cave paintings; dolmens or raising of large rocks to mark graves
4000 BCE	Creation	Stone Age; agriculture in Mesopotamia, cuneiform script and wheel invented	
3000 BCE	Noah's Ark	Bronze Age; Upper and Lower Egypt united; Egyptian hieroglyphics; pyramids built in Egypt	Mehrgarh Neolithic site in Baluchistan, Pakistan; Early days of Harappan civilisation in the Indus valley
2000 BCE	Abraham	Sumerian civilization and the composition of the Mesopotamian *Epic of Gilgamesh*, which refers to Great Flood	Final days of Harappan civilization
1500 BCE	Exodus	Horse-drawn chariot warfare first seen in the world; Pharaoh Akhenaten experiments with monotheism	Vedic semi-nomads introduce horse-drawn chariots
1000 BCE	First Temple of Solomon	Iron Age; Assyria rises in Upper Mesopotamia and Babylon in Lower Mesopotamia	Rise of kingdoms of Kuru and Panchala in Gangetic plains, and the emergence of Upanishads

	Abrahamic Lore	Historical events in Middle East and Mediterranean	Historical Events in Indian Subcontinent (South Asia)
500 BCE	Second Temple	Achaemenid Empire of Persia conquers Mesopotamia and battles Greek city states	Emergence of Buddhism and Jainism
0 BCE	Jesus	Roman Empire battles Parthians. The Second Jewish Temple destroyed by Romans	India ruled by Yavanas (Indo-Greeks), Sakas (Scythians) and Kushans (Central Asians); rise of Buddhist artwork in Gandhara and Mathura; composition of Tamil Sangam literature
600 CE	Muhammad	Byzantine Empire battles Sassanians of Persia	Gupta Empire overrun by Huns; Harshavardhan rules Kannauj; rise of Sanskrit cosmopolis and classical Hindu art

Islamic Counterparts of Biblical Names

Name in Christian/Jewish lore	Name in Islamic lore
Aaron	Haroun
Abel	Habil
Abraham	Ibrahim
Anna	Ishba
Cain	Qabil
Daniel	Danyal
David	Dawood
Elijah	Ilyas
Elisha	Il-yasa
Elohim	Allah
Enoch	Idris
Ezra	Uzair
Eve	Hawa
Ezekiel	Dhul-Kifl
Isaac	Isaq
Jacob	Yakub
Jeremiah	Urmiya
Jesus	Isa
Jethro	Shoaib
Joachim	Imran
Job	Ayyub
John	Yahya
Jonah	Yunus
Joseph	Yusuf
Joshua	Yusha
Lot	Lut
Mary	Mariam
Moses	Musa
Noah	Nu
Potipar	Aziz
Samuel	Shammil
Saul	Talut
Solomon	Suleiman

PROLOGUE

Fight over a Fruit

Every summer, when rain-bearing clouds moved from the west to the east, sailors and traders from the Mediterranean lands would sail from Arabia to India, to the ports of Chera-nadu, to buy spices, fruits and textiles in exchange for gold. They would return when the winds would shift and move from east to west in winter.

The ports belonged to queens, priestesses of the Goddess Bhagawati, who kept the sea calm at all times. Their brothers, known as Swami-Sri or Samdura-pati, sat on ivory thrones and ruled on their behalf. It was their duty to keep the ports calm.

In one such port, one day, all wasn't calm. Three sailors were arguing loudly, disturbing the peace.

The Judean yelled, 'It was a pomegranate.'

'No, an apple,' said the Roman.

'No, a banana,' said the Arab.

The argument carried on for days and nights, irritating the other sailors and merchants, some from Ethiopia, others from China. They complained to

the guards, who dragged the three sailors to the king on the ivory throne.

When questioned, the sailors revealed they were arguing over the true identity of the forbidden fruit. 'On eating the forbidden fruit, Adam was cast out of Eden,' said the Judean.

'It was the original sin, for which humanity will suffer until we accept Jesus as the saviour,' said the Roman.

'That's not quite true,' argued the Arab. Then, turning to the king, he said, 'Allah forgave Adam. But Adam had to leave Eden, as eating the fruit made his bowels move. The resulting gases and excrement have no place in paradise. Adam fell on a mountain that was closest to paradise, Sarandip, not far from Chera-nadu. You can see his giant footprint there.'

'What are you talking about? Eden? Adam? Forbidden fruit?' said the king.

The three sailors were shocked. 'Have you not heard of humanity's transgression and the message of the one true god sent to humanity through Abraham and the many messengers after him?' The king looked blank. 'Then let us tell you his tale and of the prophets and patriarchs who followed him.'

And so, in a coconut grove, on a mat made of kusha grass, three sailors sat and narrated a tale to the lord of the sea.

The king was joined by his sister, the matriarch and priestess, who rarely appeared in public, unless there was something new to learn.

The stories all took place in a land far away, a land of deserts, mountains and plateaus, and the river valleys of the Nile, Tigris and Euphrates. The king and his sister relished it all.

- The southern Indian state of Kerala was ruled by the Chera kings, hence known as Chera-nadu. Historically, it has been home to seafaring Arab merchants for centuries. The Arabs took advantage of the monsoon winds to sail towards India in summer and back home in winter. The word monsoon is derived from the Arabic *mawsim*, the season of sailing. This is why the largest population of Muslims is found in South and Southeast Asia.
- The kings of Kerala followed a matrilineal system of inheritance, seen also in Southeast Asia, where husbands visited their wives' homes, and the sister's sons inherited property.
- The Hebrew Bible does not identify the fruit in Eden. In 400 CE, when Jerome translated the Hebrew Bible into Latin on orders of Pope Damasus, he used the colloquial word *malus* that means both 'evil' and 'apple' or more specifically, 'a seed-bearing fruit'. Thus, a Latin pun resulted in the forbidden fruit being visualized as an apple. In some Jewish traditions the forbidden fruit was a fig, while in some Islamic traditions the forbidden fruit was wheat or grape. Michelangelo, therefore, shows the serpent on a fig tree, and it is only later, from the sixteenth century, that the serpent is shown on an apple tree.
- Wheat is cultivated. So, its status as forbidden fruit in some Islamic cultures suggests that humanity's 'transgression' began with the agricultural revolution, when humans learnt to cultivate the earth. In the Bengali *Nabi-bansa*, the poet Syed Sultan says that the angel Gabriel gave Adam the plough, the yoke, two oxen and seeds to help him cultivate the earth after he had been cast out of paradise.
- Bhagawati, or the goddess who embodies nature and all things material, is worshipped in every village of India as the embodiment of the village.
- In the thirteenth century, Nathan Hame'ati translated the Rambam's medical work *Pirkei Moshe* (Aphorisms of Moses) from Arabic into Hebrew, where the banana is referred to as the 'apple of Eden'. Today, some bananas are known by the Latin names *Musa paradisiaca* (fruit of paradise) and *Musa sapientum* (fruit of knowledge). Some say, the banana's identification with the Forbidden Fruit has to do with its medicinal properties, and others say it has to do with its phallic shape.

Diagrammatic Representation of the World of Abrahamic Lore
(not drawn to scale)

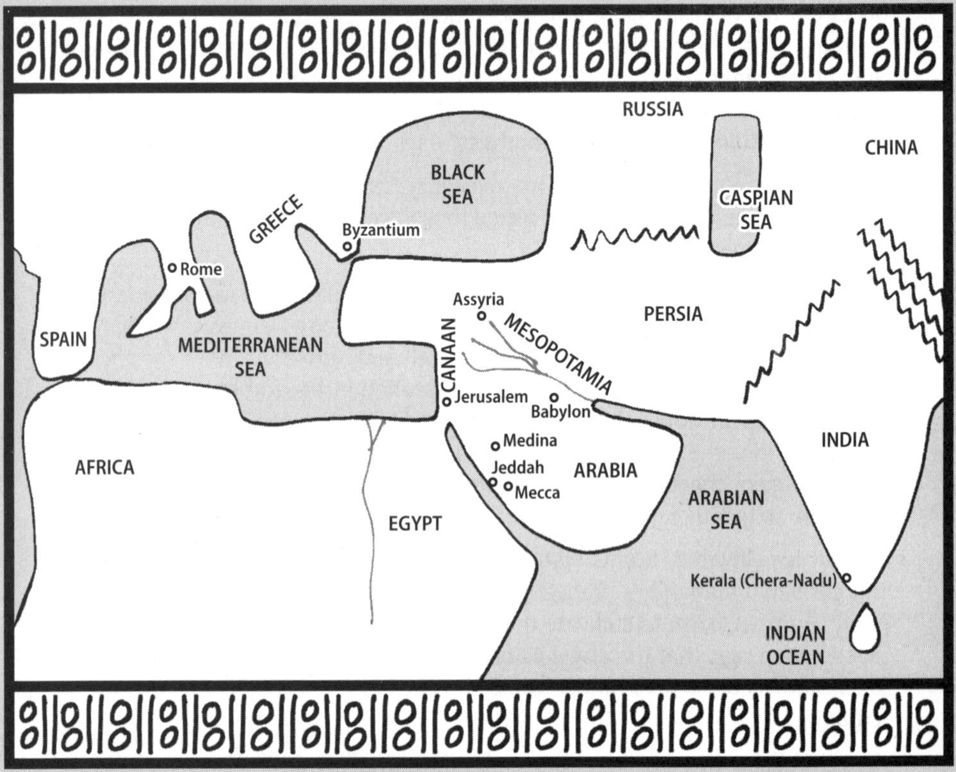

BOOK ONE

Out of Eden

Before Creation

In the beginning there was nothing but God.

God had no form or name. But God existed—conscious, sentient. Humans refer to God in the masculine, but that reveals the inadequacy of human language. God is neither male nor female, neither human nor animal, neither plant nor mineral, neither wave nor particle. He is beyond it all, an entity uncontained by measurement or word.

Before creating the world, God created seven things: God's law, God's throne, Heaven to the right, Hell to the left, God's sanctuary, an altar with the name of the first and final prophet who would tell all about God and God's law, and a voice that kept chanting, 'Come back, children of humans'.

- This story comes from Jewish tradition. It refers to a creation of God's realm before the rest of the world.
- God has no name. Words like 'El' and 'Elohim' are based on Mesopotamian gods.
- 'Yahweh', the word commonly used to refer to God in Jewish and Christian traditions, means 'I am what I am' and when spoken, sounds like an audible inhalation (Yah-) and exhalation (-weh), suggesting the role of breath in creation, as per Jewish and Christian mysticism.
- Allah literally means 'the god' in Arabic, which becomes God in Latin due to the use of capitalization, which is not a part of Arabic or Hebrew scripts.
- In some Islamic traditions, the spirit or light of the Prophet Muhammad, known as *noor*, was created long before he appeared in history. Thus, Muhammad is both the first prophet (in spirit) and the last prophet (in flesh).
- In seventeenth-century Bengali narrations of Islamic lore, Allah is identified as Niranjan (flawless, pure) and Nirakar (formless). In Gujarat, thirteenth-century Sanskrit inscriptions refer to Allah as Shunya-rupa (the embodiment of oblivion) and Vishva-rupa (the embodiment of the world).
- The Bible begins with Genesis and ends with Apocalypse, or the Final War. This is a linear worldview to be contrasted with the cyclical worldview of Hindus, Buddhists and Jains that has no beginning (*anadi*) and no end (*ananta*), with events such as Ramayana and Mahabharata repeating themselves.
- In Kabbalah, or Jewish mysticism, which became popular in the Middle Ages, Ein Sof or 'the endless one' is the name given to the abstract divine force that manifests itself through creation and various metaphysical emanations. Sufism, an Islamic mystical tradition, also speaks of God manifesting himself through creation in order to be recognized.
- Creation out of nothingness is a key theme in monotheism. Hence, the biblical phrase, 'For dust you are, and to dust you shall return'. There is no concept of past or future lives, hence no concept of karma.

Creation in Seven Days

God created the world, and life in it, out of nothingness in just six days. God's day was much longer than human days, but humans will never know as they came only later.

On the first day, he created light to illuminate what was to come later. On the second day, he created space separating the sky above from the sea below. On the third day, he caused the dry earth to rise above the waters, thus the world came into being and sprouted plants and trees. On the fourth day, the sun marked the day, the moon marked the night, and stars appeared in the sky, marking the days, the months and the years, thus the calendar came into being. On the fifth day, animals crawled, walked and ran on earth, seeking food, thus food chains came into existence, with those that eat chasing that which can be eaten. On the sixth day, humans were created in God's own image—capable of imagination, and with the power of free will to overturn the food chain.

On the seventh day, God rested and let humans discover their humanity by letting them make decisions.

- Seven is a recurring theme in Abrahamic lore. The seventh day is for rest, the year has seven major festivals, the seventh year is to keep the fields fallow, the forty-ninth (seven times seven) is the jubilee year to free all criminals and forgive all debts.
- The importance of seven, including a seven-day week, perhaps had its origin in Mesopotamia, where value was placed on the seven unblinking celestial bodies that moved amongst the blinking stars (sun, moon, Mars, Mercury, Jupiter, Venus and Saturn).
- For Muslims, the day of rest is Friday; for the Jewish people, the day of rest is Saturday; for Christians, it is Sunday. The idea of a weekend holiday emerged in America, where factories were owned by Christians and the workers were Jewish.

- James Ussher, an Irish archbishop in the seventeenth century, used information in the Bible and calculated that Creation began at 6 p.m. of 22 October 4004 BCE.
- God in Abrahamic mythologies is outside creation. So, God exists beyond our world. God is out there. Contrast this with the Hindu idea that God contains the world, and the world contains God. God is in, and around. Indian ideas of 'I have divine potential' (*aham brahmasmi*) and 'so do you' (*tat tvam asi*) are unacceptable in conventional Abrahamism, but are found in the mystic Kabbalah, Gnostic and Sufi traditions.

Adam, the First Human

The earth was a disc surrounded by water and enclosed in darkness, held aloft by a bull, which was held by a fish, which was held by an angel. On the left, there were seven layers of Hell, full of ugliness and cold and hellfire; and on the right, seven layers of Heaven, full of beauty and warmth.

From fire and light, God created the helpful angels. From fire and air, God created the mischievous ambivalent spirits known as the djinn. From smoke came the troublesome demons or shaitans. From earth, he created humans.

God asked the angels to fetch him a fistful of dirt. But each time the angels approached the earth, it recoiled from their touch. The angel Iblis asked God to grant him success on his mission to collect the dirt. Success was granted. The dirt was collected. From this dirt, God moulded Adam.

All things were created from God's word. But Adam was created from God's hand. And so, God gave Adam a special status: dominion over earth and all its creatures. He also asked all angels to bow to Adam.

All did, except Iblis, as he had participated in the creation of Adam, and was born of fire not dirt, and so felt that it made him superior. Also because he would bow to none but God, for he loved God alone.

For this act of disobedience, Iblis was cast out of God's side, out of paradise, and he swore to tempt Adam away from God's path. Iblis became the Devil. The shaitans became his horde.

- This cosmogony comes from the thirteenth-century Persian writer Zakariya al-Qazwini, who draws inspiration from local Islamic traditions. In some retellings, it is Azrael not Iblis who fetches the dirt from which Adam is made. He succeeds because he asks for God's blessings before he proceeds. For this achievement, he is made the Angel of Death, who fetches the souls of the deceased. The bull and fish that uphold the earth are considered to be Behemoth and Leviathan, monsters of chaos mentioned in Jewish and Christian mythologies. They were defeated by God to create order and the world.
- In Syed Sultan's *Nabi-bansa*, before Adam was created, there was another world full of *devas* and *asuras*, the *jann* and the *djinn*, to whom God gave his laws in the form of the four Vedas through various Hindu gods such as Brahma, Vishnu, Shiva and Hari. But God's law was not respected. And this world collapsed and Adam had to be created. In many ways, the Hindu gods are connected with the djinn. In pre-Islamic Arabia, they were equal to Allah and had knowledge of destiny. In Islamic Arabia, they were demoted and forbidden by Allah to reveal the knowledge of destiny. Hindu gods were seen not as 'false gods' in the Bengali retellings of Islamic lore, but as powerful beings who had been told to withdraw from the world and make way for Adam's descendants and the prophets.
- In Islamic lore, Adam was the first of 1,24,000 prophets (*nabi*, in Arabic) of which twenty-five are mentioned in the Quran. All nabis praise Allah. But some nabis are special: they are *rasul*; they also carry messages from God. These are Moses (Musa), David (Dawood), Jesus (Isa) and Muhammad. Some add Abraham (Ibrahim) and Solomon (Suleiman) to the list of messengers but their holy books are lost. Muhammad is considered the last prophet, the final seal.
- In Islamic lore, some argue Iblis was a djinn while others argue he was a fallen angel, an idea that resonates with Christian lore. Shaitans are considered demonic hordes who follow Iblis. But sometimes, 'Shaitan' is used as a proper noun referring to Iblis. 'Shaitan' is used as synonym for Satan in common parlance.

The Peacock and the Serpent

Iblis wanted access to paradise. But he could not get in. He saw a peacock and offered to grant the peacock immortality. The creature turned him down, stating that as it lived in paradise, he was already immortal.

The peacock then told a serpent about the charming Iblis whom he met outside. Curious to meet this angel, the serpent went and met Iblis and was so enchanted by his beauty that it agreed to take Iblis into the garden. The serpent opened its mouth and Iblis entered it. Thus, Iblis was able to enter paradise with the serpent.

For this crime of facilitating the entry of the Devil into paradise, the peacock and the serpent were made eternal enemies when cast out of Eden.

- This story comes from Syed Sultan's Bengali *Nabi-bansa.*
- In Islamic lore, Eden is simply called *Jannah*, or garden. Sometimes it is called *Jannat Adni* or 'Garden of Eden' and seen as one of the seven heavens, lower than the one of Allah.
- In the Christian Bible, the serpent is not directly linked to the Devil. This connection is made in later commentaries.
- The serpent was a popular fertility symbol linked to many gods and goddesses of Egypt and Mesopotamia. In India, too, the Naga were gods associated with fertility.
- Since the peacock is linked to paradise, brooms made of peacock feathers are used by keepers of the Sufi dargahs of India. This practice, acceptable in the Shia branch of Islam, is frowned upon in the Sunni branch.
- The Yazidis of Iran and Iraq are monotheists who believe God had seven angels. The angel who refused to bow to humans was cast in Hell. He questioned how creatures of light could bow to creatures born of dirt. His tears cooled the fires of Hell and he was allowed to rise and help fallen angels return to Heaven. This demon or shaitan is worshipped as a peacock angel by the Yazidis, who are persecuted by their Muslim neighbours, who accuse them of being Devil

worshippers. The Yazidis follow endogamy, pray facing the sun and venerate the peacock angel with fire. This leads many to speculate an ancient connect with Hindu Tamil culture, where the peacock and the serpent are associated with Murugan, the warlord-god.

Lilith

Since Adam was alone, God created a woman for him as his companion from the earth. Her name was Lilith.

Adam desired Lilith and Lilith desired Adam. But she would not lay beneath him, and he would not lay beneath her. They fought until Lilith became very angry and decided to leave God's garden and take refuge in the desert.

Angels tried to persuade her to return but she refused. Adam had to treat her as an equal or she would not return. Later, when she learned that Adam had taken another wife called Eve, she swore to destroy his children.

Lilith wandered in the darkness and became the mother of demons who cause miscarriage, stillbirth and fatal childhood fevers. She also became the mother of demons who fill men with dreams that make them spill seed outside the womb of women.

- This story comes from Jewish folklore dated to 1000 CE.
- It was clearly meant to curtail the independence of women and to explain miscarriage and masturbation.
- Jewish women believe that to protect pregnant women and their unborn

children, the many names of Lilith have to be written on walls where the delivery is taking place.

- Lilith became popular amongst feminists as an old goddess overthrown by patriarchal monotheism. Many feminist archaeologists and feminist anthropologists believe that ancient farming societies were egalitarian and non-violent clan societies that worshipped the Great Goddess in many forms until they were overthrown by patriarchal nomadic tribes that valued the male sky-god over the earth-goddess. This explains the fall of goddesses like Lilith, Gaia and Prithvi, and the rise of Jehovah, Zeus and Indra.

The Forbidden Fruit

From Adam's rib, God created a woman who came to be known as Eve, also known as Hawa. Adam fell in love with her and begged Allah to let Hawa be his wife. Allah agreed.

Adam and Hawa roamed freely in Eden, innocent, enjoying delightful fruits and fragrant flowers and the joyful breeze. The sun was not harsh, and the moon was bright. Everything was perfect. There was but one rule: to not eat of the immortal tree in the middle of Eden. If the rule was followed, Adam and Eve would live forever without hunger or fear. If they did not, they would experience hunger, fear and death.

But then the Devil, in the form of the serpent, tempted Eve to eat what was forbidden. Why was it forbidden? Are you not curious?

Eve plucked the fruit and ate a bit and offered it to Adam, who also took a bite. They were flooded with knowledge of their self, with guilt and shame, with insecurity, as well as yearnings of pleasure and pain. Suddenly aware of their bodies and their nakedness, they proceeded to cover themselves with leaves.

God saw this and demanded an explanation from Adam. Adam blamed Eve and Eve blamed the serpent. God cursed the serpent to spend all his life crawling on the ground. Eve was cursed that she would always be subservient to Adam and suffer the pain of childbirth. And both were cast out of Eden. They could not return as the gate was guarded by an angel with a flaming sword.

- The protruding tracheal cartilage in the neck of men is called Adam's apple as this is where the apple supposedly got stuck when Adam tried to swallow it.
- In Jewish lore, women are forced to cover their hair, walk behind their husband, walk in front of corpses in funerals and take care of the bread and the lamps in the house as punishment for Eve's crime of being tempted, being disobedient, and thereby, bringing death, hunger and darkness into human lives.
- In Jewish lore, Eve gave the fruit to all animals and birds. Only the phoenix refused to eat it and so was blessed with eternal life. As it ages, it shrinks in size, loses its feather and eventually bursts into flames only to rise anew, afresh.
- In Islamic lore, the Quran does not name Eve. Her name, Hawa, comes from Arabic and Persian traditions. She was punished with menstruation and Adam was punished with baldness for their disobedience.
- In Mesopotamian mythology, the human, Adapa, is summoned by the gods. Adapa is told by Enki, god of knowledge, not to eat anything the gods offer him. The gods offer him immortality. But Adapa, warned by Enki, refuses and stays mortal. This story is seen as an influence on the Abrahamic myth of the forbidden fruit, where the reverse takes place.
- In Hindu lore, the first man is Manu and so all humans are called Manavas, the children of Manu. The British equated Manu with Adam and so selected—of the many Dharmashastras available—the one called Manusmriti (recollections of the Hindu Adam) to be the foundation of the Indian legal system. Brahma, creator of Manu, chases the first woman, Shatarupa—a crime for which his fifth head is beheaded by Shiva. Shatarupa then becomes Manu's wife. In some stories, Manu's father is Surya, the sun. There are infinite Manus, not just the one, as the world keeps regenerating itself infinite times.
- The paradise of the gods, in Hindu, Buddhist and Jain mythology, has a tree that fulfils all wishes (Kalpataru). The day we have no wish that needs fulfilment, we are liberated. This concept of liberation is different from the concept of salvation or rescue found in Abrahamic lore.

- Hindus speak of the Tree of Life or Akshaya Vriksha that survived the great flood. Similar ideas are found in Mesopotamian, Persian, Turkik, even Norse, mythologies. It is the tree that connects the mortal material world with the immortal spiritual world. Norse mythology speaks of Yggdrasill, a cosmic tree that forms the axis of the universe, its branches and roots connecting to the realms of gods, giants and humans. Chinese mythology, too, speaks of a tree of life that bears the peaches of immortality, guarded by an immortal dragon and a phoenix that recreates itself from time to time.

Adam Finds Eve

Adam was cast on a mountain in Sarandip closest to Heaven. Eve was cast in the desert at Jeddah. The two wandered the earth, pining and looking for each other. Adam reached Mount Safa and Eve reached Mount Marwa. Finally, they saw each other atop Mount Arafat.

At first, Adam did not recognize Eve, for her appearance had changed greatly, as had his, until she narrated the story of their life in Eden and how they were cast out. On realizing that the woman before him was the same Eve of Eden, he wept with joy.

In gratitude, Adam and Eve built the House of God to pray to Allah. Here, angels prayed to Allah once. Here, in the future, the city of Mecca would rise.

Gabriel consoled the sad Adam and caressed his back. From his right side emerged the light of the Prophet, Nur Muhammad. From the left side emerged 1,24,000 prophets. Then, from his back emerged all creatures who would be born on earth till the end of time. They were asked if they would respect God's law. They all agreed and the contracts were placed inside a stone, brought from Eden to earth.

The angel Gabriel then taught Adam how to plough. He introduced Adam to wheat, which had been brought down from paradise. From one seed came a thousand seeds and from each of the thousand came another thousand.

Gabriel taught Adam and Eve how to harvest the wheat, dehusk the grain, grind it into flour and bake it into bread. When Adam and Eve worked, they began to sweat. When they ate and drank, they produced gas and excrement. Adam and Eve were disgusted. This never happened in Eden. They realized that as producers of this pollutant they were not welcome in Eden.

The angel Gabriel offered some liquid from Eden to Adam and Eve. Adam took one portion and Eve took nine. As a result, Adam had lesser sexual desire than Eve. Gabriel then brought three seeds for Adam and Eve. Adam ate two seeds, Eve took one and so all sons and daughters do not get equal share of property.

Gabriel taught Adam and Eve how to clean their body, perfume it and adorn it for each other. He showed them how to be intimate.

Eve became pregnant. The first child aborted itself. Thus began menstruation. When she gave birth to the second child, she was tricked by Iblis to name it. The child, therefore, fell sick and died. After that she gave birth to many children, whom she named with the grace of God and with the grace of angels, they remained protected from Iblis. They survived and thrived.

- The story of Adam and Eve being separated after leaving Eden, and finally reuniting in Arabia, comes from Arabic and Persian traditions and is unknown in the Christian world.

- The story of transgression is called Original Sin in Jewish and Christian mythology. The idea of being saved from sin is the cornerstone of the Jewish and Christian faiths. In Judaism, the saviour is yet to come. In Christianity, Jesus is the saviour. But in Islam, Allah is ever merciful. He forgives Adam and Hawa for their transgression. So, humans are not 'born in sin'. Children are born pure.
- While in Jewish and Christian traditions, Adam and Eve are cast out of Eden for eating the forbidden fruit, in Islamic tradition they are forgiven by Allah. They are cast out only because eating the fruit initiates digestion and leads to the production of gases and excrement that have no place in Eden.
- In Islamic tales, God sends Gabriel to teach farming to Adam and cooking to Eve. Adam is blessed with more property and Eve with more sexual desire. God teaches Adam and Eve how to give pleasure to each other. This is contrary to the Christian belief that sex is sin. In Islam, therefore, celibacy is frowned upon.
- Adam's Peak located in southern Sri Lanka, also known as Ratnagiri (mountain of gems) or Samanala Kanda (mountain of butterflies), has a 1.8 metre mark called Sri Pada that is identified by Buddhists as Buddha's footprint, by Hindus as Hanuman's footprint, and by Muslims and Christians as Adam's footprint.
- Adam is the first prophet in the Islamic tradition, and he is followed by 1,24,000 messengers (*paigambars*). He and all other prophets contain within them the light of Muhammad (Nur Muhammad). This light would manifest entirely in physical form as the final prophet of Allah.
- The Black Stone on the eastern corner of Mecca is believed to contain the contract of all living creatures who promised to follow God's way. On the Day of Judgement, it will 'speak' and reveal who respected the contract and who did not.
- The Red Sea port of Jeddah which welcome sailors travelling to Mecca for Hajj is said to be, as per Islamic tradition, the place where Eve was buried. Adam was buried in Mecca. Jeddah means 'grandmother' perhaps a memory of Hawa, the Islamic Eve.

BOOK TWO

Disobedience and Retribution

Cain and Abel

Adam and Eve produced many children. One of them was Cain, who tilled the soil and became the first farmer. Another son was Abel, who herded animals and became the first herdsman. Abel made tents woven from the hair of sheep, goat and camel for his family to live in.

Both brothers made offerings to God to show gratitude. Cain was measured. Abel was generous. And so, God preferred Abel's offerings over Cain's. This made him jealous.

Cain took his brother out into the wilderness and murdered him. Thus, the first farmer was also the first murderer. A raven appeared and dug its claws into the earth, showing Cain how to bury his dead brother and hide his crime. Cain realized God had seen his crime. Nothing in the world goes unseen. Nothing can be hidden.

God asked Cain where Abel was. Cain said that he did not know. 'Am I my brother's keeper?' he asked. Thus, the first murderer was also the first liar. God, who knows everything, cast Cain out of the family and forbade him from living in tents as his family did. He was also given a mark by

God so that none of Adam's descendants would kill him; he would live with the guilt of his crime till the day of his death.

Cain became the first outsider. Since he had caused blood to spill on the ground, he would never be able to farm the earth. Cast out of family, he built the first city, with houses of stone, where produce from farms and herds were bought and sold in the market.

Abel's death resulted in the first funeral mourning by Adam and Eve. Soon after, Adam and Eve had a son called Seth. He learned God's law and how to differentiate between the good and the bad. To him, Adam gave the secret knowledge that would eventually be known as Kabbalah.

- The preference for the herdsman, who lived in a house of skin and milked the udder, over the farmer, who lived in a house of mud and sprouted the seed, reveals an ancient animosity of those who herded sheep, goat, cattle and camel towards settled agriculturists who set up farms and canals and blocked the passage of their animals. Abrahamic lore favours the nomad.
- The story has its roots in Mesopotamian mythology. The shepherd Dumuzid and the farmer Enkimdu compete for the affection of the Goddess Inanna. She chooses the shepherd. The farmer-god Emesh and the shepherd-god Enten bring their dispute about which of them is better to the chief-god Enlil, who rules in favour of the shepherd.
- In Jewish lore, Cain is not the son of Adam but the son of either the Devil or a demon who raped Eve secretly.
- The 'mark of Cain' or 'curse of Cain' was considered to be a blackened face. In American lore, this was said to be the origin of the black race, a fiction introduced by European colonizers that was also used to justify slavery of Africans in the nineteenth century.
- Since Cain murders Abel with a stone, he dies when the stone house, built by his sons, caves in. In other traditions, he grows a horn that results in his grandson mistaking him for an animal and killing him by flinging a stone.
- In Christian lore, Eve had a dream of Cain drinking Abel's blood and to prevent this prophecy ensured they followed different professions and stayed away from each other. After his death, as per the Book of Enoch, Abel became the first of the martyrs crying out for vengeance against injustice.

- In Islamic lore, Eve gave birth to twins, one male and one female. Habil (Abel) was to marry Aqlima, who was the twin sister of Qabil (Cain). But Qabil wanted to marry her as she was more beautiful, and opposed this marriage and attacked Habil. Habil begged his brother to stop, warning him that the murderer carries not only the sin of murder but all the sins of the victim, for the victim is cleansed of all sins having befallen to the injustice of murder. But the words had no effect on Qabil. After the murder, Allah sent a raven to scratch the ground, to teach Qabil how to bury the corpse of his brother and hide his crime, filling Qabil with guilt and shame, for even when he thought he was alone, he had been seen by Allah. After the murder, the Devil went to Eve and told her that Abel was dead. But Eve did not know what 'dead' meant, so the Devil explained, 'he does not eat, drink, speak, move or breathe'. On learning this Eve wailed, becoming the first mourner.
- In Islamic lore, Adam and Hawa had a son called Seesh, who was taught ethics by Adam and told to fight Qabil and bring him back to God's way. But Qabil chose idolatry and built statues of Adam and Hawa and worshipped them instead. So Seesh killed Qabil and his entire clan.
- In Hindu traditions, Krishna is a herdsman and Balarama is a farmer. They are half-brothers, with a common father, who love each other. This is because both are embodiments of Vishnu and so manifestations of Atman (soul, or an expanded secure mind) that sees the other as part of the self. The creator Brahma's children always fight each other over property; this is indicative of *Aham* (ego, or a crumpled insecure mind), a failure to see the other as part of the self.

Idris Discovers Egypt

The children of Adam struggled to follow God's law. Very few, like Idris, abided by God's law as revealed to Seth. Idris, was a patient man. Late in life, God made him a prophet and he spread the word of God amongst his people. But his people, the residents of Babylon, were not interested in what he had to say. Rather than rebuke them, he decided to move away.

He travelled south from Mesopotamia and reached

the River Nile across the desert. He saw the lush fertile land on either side of the vast river that flowed north, full of date palms and papyrus reeds, and exclaimed, '*Subhan-allah*' (delightful is the creation of God). Thus, the land of Egypt came to be discovered.

Enoch followed God's law so well that he never died. He just disappeared one day and was taken by God to Heaven. But most of his followers disobeyed God's law. Tricked by the Devil, they indulged in violence and idolatry. Tired of humanity's repeated transgressions, God decided to flood the earth with torrential rain and start anew.

- This story of how Idris discovered Egypt is found only in Islamic lore. Idris is identified as Enoch in Jewish lore.
- The Book of Enoch was once part of Jewish and Christian lore. Composed around 2,000 years ago, it is not considered canonical anymore as it had too much information on demons and was seen to be inspired by dark forbidden forces. It speaks of fallen angels who copulated with humans, thus creating monsters to whom the angels taught technology. To destroy them, God needed to flood the earth. The archangel Uriel was sent to warn Noah, who would go on to build a boat to save the innocent and the faithful.

Noah's Ark

Of all humans, only one remained true to the law, Noah, who was Enoch's great grandson. He had heard of Enoch's visions—how good people are like obedient sheep and bad people are like disobedient wild animals. He tried to convince people to follow the law, but they mocked him for pretending to be a prophet and even accused him of being enchanted by the Devil.

God got Noah to build a gigantic boat that would accommodate his family and a pair of every kind of bird and animal. This was built on land, and everyone thought Noah had gone mad. Why would anyone build a giant boat on land? But Noah had faith. He did what God told him to do. He built the boat, populated it with life and lived on it with his wife, his three sons and their wives, patiently waiting for the foretold flood to arrive.

Then, the rains came like rivers gushing from the skies, covering all earth with water, drowning all those who mocked and insulted Noah, and lived life against the law. Noah's boat, which stood on land, was now afloat in water that had consumed the earth, surrounded by pillars and sheets of rain, with dark storm clouds above, witness to God's wrath.

After many weeks, the rains stopped. Noah sent out a dove to check if there was land for his boat to dock. For days, it returned home exhausted with no leaf or sprig in its beak to indicate dry land. One day, it returned with an olive branch, and Noah finally landed his boat at a spot that later, when the waters further receded, turned out to be a mountain peak named Ararat.

God promised Noah that he would never wipe out humanity. Noah was told never to shed human blood. And to mark this renewed connection between God and humans, God created the rainbow in the sky.

Noah's sons then proceeded in different directions to populate the earth. From his eldest son, Shem, came the Semites.

- Noah's three sons and their wives are supposed to have created all the peoples of the world. Noah's son Shem gave birth to the Semitic races. The term Semitic, like Caucasian, emerged in the eighteenth century. Over time, it gave rise to the word anti-Semitic, a word used for people who were ideologically opposed to Jewish people and harboured a virulent hatred for them, denying them the right to property and begrudging their success in banking and enterprise.
- In Christian lore, Noah's boat or ark is the representation of the Christian Church. He who takes refuge in it will survive the 'flood' and gain salvation. Noah was the first man who, on sight of the dove returning with the olive branch, raised his palms Heavenwards in the gesture of prayer, now called 'orans', indicative of surrender.
- In Islamic lore, Noah is called Nuh, a prophet after Adam but before Abraham. He had a fourth son, Yam, who did not believe his father. He did not board the boat and so drowned in the flood.
- Noah's wife, Namaah, was a disbeliever and did not join him on the boat.
- When the flood came to an end, Noah made a sweet dish using *nus*, dried fruit and grain. This came to be known as Noah's pudding.
- In Christian lore, Noah created the first vineyard, and was the first human to get drunk on wine. His son, Ham, saw him sleeping naked. Instead of covering his father, he laughed and told his brothers about their father's drunken and naked state. The brothers then covered their father. For his behaviour, Ham was cursed that his children would grow up to be slaves.
- In Irish mythology, Noah has a granddaughter called Cesair, who realizes she has no place on the ship. So she builds her own ships and takes men and women with her to a land to the West. Three ships with fifty women and three men reach Ireland. The women share the men among themselves. However, two of the men die and the third runs away, unable to cope with the demand. Cesair dies alone and miserable at this failed rescue. The third man named Fintan—who ran away from the women, survived the flood by transforming magically into a salmon and then a hawk and finally back into a human—tells this tale to future generations.

Hud and the Storms in Aad

From Noah's son Shem came the Semites. Shem had a son called Aram, who had a son called Uz, who had a son called Hud. Hud lived in the prosperous city of Aad, which was full of markets, buildings and temples housing idols.

But Hud grew up learning that these idols were false gods. He was told about Allah, the one true god, by his mother.

Allah made Hud a prophet and told him to reveal the truth about God to the people of Aad. Hud went about trying to convince the people of his land to turn away from idolatry and false gods and to follow God's law. But no one believed him until one day, a great wind came and blew away the people of Aad and covered the great city with sand.

- The story of Hud and the city of Aad comes from Arabic traditions. Hud has been referred to in pre-Islamic inscriptions of Arabia. There is no reference to Prophet Hud in Jewish or Christian lore.
- Verses in the Quran refer to Hud's attempts to save Aad but the people of Aad refuse to listen to the prophet's words. They see a cloud approaching the city and insist that it is simply a rain cloud and not a storm cloud that will sweep them away.
- In one Jewish legend, Solomon learns of a walled city with no gates. In it, his djinns discover an eagle which is 700 years old but he does not know where the entrance is. The djinns find the eagle's elder brother, who is 900 years old, but even he does not know the entrance. Then, the eagle's eldest brother, who is 1,300 years old, remembers that his father had said that the gate was on the western side, but it was covered by sand. When Solomon gets the sand removed and finds the gate, he enters the city and finds within a silver statue. And, under the statue are the lines that humble the arrogant Solomon, known for his wealth, power and knowledge: 'This is the statue of Shaddad, the son of Aad, builder of this city, master of a million kingdoms, friends to million vassals, conqueror of a million foes, who could not resist the angel of death.'

Saleh and the She-Camel of Thamud

Many generations later, Saleh was told by Allah to warn people against worshipping false gods and idols in the city of Thamud. The residents challenged the prophet to prove that Allah was the one true god. So, Saleh prayed to God and a miracle happened: a mountain split open and out emerged a pregnant she-camel that gave birth to a calf.

Saleh said, 'To show your faith in Allah, share the water of Thamud with this she-camel and her baby. One day, you drink the water, and allow her to drink it the next day. On the day she drinks the water, she will provide milk to quench your thirst. Maintain this discipline and all will be well.' But the people did not listen. They killed the she-camel and in sorrow, the calf howled thrice before dying. Saleh interpreted this to mean that Thamud would be destroyed in three days.

Within three days, volcanoes and earthquakes destroyed the city and all its inhabitants who did not let Allah's she-camel graze in peace even though she gave them milk.

- The story of Prophet Saleh is referred to in the Quran. It is part of Islamic lore and finds no mention in Jewish or Christian lore.
- The Quran emphasizes the importance of obedience to prophets out of the fear of God. In various verses, prophets such as Noah, Hud, Saleh and Lut say, 'Fear God and obey me'. In each case, the non-believers are destroyed by floods, storms, earthquakes, volcanoes and rains of fire.
- Recent studies have shown that domesticated single-humped camels were not used in the region of Israel and Levant, i.e., the Near East, until 1000 BCE. So, the early leaders in Biblical lore such as Abraham did not ride camels despite such popular depictions in art. Camels, first domesticated in Arabia, came to India with Arabs around 1000 CE as revealed in the Rajasthani epic of Pabuji. The double-humped camel of Central Asia was domesticated much earlier and they are referred to even in Vedic literature.

Tower of Babel

Noah's descendants settled in a land called Shinar. They all spoke the same language and lived as one community. They decided to build a great tower that would take them to the sky, to Eden.

Layer upon layer, the tower was built, reaching up to the sky. Some said this was done because the people wanted to peep into Heaven. Others said it was just a meaningless act of imaginary achievements to overcome boredom. Whatever be the case, God saw it and realized that people need to look at each other more than they look at the sky. So, he made sure that people spoke in different tongues, unable to understand each other as they did before.

Humanity split into various communities and clans and tribes and nations. Different language groups lived different lives, in different regions, pursuing different professions, finding different purposes. Diversity gave rise to collaboration in some places and competition in others. People focused on working on relationships rather than endless ambitions.

- Mesopotamians built temples atop towers known as ziggurats. They believed gods created humans to serve them. Humans could speak to the gods through priests who later became kings.
- The story of the tower is influenced by the Mesopotamian myth of Enmerkar, the king of Uruk, who finds favour with Inanna, the goddess of love and war, by building her a great 'tower'. To ensure her love, he promises to build an even greater tower. He then uses this ziggurat as an excuse to unite the kingdom around the Euphrates and Tigris rivers in a 'single tongue'. He sends emissaries to neighbouring rival kings to tell them to send him tribute, threatening to destroy their lands and disperse their people if they do not accept him as the one chosen by Inanna. The king of Aratta resists but is eventually overwhelmed by the wealth and power of Enmerkar, who is the favoured one. In this story, the emissaries are unable to remember Enmerkar's long threats and so writing is invented to facilitate political communication.
- In Islamic lore, the tower is built by the Pharaoh of Egypt to challenge God. In another version, it is built by Nimrod. People are divided as they end up speaking seventy-two languages. The original tongue is retained only by one prophet named Eber, who is an ancestor of Abraham. There are versions where there is no tower: people from every direction are brought to a place called Babil by the wind, given different languages, and then scattered again by the wind.
- The Quran also refers to Babylon as Babil. Here, in an abandoned tower, hang the angels Harut and Marut, upside down like bats, teaching humans magic, warning them that it is a test of faith, for the faithful do not submit to the charms of magic.
- Another Mesopotamian hymn suggests that while Enlil, the chief god, unites people with one language, his rival half-brother divides them with multiple tongues.
- The idea of humans building towers to reach the sky and maybe the abode of god, only to come crashing down, as well as the rise of multiple languages dividing a common people, is a recurring theme in many tribal mythologies such as that of the Kongo people of Africa and Karen of Burma.
- The Church of Jesus Christ of the Latter-day Saints (popularly known as the Mormon Church) believes that the Tower of Babel is a historical fact. According to Mormons, a man called Jared prayed to God that his language survives. He made his way via the valley of Nimrod to the Americas, where the original language continued to be spoken.

Gods of Mesopotamia

The land of Mesopotamia between the rivers Tigris and Euphrates experienced flooding every year. When the waters receded, the land was covered with silt, and so was fertile. People planted seeds and reaped a rich bounty. They also used the riverbank clay to make bricks and build cities with towers that reached the sky. In these towers they kept images of gods.

The gods were many but seven were most prominent: Anu of the sky, Enki of the water and magic and civilization, Enlil of the wind and storms, Ninhursag of the mountains and kingship, Inanna of Venus, love and war, Sin of the Moon, and Shamash of the Sun.

The people of these cities composed epics about warrior gods like Enki's son Marduk, who defeated ancient dragons like Tiamat, and turned the dragon's corpse into the land for cities above the flood waters. If Tiamat was chaos, Marduk brought order. If Tiamat caused waters to flood, Marduk caused waters to ebb.

People spoke different tongues in different cities and each city had a different god. When one city conquered another, the conqueror's god was placed atop the tower and the god of the conquered city was placed below. When a queen came from another city, her god was placed in the temples too. Thus, every city had many gods, brought in by queens and conquerors.

The gods, the people of these cities believed, created humans out of clay just as humans created idols out of clay. Gods created humans to serve them: to work in the fields, take care of cattle and make offerings to feed them. Everyone had a purpose. The blind were made musicians, eunuchs served in harems and barren women became prostitutes.

When humans angered the gods, they were punished with floods, droughts and plagues. So, humans served gods, and made sure the gods were fed and happy all the time.

The gods jealously guarded their immortality and did not share it with humans. Enki tricked Adapa into believing that the gods would poison him; so, Adapa did not eat even the fruit of immortality when the gods offered it to him in gratitude for his work and songs of praise.

Gilgamesh, the king of Uruk, was denied immortality, even though he was part-god. He had to accept that he too would die like his beloved friend Enkidu and live in the realm of shadows, eating dust and serving the gods of the afterlife.

But some were lucky, like Utnaphistim, who survived the flood and was given immortality by the gods. Others like Tammuz, loved by both Ishtar and her sister Ereshkigal, spent half the time on earth, in the land of the living, with Ishtar in summer and spring, and the rest of the time with Ereshkigal in the underworld, the land of the dead, in autumn and winter.

- Mesopotamian mythology is an umbrella term for myths that span nearly 2,000 years involving various cultures such as those of Sumeria, Akkad, Assyria and Babylon. These tales influenced Abrahamic lore a great deal. Ideas such as the jealous god, of people submitting to a god's will, of being punished by flood, drought and plague for transgressions, the value of the number seven and a god who regenerates every year can be traced to tales found on Mesopotamian clay tablets.
- The Abrahamic discomfort with polytheism and idolatry is clearly linked to the proximity of Jewish people with the great city states and empires of Mesopotamia. The monotheist communities of Canaan linked their sufferings to their interactions with polytheistic communities.
- In Judaism, Christianity and Islam, God 'writes' the law, revealing how these religions have roots in Mesopotamia, home of the oldest and most widely used script in the world, cuneiform.

BOOK THREE

Out of Mesopotamia

Abram and Nimrod

In the city of Ur lived an idol-maker and idol-worshipper named Terah, also known as Azar. He had a son called Abram, who carried the idols in a cart to be sold in the market. One day, the idols fell to the ground and Abram realized that these idols could not put themselves back together. He doubted the power of idols as they could not fix themselves when broken.

Abram wondered who God truly was. Who was a true god? Was God a star? But stars set, as did the sun and the moon. He sought the one who caused the stars, the sun and the moon to set. Pleased with his doubt and curiosity, Allah appeared before him and identified himself. Abram bowed and surrendered completely to God, and was asked to tell the whole world about the one true god, who is Allah. Abram agreed wholeheartedly.

No one believed Abram's claim that there was only one true god, and that there was no need for worshipping idols. The local king, Nimrod, told him that as king he had the power to punish people, kill enemies or forgive them, and let them live. Abram argued that despite all his power, a human king could not make the sun rise from the west. Nimrod then ordered Abram to worship fire. Abram said that he would rather worship water, which douses fire. So Nimrod told him to worship water. Abram said he would rather worship the clouds, which carry all the water. Nimrod told him to worship clouds. Abram said he would rather worship the wind, which pushes the clouds. Nimrod told him to worship wind. Abram said he would rather worship humans, who withstand the wind. Exasperated, Nimrod threw Abram in the fire. But to everyone's surprise, the flames became cool and did not harm Abram, for he was protected by God.

Nimrod then attacked Abram with a huge army, but Abram was protected by a swarm of mosquitoes that dispersed Nimrod's army. A lame mosquito entered Nimrod's ears and drove him mad.

Thereafter, no one bothered Abram, though no one believed what he had to say either.

But the public humiliation of Abram caused him to leave Ur. He left with his father, his brother, and his wife, Sarai.

- The story of Abram's confrontation with Nimrod comes from Jewish and Islamic traditions. In the Quran, Nimrod's name is not found, but he is probably the 'king' who keeps arguing with Ibrahim against monotheism.
- In popular understanding, Nimrod is considered to be a strong but dim-witted person. He is also associated with the building of the Tower of Babel.
- In Jewish lore (*Midrash Rabba*), Abram's brother Haran is depicted as an opportunist, who cannot decide whether to follow Abram or Nimrod. He plans to declare that he is a follower of the winning side. When he declares that he is the follower of Abram, Nimrod has him thrown in fire, and he is burnt alive as he lacks faith in God. In the Christian Bible, this story is not mentioned. It is only said that Haran dies before his father, Terah.
- The story of the mosquitoes driving Nimrod mad and destroying his army comes from Islamic traditions.
- In the Church of Latter-day Saints, the Book of Abraham is a canonical text. Published in the nineteenth century by the founder of the church, Joseph Smith, it is allegedly based on the Egyptian papyri that record the story of Abraham's early life, including how he was rescued by angels when pagan priests tried to sacrifice him, and how Abraham was exposed to astronomy. Non-Mormon Egyptologists as well as biblical scholars find this claim inauthentic.

Abram Marries Sarai

Ur was located near the delta of Mesopotamia. Abram first moved upstream towards the source of the rivers Tigris and Euphrates. There, near the city of Harran, his father died. His brother decided to settle there, but Abram continued his journey, moving south along the Mediterranean to Canaan.

A famine in Canaan forced Abram and Sarai to move south to Egypt. Fearing that people would kill him in order to claim Sarai for themselves, Abram told everyone that Sarai was his sister. The pharaoh of Egypt liked Sarai; so he gave Abram gifts of goat and sheep and camel, and took his 'sister' Sarai to his palace to be part of his harem. But then Egypt was struck by a series of plagues. On investigation, the pharaoh learned that Sarai was Abram's wife and God was unhappy that the king had coveted another man's wife. Abram was accused of lying, but he clarified that Sarai was his wife, as well as his sister, for they had a common father but not a common mother. So, the pharaoh let Sarai go and asked Abram to leave his land with the many gifts of goat, sheep and camel that he had received. Amongst his many gifts to Abram and Sarai was a woman called Hagar.

- Abram is the older name of Abraham and Sarai is the older name of Sarah. God changes their names later.
- This story reveals the transformation of Abram, from a city dweller to a nomad with no land to his name, a transformation inspired by his faith in the one true god who created nature and rejection of false gods. He moves around with his herds and his family, and is often at odds with settled communities.

- The incident of the pharaoh wanting to marry Sarah, assuming she is Abraham's sister, happens again with Abimelech, the king of Gerar, indicating how beautiful Sarah was.
- These early stories of Abram do not refer to chariots pulled by horses, which were invented around 2000 BCE in Central Asia. People rode carriages pulled by mules. The earliest recorded battle involving horse-drawn war-chariots takes place in 1300 BCE, between the Hittites and Egyptians, in the region of Canaan. This is also the time when we get the first epigraphic evidence of the Vedas in the form of a clay inscription of the Mittani people referring to Vedic gods Indra, Varuna and Natasya. Abram's story clearly belongs to this early time, before 1500 BCE. Chariots are very much part of the story of Moses taking people out of Egypt four centuries later.

Abram's Well

Abram moved to the city of Gerar in Palestine. Here, too, he told everyone that his wife was his sister for her protection as well as his. Here, too, the local king, Abimelech, took Sarai into his palace but let her go as soon as dreams and plagues revealed that Sarai was Abram's wife. Here, too, the king gave cattle, goats and sheep as appeasement, and here, too, Abram's prayers ensured that the land was no more afflicted by plagues.

In the land of Gerar, Abram dug a well for his family and flock. This got him in trouble with the king's servants over who owned the well. Abimelech came with his army and saw Abram stake his claim forcefully, so unlike the Abram who had meekly surrendered his wife earlier, and so, he recognized Abram's ownership of the well. Abram was a changed man, ready to claim what was rightfully his.

- The escape to Egypt and wives being presented as sisters in foreign lands are recurring themes in the Bible. Abraham's son Isaac also has similar experiences.
- The idea of Abram's well connects him with the land. He is not simply one who takes; he also adds value wherever he goes.
- Those who wish to see biblical lore as historical accounts have identified a well in Beersheba, Israel, as Abraham's well, which was later restored by Isaac.

Abram and Lot

Abram returned to Canaan. In fact, he and his nephew, Lot, had so many sheep and goats that there was not enough pasture for all. This led to fights within the family, and so Abram requested Lot to move to another land.

Abram gave him the choice of travelling north or south, but Lot chose to travel east towards Jordan, where there was a large waterbody and much-irrigated pastures, and where stood the twin cities of Sodom and Gomorrah.

But separation did not mean the end of relationships and responsibility. For, when the king of Elam attacked Sodom and imprisoned its people, including Lot, Abram came to their rescue with his army.

- In Islamic lore, Lot is a prophet. His name is Lut. He tries to convince the people of Sodom and Gomorrah to follow the path of Allah. But they indulge in idolatry.
- The story draws attention to how prosperity brings conflict between brothers, leading to separation; yet, there is need for alliances.

Sodom and Gomorrah

Once, two angels came to visit Lot. He invited them to his house for a meal. At night, a mob of men from Sodom knocked on Lot's door, demanding to have sex with the two handsome strangers. Lot did not open the door and offered to give them his two daughters instead. But the men refused. They knocked and knocked on the door, scaring Lot's family, but he refused to open the door, determined to protect his guests at all costs. The mob finally dispersed.

The two angels told Lot to leave the city of Sodom immediately for God planned to destroy it with fire and brimstone. 'And do not look behind to look at the burning city after you have escaped,' they warned. Lot, his wife and his two daughters did as advised. But Lot's wife turned back to see the burning city and was turned into a pillar of salt.

Lot and his daughters escaped to the hills, where his daughters got Lot drunk, had sex with him and bore his children.

- Historically, Sodom and Gomorrah have been used as metaphors for homosexuality. The word 'sodomite' was used pejoratively for men who indulge in oral and anal sex.
- People have argued that the sin of the people of Sodom that angered God was them not treating guests and strangers with respect, and not homosexuality.

- Those who condemn the homosexual desires of Sodom are not so forthcoming in condemning incest, which is also part of the story.
- The Dead Sea, with its high salt content, is associated with Lot's wife, who turns into a pillar of salt.
- Islam does not accept the story of Lot committing incest with his daughters. The acceptance of incest, and even heterosexual rape, but condemnation of homosexuality, has been the cause of many debates in Jewish and Christian circles.
- In Islamic lore, Lot's wife, who turns into a pillar of salt, and Noah's wife, who drowns in the flood, are examples of women who do not listen to their husbands and so are punished by God.
- The Hindu Puranas also tell the story of cities being destroyed. Krishna's city of Dwarka was cursed to be swept away by the sea. Shiva destroyed three magical flying cities (Tripura) with a single arrow, as the asuras who resided there, as per different retellings, were either too hedonistic or too monastic.

Abram becomes Abraham

Three angels visited Abram and told him that he would be the father of as many nations as there are stars in the sky. But Sarai was old; her womb withered. She doubted if this would happen. As she doubted God, the angels said her son's rights would be contested, and this would result in generations of rivalry.

The doubtful Sarai passed on her handmaiden, Hagar, an Egyptian, to Abram so that he could father the prophesized children with her. Thus was born Ishmael. But a few years later, to everyone's surprise, Sarai did bear a child in her hundredth year. The boy was named Isaac.

Abram realized that God always keeps his word. He, too, had to keep his word. So, Abram sacrificed heifers, rams, goats and birds to God. Each was cut into two pieces to represent what should happen to him if he lost faith in God and transgressed God's law. God, in turn, passed between the pieces in the form of a flame, informing Abram that his numerous children would one day inherit the land on which he stood, between river and sea, but only after 400 years of wandering, suffering and exile in a foreign land, provided they worshipped him alone, and not false gods. This was the 'covenant of pieces' between Abram and God.

God then renamed Sarai as Sarah, which means princess, and Abram as Abraham, which means father of many nations. A new era started.

- In Islam, Abraham is referred to as Ibrahim. He is the first monotheist (*hanif*, in Arabic) and the first to submit to God's love and law (Muslim). He is most referred to in the Quran, after Moses. His father is often identified as Azar, not Terah, though some say Azar is his uncle.
- In Islamic lore, Sarah is not the daughter of Terah but his niece. This makes her Abraham's cousin.
- In an attempt to show all religions as the same and from the same source, some Hindus argue that the name Abraham comes from 'Brahma'—the Hindu god of creation—and the name 'Sarah' comes from Saraswati, Brahma's consort, knowledge. Also, the story of Abraham being saved from fire is seen as mirroring the story of Prahlad, who is saved by Vishnu from the fire into which he is thrown by his own father, Hiranyakashipu.

Waters of Zamzam

Soon after Isaac's birth, God told Abraham to institute the practice of circumcision amongst all men in his family. This was the covenant of blood to establish a bond between God and man. So, Abraham circumcised himself and all the men of his tribe. Ishmael was fourteen then. Isaac was barely eight days old when he was circumcised. Ishmael would taunt Isaac that he was a lesser man as his covenant was involuntary, forced upon him when he was just a baby.

Sarah became insecure that her son, Isaac, would lose his inheritance to Ishmael, who was the firstborn. So, she forced Abraham to send the mother and son to the desert.

Abraham took Hagar and Ishmael to Arabia. Near the ruins of Kabah, the House of God once built by Adam and Hawa, Abraham gave Hagar bread and water and turned away. When Hagar asked him why he was abandoning them, Abraham refused to answer. She then asked if this was the will of God. He nodded. So, she accepted his decision for she was sure that God would provide for her.

The water soon ran out and mother and son were soon consumed by intense thirst in the searing heat of the desert. Ishmael fainted and Hagar ran between two hills, Safa and Marwa, seven times, looking for water. But found none. This was the place where Adam and Hawa once stood, where they were united after a period of separation upon being cast out of Eden.

Hagar feared Allah had forsaken her but then the angel Gabriel appeared and asked her to dig just under where Ishmael lay exhausted, dehydrated. Sure enough, she found water oozing out of the ground. She dug and found a spring.

That water, the Zamzam, formed an oasis, where many caravans and traders came, creating a prosperous city where Hagar lived happily with her son.

- In Islamic lore, Hagar is referred to as Hajar. She is the daughter of the Pharaoh and the wife of Abraham, not Sarah's handmaiden.
- The Hajj pilgrimage involves the Sai (seeking), when people walk between the two peaks of Safa and Marwa seven times, running in between (when Hajar could not see her son) and walking towards the end (when Hajar could see her son from the slopes). This is located right next to the Kabah.
- The name Zamzam comes from the phrase '*zome, zome*', which means 'stop flowing' as Hagar/Hajar tried to contain the water from the spring that appeared to quench her son's thirst. The well is located sixty feet to the east of the Kabah. The water is collected by the faithful.

Ishmael's Wives

God had not abandoned Hagar. He sent the celestial winged beast, Buraq, so that Abraham, having spent the day with Sarah, would travel through the skies and spend every night with Hagar. Abraham continued to travel from time to time after both his wives died, to ensure the welfare of his sons.

Once he came and found no one in Ishmael's tent except a strange woman who identified herself as Ishmael's wife. She kept complaining a lot, was unhappy with what she had and had no faith in God. Abraham had to leave before Ishmael returned, but he asked Ishmael's wife to convey a message to his son: change the threshold. Ishmael on hearing this message realized his father wanted him to divorce this woman, who Abraham felt was not a good wife.

A few months later, Abraham returned and found another woman in Ishmael's tent. She did not complain, was happy with what she had and had faith in God. Abraham had to leave before Ishmael returned but he asked Ishmael's new wife to convey a message to his son: keep the threshold. Ishmael on hearing this message realized his father was happy with his wife, who was a good woman.

- The Jurhum tribe wanted access to the water of the Zamzam well and so gave wives to Ishmael. The Jurhum was an Arab tribe from the north, and that is how Abraham's son became an Arab.
- The Jurhum tribe became the guardian of the Kabah and the Zamzam. When ousted by the Khuza tribe, they collected all the treasures offered to Kabah, filled the well of Zamzam and fled. Many generations later, Prophet Muhammad's grandfather rediscovered the Zamzam well.
- Prophet Muhammad's lineage is traced to Ishmael through Adnan, and before that through Qedar. The Arabs even today categorize themselves into two groups: those who are native to Arabia and those who are settlers, descended from the immigrant Ishmael. The Arabs were further classified into those who lived in tents and travelled as nomads across the desert, and those who lived in houses of stone and in houses near oases.

Building the Kabah

Abraham helped Ishmael rebuild Kabah, the first mosque built by Adam, which was now in ruins. This is where angels had prayed before creation.

Abraham stood on a rock, and Ishmael sat on his shoulders, to complete the building. When it was ready, he placed there a black stone, originally transparent when it came from Eden, but now black due to the sins of man. It contained all the promises humans and prophets made to uphold God's law at the beginning of time. Abraham put it in the eastern corner of the Kabah so it could face the rain-bearing east wind.

This stone was once the angel under whose watch Adam and Eve had eaten the fruit of the forbidden tree. For his negligence, the angel had been turned into stone and cast down to earth. The stone fell on earth like a flaming meteor, helping Adam locate Eve in Mecca. This rock was situated on a mountaintop and could speak, but it would stay silent until the Day of Judgement, when it would separate the believers from the non-believers.

- The rock on which Abraham stood to help Ishmael build the upper part of the House of God (station of Ibrahim, with marks believed to be his footprint) and the black stone in the eastern corner are the only fragments from the original Kabah that still survive.
- Originally, the room contained the horns of the ram that God sent for Abraham's sacrifice in place of his favourite son.
- The Kabah was even venerated as the shrine of Allah even before Islam was founded in the seventh century CE. Allah, or Al Lah in pre-Islamic times, referred to one of the most powerful and the highest god of all Arabic tribes. But over time, people filled the space within and around the Kabah with idols of various gods, including one Hubal, who was associated with fortune-telling. Some have speculated that there were 360 images, one for each day of the traditional Arabic year. They have also speculated that the practice of going around the Kabah in a counter-clockwise direction was practised even before Muhammad's time. So sacred was Kabah that war was forbidden in the region around it even in pre-Islamic times.
- The Kabah is covered with a black cloth that carries a strip of gold embroidery. It is replaced every year. The old fabric is torn and distributed. Earlier, it was draped with a different coloured cloth several times a year. There were many disputes over the colour of the cloth, and how much cloth could be put on the structure and when, until a decision was taken to regulate and restrict the practice.

Binding of Isaac

One day, God told Abraham to sacrifice his son. Abraham did not question the decision. He climbed a mountain with his son, an axe and some wood. Atop the mountain he gathered some stones to form an altar and placed the wood on the stone altar. He then bound Isaac's hands and feet as one binds a sacrificial animal and placed him atop the wood.

Isaac realized he was the sacrifice, and though his heart was filled with fear, he accepted his father's decision—a voluntary act of faith in God.

As Abraham was about to cut his son's throat, God stopped him. Pleased with his display of unconditional obedience, Isaac was released and Abraham found, rather miraculously, a mountain goat, trapped in the bushes. This was offered to God in Isaac's place.

- In Jewish and Christian traditions, the son offered for sacrifice is Isaac but in Islamic traditions it is Ishmael. The argument offered is that God asked for Abraham's favourite son. The son was not named. Hence, the difference in traditions.
- The story of the sacrifice of the favourite son is linked to the festival of Bakra Id, where Muslims commemorate the event by sacrificing (*qurbani*) a goat to God.
- In Islamic tradition, Ibrahim was tempted three times by the Devil during this incident: first, appealing to the father not to kill the son; the second time, appealing to the mother to stop the father from taking her son; and the third time, appealing to the son to stop the father. Each time stones were hurled at the Devil. So, 'stoning the Devil' is a ritual act performed during the Hajj.
- Many ancient cultures did practice child sacrifice. Stories such as these come from a time when these practices were frowned upon. The Israelites do accuse their neighbours of sacrificing children to idols and false gods. The Hindu Puranas tell the story of one Sunahshepa, who is offered as sacrifice by his own father in exchange for payment and how at the last moment the gods stop the sacrifice of the boy.

The Death of Sarah

When Sarah saw Abraham taking her son Isaac to the mountain, she realized why and she died instantly, unable to bear the shock. Abraham bought a cave to bury her.

The Hittite who sold the field in which the cave was located first offered it for free; but Abraham, who was a nomad and had no land, wanted to take no chances. For a land given as gift can be reclaimed in the future. He and Isaac buried Sarah in the cave that would one day also be his own resting place and that of his son and his son's son.

- In Jewish lore, the news that Isaac had been sacrificed by Abraham caused Sarah to wail. But on learning Isaac had been spared, she was filled with so much happiness that she died. Thus, her request that Ishmael be sent to the desert comes much before the story of the sacrifice.
- Many characters in the Bible have very long lives. Adam lives for 930 years, Noah for 950. Adam's grandfather, Methuselah, lived the longest, 969 years. Rationalists argue that these numbers refer to months, not years. So, these ages would refer to men in their eighties. Others argue that before Noah's flood the world was filled with special elements that allowed humans to live longer. With the passage of time, lifespan fell, and so Sarah lived till just 127.
- That in ancient times humans lived longer and were taller are themes found in Jain mythology too. As time passed, people became shorter and lived shorter lives. This makes the forefathers literal not just metaphorical 'giants'.
- The Cave of the Patriarchs is where Abraham and Sarah, Isaac and Rebecca, and Jacob and Leah are buried. In the ancient times, land rights were established by claiming, 'This is where our ancestors were buried.' Located in Hebron, it is a site where a mosque was built a thousand years ago. Christian Crusaders built a church over it. This was again replaced by a mosque when the Muslims took over the city in the twelfth century. The state of Israel divided the mosque and built a synagogue there in 1967.

BOOK FOUR

Refuge in Egypt

Rebecca

Isaac was thirty-seven at the time of his mother's death. He mourned her for three years. At forty, he had no wife, and so Abraham sent his servant to find a wife for him. 'Choose not one from the Canaanites for they worship idols. Choose from my own people in the east, in Mesopotamia. Choose wisely.'

The servant travelled to Mesopotamia, to the land from where Abraham had migrated a long time ago, and looked for a woman who was generous and kind, one who would offer water to a stranger without hesitation and water to his animals too, even though that required a lot of effort.

He found such a woman in Rebecca, who was kind and generous to him even though he was a stranger. It turned out that she was the grand-niece of Abraham, who had settled at the spot where Abraham's father had died, at the source of the Tigris and Euphrates.

Abraham's servant gave her gold bracelets and a nose ring as gifts of betrothal. Rebecca accepted and was brought to wed Isaac. When she arrived at Abraham's camp, she saw a man praying in the afternoon. She was touched by his spiritual aura. 'Who is he?' she asked. And the servant said that he was Isaac, her husband to be. Much pleased, she covered her face with a veil that he would unveil on the wedding night.

Like in the case of Sarah before her, three miracles marked Rebecca's tent: a cloud always hovered above it creating shade; the bread she baked never spoiled; and a candle burnt on its own through the Sabbath to mark the day of rest.

Like Abraham, Isaac was forced to leave Canaan because of a famine, but God did not let him go outside Canaan and made him take refuge on the border of Egypt, in Palestine, in the city of Gerar.

Here he re-dug the wells his father had once dug. Like his father, he told everyone that Rebecca was actually his sister. Like Sarah, Rebecca, too, did not bear children for many years, and when everyone lost hope, twenty years after her marriage, she finally became pregnant with twins.

- Rebecca like Sarah is very beautiful and needs to be protected from kings of neighbouring lands. Like Sarah, she bears children when she is old. But she does not doubt God. Like Sarah, she is linked to abundance and fertility, which is why both their tents are linked to clouds, bread and lamps.
- Rebecca's arrival in Isaac's life marks Abraham's reconnection with his old family.
- As per Jewish writers, Rebecca veils herself before her marriage on seeing the man she would wed, thus asserting her independence. If she wore the veil after her marriage, she would be declaring her complete submission to him.

Jacob and Esau

Rebecca's unborn twins started fighting when they were still in her womb, causing her great distress. The one who would be named Esau would try to leave her womb when she passed an idol, and the one who would be named Jacob would try to leave her womb every time he heard discussions on God's law.

Esau was protected by the angel Samael and Jacob by Michael, and their fights inside the womb were repeated in God's presence by the two angels. Esau valued the material world of pleasure and conquest. Jacob valued the spiritual world that would follow this material world. They argued over who should be the firstborn; Jacob finally let Esau be born first after Esau threatened to kill their mother. Esau was born covered in filth, too weak to be circumcised, but Jacob was born clean and pure, already circumcised.

Rebecca saw the flaws in Esau but Isaac loved Esau to a fault, overlooking his flaws because Esau would always say the right things and bring him food to eat. Isaac never realized that the food being served was wild game meat forbidden by God's laws.

- The tension between Esau and Jacob mirrors the tension between Cain and Abel, Nimrod and Abraham, Ishmael and Isaac. The idea of brothers fighting over inheritance is a key theme in Hindu mythology, too; for instance, in epics such as the Ramayana and the Mahabharata.
- In Islam, Jacob is called Yakub and is mentioned as a venerable prophet along with his grandfather Ibrahim, his father Ishaq, his uncle Ismail and his son Yusuf (Joseph). He was taught monotheism by Ibrahim himself. The story of his rivalry with Esau is not found in the Quran but is found in Islamic commentaries.

The Death of Abraham

Esau broke so many of God's laws, from adultery to murder, that God decided that the old man Abraham had to die to be spared the pain of learning that his own grandson did not value God's law.

One day, when Esau returned from his hunt, he was hungry and found Jacob cooking lentils. 'Why not meat?' he asked. Jacob informed him that this was the food of mourning and the family was mourning Abraham, who had died while he was away hunting. Esau mocked this tradition, and the belief in resurrection of the dead and the idea of an afterlife.

Esau then asked his brother to give him the lentil soup as he was very hungry. Jacob agreed to feed him but on a condition: 'If you do not believe in God or his laws or the spiritual life that follows the material life, or in resurrection of the dead, why do you not give away your birthrights, as a scion of Abraham, over these to me?' Esau agreed with a scoff, not realizing what he had done.

- After the death of Sarah, Abraham took another concubine and had many children by her. Polygamy is referred to nearly forty times in the Bible, but the practice came to be frowned upon by later Jewish and Christian communities. Monogamy became the norm in ancient Greek, Roman and later European societies, though the rich and powerful did have mistresses and visited brothels. The Mormon community of America, in its early years, tried to reintroduce polygamy, but this practice was condemned and finally rejected by later members.
- The phrase 'mess of pottage' is used to refer to something cheap that is bought carelessly in exchange for something of much greater value. It refers to Jacob's lentil soup (or 'pottage') meal (or 'mess') that cost Esau his birthright.
- Jacob's red lentil soup is recreated as a popular dish in Jewish communities even today.
- Since Abel loses his life to violence, we find different methods used by brothers to prevent confrontation. Negotiation is used to separate Abraham and Lot; rules are used to separate Isaac and Ishmael; trickery is used to separate Jacob and Esau.

Esau Loses His Birthright

As Isaac grew older, he became blind. He feared he would die soon. So, he prepared to pass on his blessings, all his inheritance, to his firstborn. He told Esau to bring him some venison to eat.

Rebecca realized that after eating this meal, in gratitude, her husband would give his blessings to Esau. So, she told Jacob to bring her two baby goats so that she could prepare a dish that Isaac would enjoy. She then dressed Jacob in Esau's robes and covered his soft arms with animal skin to make them rough and hairy like Esau's. She told Jacob to serve this meal to Isaac pretending to be Esau.

Jacob hesitated as this was trickery. But Rebecca told him this was necessary as Esau did not believe in God and was not worthy of the blessing. Jacob feared that his father would curse him. Rebecca told him that she would receive the curse on his behalf. Thus convinced, Jacob offered the meal to his father while pretending to be Esau.

Isaac was a bit suspicious for the meal had come too soon. Also, Esau's voice sounded softer, more like Jacob's. So, Isaac smelt the robes of the man who served him his meal and felt his hairy arms. They smelt like Esau's robes and felt like Esau's arms and so he blessed Jacob, thinking him to be Esau.

'May God give you the dew of Heaven and the fat of the earth, abundance of new grain and wine. May peoples serve you, and nations bow to you. Be master over your brothers, and let your mother's sons bow to you. Cursed be they who curse you, blessed they who bless you.'

Thus, the blessing that Abraham passed on to Isaac, not Ishmael, now came to Jacob, not Esau.

- Angels wept when Abraham was about to sacrifice Isaac. Their tears fell into Isaac's eyes, which is why his eyesight was weak.
- Esau does not follow God's way. He marries Canaanite women who worship idols, thus upsetting Rebecca. Later he marries a daughter of Ishmael.
- Esau is portrayed as hairy, rough and rude, while Jacob is shown as soft, gentle and kind. They are opposites of each other.
- Esau is also called Edom, and so his descendants are called Edomites. In the Jewish tradition, Edomites eventually gave rise to Romans and all Europeans; so, European anti-Semitism can be traced to the rivalry of Esau (father of the Europeans) and Jacob (father of the Jewish people).
- Islamic tradition does not accept the story of Jacob (Yakub) tricking Esau out of his birthright and blessing. Yakub is seen as a prophet chosen by and beloved of Allah, just like his father Isaac and his grandfather Ishmael.

Jacob's Ladder

Fearing the wrath of Esau who had been deprived of both birthright and blessings, Jacob ran out of his father's house. On his mother's advice, he journeyed towards Mesopotamia, to the source of the rivers Tigris and Euphrates, where lived his mother's family. On the way he slept on the ground, using a stone as pillow. That is when he had a splendid dream.

He saw a staircase connecting earth to Heaven, and saw angels going up and coming down.

When he awoke, he realized he was safe. Yes, his world was changing from the familiar security of his father's house to the unfamiliar world of his uncle's house. But God was with him. Older guardian angels were returning to Heaven and newer angels were coming down to help him.

Jacob marked the spot with the stone on which he had rested his head. Here, one day, would rise the city of Jerusalem.

- The Temple Mount and the Dome of the Rock in Jerusalem mark the spot where Jacob (Yakub, in Arabic) rested his head on a rock and dreamt of the ladder.
- Jacob's ladder is a popular theme in art.
- Jacob's ladder is interpreted in many ways. The angels are the children of Adam

and Eve who had been cast out, and so were going down the ladder, but would eventually go up, meaning they would return to God. Some who are returning are visualized as slipping and falling, indicating some returns would be delayed due to doubt and transgression.

- In Jewish mysticism (Kabbalah), Jacob's ladder represents the map of our journey towards God. It connects the earth to Heaven. There are seven rungs, or levels, to be attained through initiation and practice. It mirrors the Tantrik concept of chakra. In Zohar, the medieval Kabbalah text, the act of experiencing pain and suffering through fasting marks the raising of the ladder towards spiritual upliftment.
- The story of the ladder is not found in the Quran but is part of the Islamic commentaries. The ladder indicates the 'straight path' to God, which starts at the very beginning of time. The ladder marks the path taken by Prophet Muhammad when he flew to Heaven in one night from Jerusalem.
- Buddhist literature speaks of the paradise of the thirty-three gods connected to the earth by a spiritual ladder of thirty-three levels, which Buddha ascends after attaining supreme awareness. He then returns to the earth to begin his preaching. This has been connected with Jacob's ladder.

Laban's Daughters

Jacob took shelter in the house of his mother's brother, Laban. There he met Laban's daughter Rachel and sought her hand in marriage. 'You can marry her if you serve me for seven years,' said Laban. Jacob agreed and served Laban for seven years, but on the wedding night was shocked to find Leah, Rachel's elder sister, in his wedding bed.

When accused of cheating, Laban argued that he could not get the younger sister married before the elder. 'You can marry Rachel, too, but you have to serve me for another seven years,' said Laban. Jacob agreed and was forced to stay with Laban for seven more years. Thus, the man who tricked his brother ended up being tricked by his father-in-law.

- Laban's world is full of trickery and deception. Jacob has to endure it as he, too, has indulged in trickery and deception. Laban revels in this world but Jacob engages with it reluctantly.
- In Isaac's world, the elder son, Esau, is bypassed and Jacob is favoured. In Laban's world, the elder daughter, Leah, is not bypassed. But this seemingly fair world of Laban is full of trickery.
- As per some stories found in the Black Muslim movement of America, such as the Nation of Islam, the world was originally full of black people till white 'devils' were created by the mad scientist Jacob/Yakub, who was born in Mecca and who lived on an island in the Mediterranean. The white creations of Jacob lived in the caves of Europe without God and learned savage ways of conquest and slavery, which they used against black people.
- As per Jewish lore, before the wedding ceremony, the groom removes the bride's veil to check if he is marrying the right woman to avoid being tricked as Jacob was tricked by Laban into marrying Leah.

Laban's Goats

After serving his father-in-law for fourteen years and having finally secured Rachel as his wife, Jacob wanted to leave. But Laban begged him to stay, for he saw that Jacob's presence brought prosperity. He was clearly blessed by God.

For all the extra time that Jacob stayed with Laban, he demanded payment. 'Give me all the goats that are speckled and you keep all that are solid in colour, fully white or black,' he said. Laban agreed as there were fewer speckled goats. Jacob added, 'And let all black goats and all white goats that my speckled goats bear be yours and all speckled goats that your black goats bear be mine.'

Laban told his sons to keep all the white and all the black goats away from the speckled goats. That way, speckled goats would give birth to speckled kids, black goats would give birth to black kids and white goats to white kids. Jacob saw this and put a speckled staff in the water trough used by all the goats.

God ensured that all the speckled goats gave birth to speckled kids and many of the black goats gave birth to speckled kids and the white goats gave birth to speckled kids too. Over time, despite Laban's tricks, Jacob ended up with many goats and became rich and prosperous, and acquired more helpers and servants, and followers.

- In America, where there are tensions between the biblical schools and the scientific schools, the story of Jacob's goats is seen as proof of knowledge of genetics in biblical times. Others argue that Jacob's use of the 'speckled staff' reveals belief in magic.
- Most tribal mythologies separate fertility myths (related to production of wealth) and guardian myths (related to securing and distributing wealth). In Abrahamic lore, all these functions are transferred to a transcendental God.

Death of Rachel

Leah gave Jacob six sons while Rachel gave him none. So, Rachel gave her servant, Bilha, as a concubine to Jacob and he fathered two sons by her. To compete, Leah also gave her servant, Zilpah, as a concubine to Jacob, who gave him two sons too. Thus, Jacob fathered ten sons. But not one by Rachel. Then, at the ripe old age of sixty did Rachel become pregnant and give birth to Jacob's eleventh son, Joseph, who would become his father's favourite.

When Rachel was pregnant the second time, Jacob decided it was time to return home to Isaac. Jacob knew that his father-in-law would not give him permission to leave, so he slipped away in the night with his wives, concubines, children, servants and flock. Unknown to him, his wife Rachel took her father's idols with her.

Laban gave chase to Jacob and caught up with him, accusing him of stealing his idols. Jacob rejected the accusation, telling Laban to check for himself. He asked Laban to affirm his innocence and publicly declared that any member of his household who had taken anything that was not his or her to take would die.

Laban searched all of Jacob's tents and did not find the idol, for Rachel sat on the idols and did not get up, informing her father that she was menstruating. Laban returned home frustrated.

But because Rachel deceived her father, Jacob's curse fell on her. She died shortly thereafter, while giving birth to her second son, Benjamin.

- The tension and jealousy between the sisters Leah and Rachel are an extension of the tension between brothers such as Cain and Abel, Isaac and Ishmael, and Jacob and Esau. Similar stories are found in the Mahabharata, where Kunti fears her co-wife Madri will have more children than her.
- There is no explanation given as to why Rachel carries her father's idols. Does she not follow Jacob's monotheistic ways? Maybe that is the reason she dies in childbirth and is not buried with Jacob in the Cave of Patriarchs. That privilege goes to Leah.
- The story clarifies that Abraham's descendants, which includes Jacob, follow monotheism. But the descendants of Abraham's brothers, which includes Laban, do not.

Jacob Is Renamed Israel

Jacob was terrified of returning home and facing the wrath of Esau. So, he sent in advance a gift of goats and sheep and camels to appease his brother. And he travelled keeping his favourite children, those of Rachel's, at the rear end of the caravan.

But one night, Jacob decided to pray alone on the banks of the River Jordan, after his family had crossed the ford to the other side. As he was about to join his family, his path was blocked by an angel and the two wrestled all night. In the morning, the angel disappeared. Jacob realized that his opponent was no man, but a divine spirit, an angel, maybe God himself. It filled him with confidence to meet his brother, for if he could survive fighting an angel, he would surely survive a hostile brother.

Following this incident, Jacob was named Israel, he who has wrestled with an angel. His children and their children would be known as the children of Israel.

- This story is found in Jewish and Christian but not Islamic lore.
- Jacob develops a limp after this event as the angel touches his hip. This is why Israelites to this day while consuming meat avoid eating the sinews of the hip joint.
- Angels in the Bible are not described as having wings. This practice starts from the fourth century CE. In the Bible, angels are simply messengers who talk to humans and convey the word of God. They look like humans. The importance of angels in Abrahamic lore rises following the official recognition of the Roman Church by the Roman emperor 1,600 years ago. The Sassanian kings, who followed Zoroastrianism, were the rivals of Christian Rome. So, Rome was strongly influenced by Zoroastrian ideas of archangels (Amesha Spenta, who serve Ahura Mazda) and guardian angels (Asho Farohar or Fravashi) and their depiction as winged creatures. Over time, a whole hierarchy of angels emerges:

some with wings, some without, some archangels, some warrior angels, some messenger angels, some child-like cherubs inspired by the Greek god Eros, and some musicians. There are also fallen angels, who have angered God.

- While the Hebrew and Christian Bible mentions only two archangels—Gabriel, who communicates, and Michael, who fights—over time, a host of angels emerge like Raphael, who heals, and Azrael, who is the angel of death in Islam. The concept of seven archangels gains popularity and they are linked to various roles, and serve as knights of God, associated with seasons, or with days of the week.

Jacob Reconciles with Esau

Jacob expected his brother to be hostile, still bearing a grudge against his younger sibling who had stolen his birthright. But Esau was not angry. He had received Jacob's gifts with joy and had travelled ahead to meet his brother. The union was an emotional one.

They were together when their father died. Together they buried Isaac in the Cave of the Patriarchs, alongside his parents, Abraham and Sarah.

- Abraham travelled from Mesopotamia through Canaan to Egypt. Jacob, too, travels from Canaan to Mesopotamia and will eventually go to Egypt. But Isaac stays in Canaan all his life. As per Jewish lore, this is because he was offered as sacrifice and so was sacred and would always stay in the Holy Land.
- As per the *Book of Jubilees*, a collection of Abrahamic lore, Esau promised Isaac before the latter's death that he would not quarrel with Jacob. But after Isaac died, goaded by his sons, Esau attacked Jacob to seize all of his share of the inheritance. In the fight that followed, Jacob released an arrow that killed Esau.

Jacob's Daughter Dinah

Jacob had two wives and two concubines. They gave him twelve sons, who would become patriarchs of the twelve tribes of Israel. Jacob also had a daughter called Dinah by Leah. Shechem, a local prince, fell in love with her and took her to his house, and claimed her as his wife. His father went to Jacob and sought her hand in marriage.

Dinah's brothers, Simon and Levi, did not appreciate a worshipper of idols claiming their sister by force. They said they could agree if Shechem, his father and all the men in their city agreed to circumcise themselves. Shechem agreed and so did his father and so did his people. They circumcised themselves, and while they rested to let the wound heal, Dinah's brothers attacked the city, killed the men, plundered its wealth and brought back their sister.

Jacob did not approve of this action, for they risked the friendliness of the city-dwellers. Simon's descendants would dwindle over time while Levi's descendants would serve as priests and rely on the generosity of others. Simon and Levi did not care. They believed they were upholding the family honour. No one asked Dinah what she wanted.

- In Jewish retellings, when Jacob met Esau, he hid Dinah in a box because he feared Esau may want to marry Dinah. For this action, he was rebuked by God and warned that she would break God's law and follow her own path that would bring shame.
- Some Christian commentators have used this story to argue about the dangers of women being allowed to wander in public rather than being kept segregated in private.
- Modern scholars have conjectured whether Dinah is raped or whether she chooses her lover, who wants to marry her. In biblical times, and in orthodox communities, the idea of women having agency is never acknowledged. It is

feared and frowned upon, seen as the ways of Lilith, God's first creation, who, unlike Eve, chose freedom over submission.

- During the American Civil War, African American slave women were referred to as Dinah.

Jacob's Son Judah

Judah was also Jacob's son by Leah, younger than Simon and Levi. Judah had many sons. Er, his eldest, married Tamar. But Er died before he could give Tamar children and so, she was given in marriage, as tradition demanded, to Er's younger brother, Onan. But Onan also died young, punished for not shedding his seed inside his wife. By law, the widow Tamar had to be given to Judah's third son Shelah in marriage, but Judah did not give his consent as he saw this woman as a husband-killer.

To prove her father-in-law was wrong and being unfair, Tamar disguised herself as a prostitute and seduced Judah when he was travelling to get his goats sheared, thereby becoming pregnant.

Tamar was accused of adultery, until she revealed who had made her pregnant. She gives birth to twins, one of whom, Perez, is the ancestor of King David and, eventually, Jesus Christ.

- Onan is associated with coitus interruptus, where a man does not shed semen in a woman so as to avoid pregnancy. But in Protestant commentaries, Onan is accused of masturbation and the story is used to explain why the practice of self-stimulation is sinful. Many gay writers argue Onan was gay.
- Ancient Hindus also practised *niyoga* or levirate marriage, when a widow was allowed or obliged to marry her brother-in-law.

Jacob's Favourite Son

Of his twelve sons, Jacob loved Joseph the most. Joseph's brothers resented this.

Joseph would share his dreams with his brothers, despite Jacob forbidding him from doing so. In one dream, the bundles of corn Joseph's brothers gathered bowed to the bundles of corn Joseph gathered. In another, the sun, the moon and the stars bowed to Joseph. Joseph interpreted the dreams to mean that one day his brothers would bow to him. Joseph's brothers were not amused.

Matters got worse when Jacob gave Joseph a robe of many bright colours.

Tired of the disproportionate love and attention Joseph got, and convinced that he was not as innocent as he pretended to be, Joseph's brothers wanted to kill him. Reuben, however, was against this. He convinced his brothers to throw Joseph in a pit instead and leave him to his fate. When the brothers finally agreed to this, Simon stripped Joseph of his robe, pushed him into a pit, tore his robe and smeared it with blood.

On returning home, he showed the blood-smeared torn robe to Jacob as proof that a lion had killed Joseph. Jacob believed their story and mourned his loss. He wept so much that he became blind and refused to let his son Benjamin leave his side, fearing the same fate would befall Rachel's second son. As a punishment for his role in the crime, one of Simon's hands withered and became unusable.

Meanwhile, a caravan found Joseph in the pit and decided to sell him as a slave in Egypt.

- In Islamic lore, Joseph is referred to as Yusuf and there is a whole chapter in Quran related to his story, making him the only prophet to have a chapter devoted to him. Ironically, he is not much discussed in Hadith literature.
- Yusuf of Islamic lore is described as being very handsome. Half of the world's beauty belonged to him and his mother, and the other half to the rest of humanity. He is raised by Jacob's sister, who refuses to let him go. In fact, to ensure he does not leave her side, she accuses him of stealing a belt that belongs to her and as repayment demands that he stay with her.
- In Islamic lore, Joseph obeys Jacob and does not tell his dreams to his brothers. Still, his jealous brothers throw him in a dry well. There he is found by a caravan of merchants, who make him their slave. Yusuf is enslaved and taken to Egypt as punishment for a crime of his great grandfather, Abraham, who had not dismounted from his horse and walked with his slaves as an equal, while leaving Egypt.

Joseph and Zulekha

The man who bought Joseph was Potipar, the captain of the pharaoh's guard. He discovered that Joseph was good with numbers and letters, and that he was a good manager of people and the estate. In a few years, Joseph became the head of his household, managing his fields, his cattle and his slaves and bringing him great prosperity. Joseph, who came in as a slave, had risen up the ranks to be a trusted servant and was almost a son to Potipar.

Potipar's young wife, Zulekha, fell in love with Joseph. Her friends found it amusing that she was infatuated with a servant. So, she invited them to her house, served them apples to eat and gave them knives to cut the fruit. While they were peeling the apples, she made Joseph walk past the room. Such was his beauty that the assembled women ended up cutting their hands instead of the apples.

One day, unable to resist his beauty, Zulekha

forced herself upon Joseph. But he ran away. She tried to catch him by his robes, but ended up tearing them. That is when Potipar entered the house. To save herself, she accused Joseph of attempting to rape her. Potipar checked Joseph's robes. The back was torn, not the front, indicating it was torn when he was running away. Joseph was innocent. Still Potipar had Joseph thrown in jail, for shaming his wife would bring shame upon him.

- In Islamic lore, the story of Yusuf and Zulekha is very popular and retold in many Arab and Persian ballads.
- Potipar is known as Aziz in Islamic lore. The stories of the apples and Joseph's torn robes are not part of Jewish and Christian lore.
- Yusuf's story is one of the rare ones where male beauty is celebrated and women's desires acknowledged.
- In Sufi tradition, Yusuf's love for God is the mystical love and Zulekha is an allegory for the earthly temptation that takes us away from God.

Joseph Interprets Dreams

In jail, Joseph met two men who had once served the pharaoh before displeasing him. They had been the pharaoh's cup-bearer and baker. Both saw dreams at night that Joseph interpreted.

The cup-bearer saw images of a vine that bears grapes from which wine pours into a cup. 'You will be forgiven,' Joseph said. The baker saw three loaves of bread in a basket being eaten by birds. 'In three days you will be executed,' Joseph said. Both these interpretations turned out to be true. The cup-bearer was released, and the baker was killed.

Joseph asked the cup-bearer to remember him when he had been freed and help in his release. The cup-bearer promised he

would, but forgot all about Joseph when he came out of prison. So, Joseph languished in jail.

A few years later, the pharaoh dreamt of seven fat cows being eaten by seven thin cows that emerge from the Nile. His oracles were not able to make sense of it. So, the royal cup-bearer told the pharaoh to send for Joseph, who was still in prison. Joseph told the pharaoh, 'The seven fat cows represent seven years of good harvest that Egypt will experience, and the seven thin cows represent the seven years of famine that will follow and ravage the land.'

A startled pharaoh wondered what he could do to prevent this from happening. Joseph said, 'You cannot stop the eventuality. But you can manage things to minimize damage. Store grain during the healthy years to feed the hungry during the famine years.' The pharaoh liked the idea and gave Joseph all the powers to make this happen. He was released from prison, made a royal courtier and given an Egyptian wife.

- Dream interpretation is a recurring theme in Abrahamic lore. Jacob knows that of all his sons, Joseph alone is special as he has the gift of dream interpretation and prophecy.
- Islamic commentaries state that since Joseph asked the cup-bearer for help with his release, rather than just trusting Allah, he endured imprisonment for a longer duration.
- In Persian retellings, when Joseph is released from prison, he returns to the house of Aziz and learns that Aziz has died. In his kindness, he bears no ill feeling towards his former master or his widow. After years of suffering and longing, Zulekha follows the path of Islam that Yusuf had pointed her towards. Eventually, many years later, in some retellings, Yusuf is directed by Allah to marry Zulekha. Thus, desire is not condemned though it is seen as socially disruptive and as an obstacle to the spiritual path.

Joseph, the Saviour of Egypt

Joseph went about measuring the land, weighing the harvest and ensuring that every crop was accounted for. He also built gigantic granaries where grain collected as tax from the people during the prosperous years was stored carefully. Then, during the famine years, he sold the grain to the people.

Foreigners had to pay in gold. Egyptians had to give their land to the pharaoh and take grain. As the pharaoh now owned the land, the people were forced to pay a fifth of their produce to the king as rent. Thus, Joseph made the king of Egypt a very rich man and the king never forgot that. He made Joseph his vizier, the most powerful man in the land, second only to the pharaoh.

- Until they were identified as tombs, the pyramids of Egypt were considered the granaries of Joseph by Christian pilgrims.
- Historically, Egyptian kings came to be officially known as 'pharaoh' from roughly the fourteenth century BCE, during the reign of Akhenaten, the pharaoh who introduced the idea of one God, Aten, to Egypt and rejected polytheism. Yusuf's story refers to the king of Egypt as 'malik' and the word 'pharaoh' is used in the story of Moses in the Islamic retellings. The same difference is noticed in Hebrew retellings. This suggests that the migration of Jacob's sons occurred before the thirteenth century BCE and the exodus from Egypt happened after the thirteenth century BCE.
- Just as Jacob's presence brings prosperity to his uncle, Laban, who does not want to let him go, Joseph's presence brings prosperity to the pharaoh, who ensures that Joseph never leaves Egypt. Thus, God's messengers are also harbingers of material fortune.

Joseph Reconciles with His Brothers

Amongst the foreigners who came to Egypt looking for grain were the ten sons of Jacob. Joseph recognized his brothers who had sold him into slavery but they did not recognize him. He invited them to his palace and asked about them. They told him that they were twelve brothers, and then lied that one of them died of starvation, and the youngest was left behind with their blind father.

Joseph demanded that his brothers bring Benjamin to Egypt if they wanted grain. He held Simon hostage to ensure their return. So, the brothers were forced to return home and, despite Jacob's protests, bring Benjamin to Egypt and present him to the powerful Egyptian vizier.

Joseph was overwhelmed by emotion on seeing Benjamin. But he restrained himself. He gave the sons of Jacob all the grain they wanted and let them go, but secretly put his silver cup in Benjamin's bag. When the brothers were leaving, Egyptian guards stopped them, checked their bags for stolen goods, found the vizier's silver cup in Benjamin's bag and arrested him.

The brothers ran to Joseph and begged him to release Benjamin. 'He is innocent, incapable of such an act.' Joseph refused to let Benjamin go. The brothers refused to abandon Benjamin. 'Our father will die without his beloved son. We caused him the loss of one son; we cannot lose another. Take any one of us, but not him.' When they spoke these words, Joseph realized that his brothers had atoned for their crime and were willing to sacrifice themselves for Benjamin. He ordered the brothers to bring their father to Egypt if he wished to see Benjamin. He gave them a shirt of his as gift for their father.

As soon as Jacob held the shirt gifted to him by the Egyptian vizier, he felt it could only be Joseph's. He placed the shirt on his eyes and his eyesight was restored. He rushed to Egypt with his sons, eager to see this mysterious vizier and at first glance recognized him as Joseph. His identity revealed, Joseph embraced his brothers, reconciled with them and invited all the sons of Jacob, and their descendants, to stay in Egypt for as long as they wished.

- The shirt that Joseph sent to Jacob was the one passed on from Abraham to Isaac to Jacob and given to Joseph as a child. It was woven in paradise, as per Islamic lore, and had protected Abraham when Nimrod had cast him in fire.
- When Jacob died, his body was taken out of Egypt to Canaan to be buried in the Cave of Patriarchs. As per the *Babylonian Talmud*, Esau tried to stop the burial claiming it was his right to be buried there. The sons of Jacob argued that Esau had sold his rights for gold and silver. To prove it, one of the sons travelled back to Egypt to get the sale deed. But Hushim, one of Jacob's grandsons who stayed back, was irritated that his grandfather's body had to be kept waiting for a respectful burial. He swung his club at Esau and killed him.
- The twelve sons of Jacob, who establish the twelve tribes of Israel, are born of two wives (Leah and Rachel) and two concubines (Zilpah and Bilha). The sons of Leah are Reuben (Jacob's firstborn), Simon, Levi, Judah, Issachar and Zebulun. The sons of Rachel are Joseph and Benjamin. Gad and Asher are the sons of Zilpah. And Dan and Naphtali are the sons of Bilhah. While no tribe bears the name of Joseph, two tribes are named after Joseph's sons, Manasseh and Ephraim. Ten of these tribes are eventually sent into exile by the Assyrians and they came to be known as the ten lost tribes of Israel, found since in almost every corner of the world, including India.

BOOK FIVE

Out of Egypt

The God-King of Egypt

The people of Egypt, blessed with the River Nile, believed that their king was a god who would lead them to an eternal afterlife. He descended from Horus, the son of the first god-king, Osiris. Osiris descended from ancient gods who gave rise to nature. Osiris, along with his wife, Isis, created culture.

In the beginning, Atum made love to himself and gave birth to breath and moisture, Shu and Tefnut, who created the sky-goddess, Nut, clad in stars, above and the earth-god, Geb, below. The sky and earth made love and it rained, and the River Nile came into being. The Nile flooded its banks, and when the flood waters receded, plants sprouted and supported animal life.

Osiris then gave birth to civilization, winning the admiration of all gods, except Seth. Just like Cain, who was jealous of Abel, Seth murdered Osiris, cut his body into pieces and cast them into the river. Isis found the fragments of her husband's body and with her magic revived him for long enough to become pregnant with his child. Thus was born Horus, the hawk, who fought and overpowered his jealous uncle Seth, driving him to the desert, and became king of the Nile.

Horus ruled life. His father ruled the afterlife. All pharaohs spent their lives preparing to enter the afterlife, a world without flood, without the desert, without hunger, without fear. Their bodies were mummified in an elaborate ritual and placed in stone tombs like the pyramids, awaiting the jackal-headed Anubis to take them to the Hall of Judgement, where the ibis-headed Thoth would weigh their heart against the feather of goodness, Ma'at. The bodies of the bad were devoured by a monster goddess called Ammit, who had the head of a crocodile, the torso of a lion and the back of a hippopotamus. The bodies of the good were revived and sent to the world of Osiris.

These were the stories that the children of Joseph heard when in Egypt. Here, they found many gods, not just one. Here, the gods spoke through priests. The many gods had human and animal forms. But all these many gods submitted to the one and only sun-god Amun-Ra, who died as Osiris at dusk and rose as Horus at dawn. The whole night Amun-Ra fought the serpent of night, Apep, just as Horus fought Seth. Every dawn, Amun-Ra as Horus rose like the sun, took the form of the pharaoh and ruled over the Nile. None was greater than or equal to the pharaoh, who united the river and the delta, the vulture and the cobra, and who held the crook in his hand to restrain errant animals and a flail to dehusk the grain.

The Egyptians also heard the stories of the children of Jacob. Of one God, without form, without family, who spoke only through prophets. So similar yet so different. They could have been friends, but the Egyptians chose to enslave them.

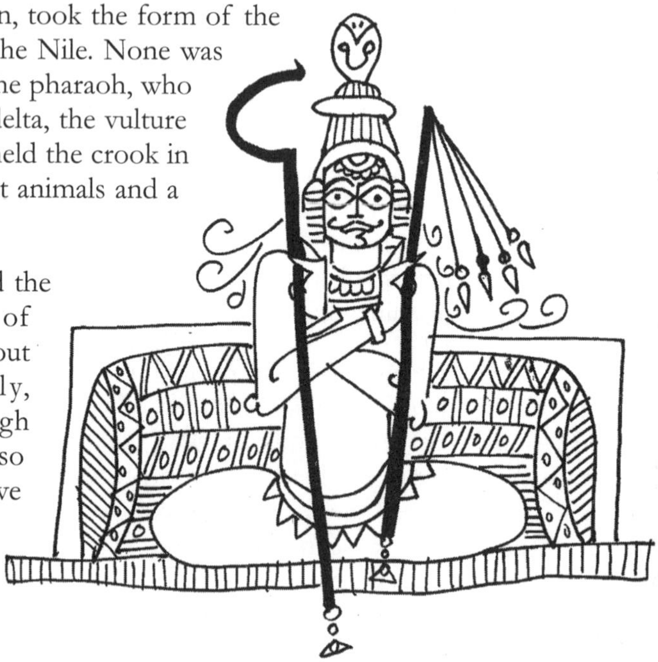

- In Islamic lore, the king of Egypt listens to the wisdom of Joseph and becomes Muslim.
- The Egyptians had many gods, almost one for each city, and all of these would eventually bow to the pharaoh, who was seen as the embodiment of the mightiest of gods: Horus, Osiris, Amun-Ra and even Ptah, the god of craftsmen.
- The idea of judgement and justice is strong in Egyptian mythology as visualized in the weighing of the heart on the pan scales against Ma'at, the ostrich feather of righteousness.
- Like Mesopotamian mythology, Egyptian mythology speaks of man existing to serve the gods. Both refer to one life followed by one afterlife. Egyptian mythology speaks of gods dying and resurrecting themselves, but in Mesopotamian mythology, gods are immortal and they deny immortality to humans. In Mesopotamian mythology, the afterlife is the 'Great Below'—it is neither punishment nor reward but a place of listlessness and darkness, occupied by the spirits of all people, who feed on dust and clay. By contrast, Egyptian mythology speaks of judgement in the afterlife with only a few souls entering the eternal world of Osiris and the rest being eaten by the crocodile-headed monster, Ammit. Thus, Mesopotamian mythology has no Heaven or Hell while Egyptian mythology has Heaven but no Hell. Jewish tradition is strongly influenced by Mesopotamian mythology and does not speak much about Heaven or Hell.
- If the idea of paradise in the afterlife comes from Egyptian mythology, then the idea of Hell as a place of punishment comes from Greece, where the Olympian gods cast those whom they don't like into the dark and miserable Tartarus. The Greeks do not have a clear Heaven: the heroes are sent to Elysium, or invited to Olympus, and the mediocre masses are sent to Asphodel. Zoroastrian mythology speaks of Heaven and Hell clearly as places for good and bad people, which was adopted by Christians and Muslims.
- The idea of the king being identified with a lion emerges from ancient Egypt. The idea spread to Persia and thence to India and China, and even Europe. So, lands without lions, such as China, Sri Lanka and Singapore, also identify royal authority with lions.

Moses, the Foundling

The children of Jacob prospered in Egypt and carried on with their faith. Over time, most forgot about Canaan and only a few remembered stories of Abraham, Isaac, and Jacob and his twelve sons. Generations passed. Centuries rolled by. New pharaohs did not remember the contribution of Joseph during the great famine. They did not like the Israelites, who worshipped the God of Abraham and saw Amun-Ra and Osiris and Ra as false gods. They feared their numbers. The only way to control them was to enslave them. Those who did not bow voluntarily were made to bow forcefully.

The pharaoh decided that Israelite children born one year would be spared and born the next year would be killed. This mass culling was meant to control the community's numbers. Amram and his wife Jochebed had a daughter called Miriam and a son called Aaron, both born in the years when the infants were spared. But then in the year of purge, Jochebed gave birth to a third child, a son. Fearing for his life, she put him in a basket of reeds and left him to the whims of the River Nile. Miriam swam behind the basket, protecting it from crocodiles and hippopotamuses.

The pharaoh's wife, Asiya, who had no children, found the basket with a boy in it, and she decided to adopt this child. She noticed the child was circumcised, hence, an Israelite. But she decided to adopt him nevertheless. She named him Moses.

The baby, however, would not drink milk from any of the Egyptian nursemaids. Miriam, who kept hovering around the palace, heard this and offered the queen the services of her mother, who had recently lost her child. The queen let Jochebed nurse her child, not knowing this was the baby's biological mother.

- In Jewish and Christian retellings, the pharaoh kills Israelite children as his oracles state that one such child would overthrow him. Islamic lore gives an economic reason for the killing of babies and keeping the Israelite population in control.
- In Islamic tradition, the pharaoh's wife, Asiya, believed in Allah, which is why she was chosen to be the mother of Moses. She was humble and generous, unlike her husband. When she saw her husband torturing a man for his monotheistic beliefs, she tried to prevent it by declaring her faith. The pharaoh ordered her to give up her faith. She refused and so was tortured to death. She was received into Allah's paradise and is much venerated in the Islamic world.
- In Jewish and Christian retellings, Moses is adopted by the pharaoh's daughter. Jewish lore refers to her as Bitiah or Thermutis.
- The stories of a child being left in a basket to the river's whims and surviving and eventually growing up to be a hero are part of a recurring theme. This theme is found in the Mesopotamian legend of Sargon, king of Akkad. Stories of Karna and Krishna in Hindu mythology also reflect this theme.
- The pharaoh's wife, Asiya, who adopts Moses, is considered one of the four noble women of Islam, the other three being Mary, the mother of Jesus Christ, Khadija and Fatima, the first wife and daughter of the Prophet Muhammad.

Burning Coal

Moses grew up as an Egyptian prince in the pharaoh's house. One day, while sitting on the pharaoh's lap, he grabbed the royal crown and put it on the ground. The oracles saw this and said the child posed a threat to the pharaoh and that he should be killed. Asiya argued it was only the action of a child.

To check if the action was intentional or unintentional, a plate was brought before Moses with a ball of gold and a ball of burning coal. If the child picked up the gold ball, he was clearly someone with ambition and hence, was a threat. Moses was about to pick the gold ball when the angel Gabriel pushed his hand and made him pick up the piece of burning coal and put it in his mouth.

This proved to the pharaoh that Moses was an innocent child, and therefore no threat, much to the queen's relief. However, the coal burned Moses's tongue and he was left with a speech defect.

- This story comes from the Islamic folklore.
- In the Jewish retelling by Josephus, who lived in Roman Judea 2,000 years ago, Moses was sent on an expedition to Ethiopia, where a Cushite princess named Tharbis fell in love with him and secured him as a husband. She would not let him go till he gave her the ring of forgetfulness. Some people read Cushite as a black woman, and say Moses's wife belonged to the sub-Saharan regions of Africa.

Jethro

Moses grew up as a prince, but with a deep sense of justice, especially for the descendants of Jacob who were enslaved, and who saw their children die every other year.

One day, he saw an Egyptian beating up an Israelite. While trying to stop the Egyptian, Moses killed him. The next day, Moses saw two Israelites fighting. When he tried to stop them, one of them barked, 'Who made you ruler and judge? Will you kill me as you killed the Egyptian?' Moses realized his actions had not gone unnoticed. Fearful of the repercussions, he ran away to Midian.

Here in the wilderness, he mingled with those who herded sheep, goats, cows and camels. One day, he found a group of men pushing away seven women from a well so that they could water their animals first. Moses intervened, and ensured that the seven women, who had arrived first, watered their animals before the latecomers. The women were much pleased and introduced themselves as the daughters of Jethro.

Jethro invited Moses to have a meal in his house. He took Moses to his garden and showed him a staff there which had been planted in the ground. Jethro asked Moses to pull it out. This staff belonged to Abraham. On it was carved the four letters that constitute the name of Abraham's God. No one had ever been able to pull it out, but Moses uprooted it effortlessly. This proved he was no ordinary man. He was a prophet and God's messenger. Jethro, therefore, gave him in marriage his daughter Zipporah.

Moses, not yet initiated into the ways of monotheism entirely, did not circumcise his firstborn. Then, one day, he was caught by a python, which began swallowing him. To save him, Zipporah circumcised their firstborn and instantly the python disgorged a rather shaken Moses.

- In Jewish tradition, the pharaoh called three oracles—Jethro, Balaam and Job—to decide the fate of the Israelite children. Jethro ran away without giving an answer; Balaam ordered their killing; and Job remained silent.
- The rod of Abraham had been passed on through Isaac and Jacob to Joseph and had been claimed by the pharaoh. Jethro stole the rod of Abraham from the pharaoh's palace before leaving.
- Jethro is seen as the founder prophet of the secretive mystical Druze religion, a monotheistic faith based on Islam from the Middle East. It sees itself as distinct from Islam based on its belief in rebirth. Humans are reborn as humans. Men as men. Women as women. And when wisdom is attained, the soul joins the cosmic mind and is never reborn again.
- In Islam, Jethro is addressed as Shoaib.

The Burning Bush

One day, while herding Jethro's flocks, Moses was drawn to climb a mountain. There he saw a vision that would change him forever.

He saw something burning atop a hill. On investigation, he saw it was a burning bush: only the leaves were not burning, and there was no smoke. He realized there was something special about this vision. He removed his footwear and approached the bush, when he heard a voice. 'Who are you?' Moses asked. And the voice replied, 'I am what I am.'

Was this the voice of God? Moses was not sure. The voice asked, 'What do you hold in your hand?' Moses said he held a staff but when he turned to see, it turned into a serpent and then a staff once again. Moses bowed for he realized he was in the presence of a powerful force—the one true god, the God of Abraham.

Moses was told that he had been chosen to lead the enslaved children of Jacob out of Egypt. He had to go back and ask the pharaoh to let God's people go.

Moses was suddenly afraid. For he feared the pharaoh and could never speak before him. The voice also told him to take the help of Aaron, his elder brother, who would speak on his behalf until he found the confidence to speak himself.

- The Hebrew bible identifies the mountain with the burning bush as Mount Horeb. Most people identify it as the same Mount Sinai on which Moses receives the commandments. Some say Horeb and Sinai are two sides of the same mountain. Others say they are two peaks of the same mountain.
- In Islamic tradition, Moses works for Jethro as payment for marrying his daughter. He sees the burning bush on his way back to Egypt. Moses enters the valley of Tuwa, where Allah tells him to remove his footwear as he has entered a sacred

space. That is why Muslims always enter the mosque barefoot.

- In Eastern Orthodox churches, the burning bush is often identified as the unburnt bush. It is seen not as a miracle (hence, impermanent event) but as God's uncreated glory (hence, eternal).

Plagues in Egypt

Moses had no doubt he had witnessed the presence of God. He returned to Egypt, reconnected with his brother Aaron and his sister Miriam, and told them all that he had witnessed.

With faith in his heart, staff in hand and Aaron by his side, Moses marched to the palace and spoke to the pharaoh. 'You are the king of Egypt and the Nile,' they said. 'But we represent the Lord who is the one true god, creator of the sky, the earth and everything in between. He who is the lord of all rivers and seas commands you to free the descendants of Jacob and return them to whence they came.'

The pharaoh laughed and asked Moses to prove he was indeed the representative of the one true god. So, Moses asked Aaron to drop his staff to the floor and it turned into a serpent. The pharaoh's sorcerers threw their staffs on the floor, and these too turned into serpents. But then Aaron's staff-turned-serpent ate the sorcerers' staff-turned-serpents.

This made the pharaoh nervous, but he refused to release the Israelites. So, Moses said, 'If you don't do as God has demanded then he will strike your kingdom with plagues, until you concede.'

And so, Egypt was struck by plagues. The waters of the Nile turned into blood. Frogs covered the land. The air was filled with flies. Locusts ate the crops. Cattle fell sick. Lice covered people's bodies. Their skin was covered in boils. It started to hail. The sun did not shine. But still the stubborn pharaoh refused.

Finally, God did to the pharaoh what the pharaoh did to the children of Israel. He declared he would kill every firstborn in Egypt. Moses was told to warn those who believed in him to mark their houses with blood so that death would pass over these houses and strike the houses without the mark of faith.

The believers did as they were told. The non-believers did not. Death came silently and killed every firstborn in Egypt, even in the house of the pharaoh. A terrified pharaoh told his slaves to leave Egypt immediately.

- The story of the confrontation between Moses and the pharaoh mirrors stories of confrontation between Abraham and Nimrod. Abraham had to leave Mesopotamia after this confrontation. He found a home in Canaan. Moses leaves Egypt and returns to Canaan.
- Islamic retellings state that the tower of Babel was built by the pharaoh so that he could see the Moses's God.
- In Hindu mythology, a confrontation between a believer and a non-believer takes place in the *Vishnu Purana* between Prahlad and his father, the Asura-king, Hiranyakashipu.

The Parting of the Sea

The children of Israel cheered when they heard the news. They were being set free. But where would they go? To the Promised Land, said Moses, to the land whence Jacob and his children came. To the land that was home to Abraham.

So, the children prepared to leave. They left with all their belongings. Thousands of men, women and children travelled, eager to live as free people, in a land of milk and honey. They took with them the mortal remains of Joseph, too, that was kept in a sarcophagus within a cave. Though long forgotten, Moses managed to retrieve it.

A pillar of cloud led the Israelites all day, which turned into a pillar of fire all night. But it did not take the short route along the Mediterranean Sea; instead the people were taken by another route—towards the Red Sea. Why? Moses did not question God. He just followed the cloud. People assumed it was because the short route had garrisons of Egyptian soldiers who could arrest them if the pharaoh changed his mind.

Suddenly, the children of Israel found themselves with Egypt behind them and the sea in front. How would they cross the sea? To their horror they discovered that the pharaoh had changed his mind, as they had feared, and was riding with 600 chariots, towards them, determined to take them back as slaves.

Moses struck his staff and a miracle occurred. The winds pushed the sea in one direction, the tides moved the sea in the other, and that ripped the sea causing it to part, and the children of Israel were able to cross to the other side over the dry seabed.

Then the parted sea came together again, and drowned all the 600 chariots that were giving the children of Israel chase. The horses and the soldiers drowned along with the pharaoh. Finally, the children of Israel were free. The men led by Moses and Aaron sang songs, and the women led by Miriam danced.

- The explanation of why the route along the Mediterranean was not taken comes from Jewish lore. What they did not know is that they were being taken by the long route to spare them the sight of the bones of their ancestors who had long ago tried to leave Egypt, carrying only gold with them, but who had died of starvation as no one gave them provisions, and no one had buried their remains.
- There are Jewish tales of how the body of Joseph lay buried deep in the ground and how it rises to the surface when Moses speaks of the exodus, despite attempts by Egyptian sorcerers to hold it down as many Egyptians believed Joseph's remains ensured the prosperity of Egypt.
- When Moses struck his staff on the seashore, the sea did not immediately part. But Aaron's brother-in-law, Nahshon of Judah, did not wait for the waters to part. He kept walking into the sea and when the waters reached his nose, the parting began. Hence, he was seen as one of great faith and his tribe was allowed to make the first offering to God after the exodus.
- The Song of the Sea that was sung after the exodus is still sung as a part of Jewish prayer.
- Just as there are many Hindu lobbies bent on identifying historical evidence of Ram's bridge to Ayodhya that is mentioned in the Ramayana, there are Jewish and Christian lobbies that argue for the historicity of the exodus and claim to have found scientific evidence of the Red Sea parting. Sacred texts use metaphors

to drive home a point, but for many, the material measurable world remains the only true reality.

- The 4,500-year-old pyramids were built in Egypt during the period of the Old Kingdom. The 3,500-year-old New Kingdom that saw horse-drawn chariots preferred tombs over pyramids.
- Climate change (Meghalayan Age) marks the fall of the Old Kingdom, as well as the collapse of many other civilizations such as the Akkadian Empire in Mesopotamia and the Harappan civilization in South Asia. It also accounts for the movement of nomads such as the Semitic people to Egypt and Steppe pastoralists to Europe and India.
- The use of horse-drawn chariots in the story of Moses indicates that the departure of the Jewish people from Egypt took place after the Hyksos invasion that introduced horse-drawn chariots to Egypt around 1500 BCE.

Golden Calf

At Sinai, where Moses had seen the burning bush, the Israelites saw a mountain covered with cloud and thunder. Moses went up the mountain to talk to God while the newly liberated slaves waited on the slopes, for the laws to arrive.

After forty days and forty nights, Moses finally came down the slopes with the tablets on which commandments were written by the finger of God. He was shocked by what he saw.

His people had built the image of the golden calf, had made offerings to it and were singing, dancing and feasting around it, thus indulging in idolatry and worship of a false god, explicitly forbidden by God.

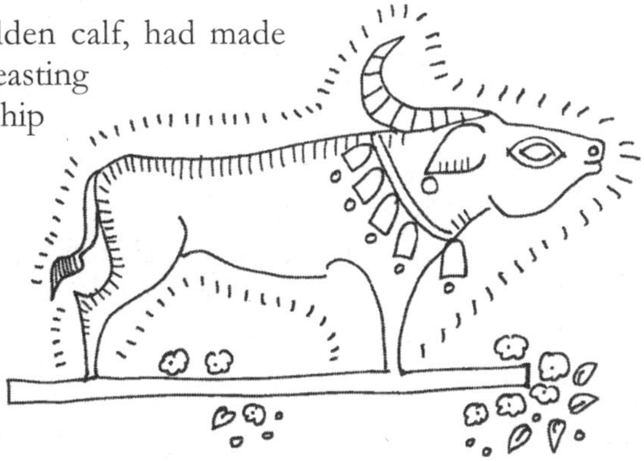

In his fury, Moses threw the commandment tablets on the ground, and yelled in a thunderous voice, commanding the people to stop. Aaron explained that the people

were nervous, anxious and insecure in the absence of Moses. In their impatience Samiri had suggested that they create a god of gold, imitating the ways of the Egyptians, in order to express gratitude and celebrate their freedom. Hur, the son of Miriam, had tried to stop them but the people had killed him. To prevent more killing, Aaron had agreed to create the golden calf for the people.

God threatened to destroy the Israelites. Moses begged God not to do so, 'Otherwise everyone will say the God of Abraham led the slaves of Egypt across the sea into the wilderness only to kill them. Do not forget your promise to Abraham that his people would one day inherit the Promised Land.'

Moses then asked the Israelites. 'Who is with me and God?' The Levites said they were. So Moses told the Levites to smash the image of the golden calf, powder it, mix it with water and make the Israelites drink it. He then ordered the Levites to kill all the men who danced around the image, all 3,000 of them.

The rest bowed in shame before Moses. 'Will you follow me? Will you submit to God's law? Will you accept he is the one true god, and not worship false gods and idols in his stead?' Much chastised, they agreed.

The stone tablets with the commandments of God were placed in a box covered with gold, with the image of winged angels on it, who spread their wings to shelter the contents within. This was the Ark of the Covenant that would never be placed on the ground, always be hidden by a veil and be carried in front of the twelve tribes of Israel until they reached their new home.

- The Quran describes this incident in the second chapter, known as 'Heifer'. Moses had to fast for forty days in preparation for receiving God's law, hence, the long wait. Samiri is identified as the man responsible for initiating the worship of an idol. Aaron is thus not linked to idol worship. He argues that he supported the venture in order to prevent divisions amongst the Israelites.
- Moses asks seventy men to pray to Allah alongside him for forgiveness for all those who indulged in idolatry (known as *shirk* in Arabic). The seventy men see Moses talking but cannot see God and so refuse to believe Moses when he says he was talking to God. Angry, God strikes the seventy disbelievers with lightning and kills them. Moses prays and begs Allah to be merciful and the men are resurrected. And they continue their journey.
- The story of Hur comes from Jewish retellings and is not found in the Bible.
- Metaphorically, the golden calf represents Mammon, the personification of wealth in the New Testament of the Christian Bible.

Doomed to Wander

Moses sent twelve spies from Sinai to Canaan to scout the land that would eventually be their home. When they returned, ten of the twelve men told the Israelites that the place could not be home. It was not rich enough to support them. It was guarded by giant hostile tribes in walled cities. It was best to turn back and return to Egypt.

But two of the spies, Jacob and Caleb, said the opposite. They said that it was indeed a fertile land, full of water and orchards and fields and vineyards, with people who were friendly and opponents who could easily be overpowered. In that land, there was freedom, which they never had in Egypt.

Most of the Israelites agreed with the ten spies and wanted to return home. They wept that they had left Egypt only to face misery and defeat.

So, God said that all those who did not trust his word, those who were unwilling to move forward, would never see the Promised Land. They would also never be able to return to Egypt. Instead, they would be trapped in the desert and they would wander for forty years in the wilderness till they learned the value of what was being given to them.

Those who had experienced both the slavery and the luxury of Egypt would not see the Promised Land. The next generation, born in the wilderness, toughened by the experience of wandering, would see the Promised Land. As would the two spies who spoke well of Canaan and encouraged people to proceed, not retreat.

Thus began the great wandering in the desert for forty years.

- This story provides an explanation for why a journey that should have taken a fortnight took forty years.
- This story is a reminder that the change demanded is not of a place but of mindset. Those who do not trust, wander. For mindsets to change, one needs time, and perhaps a shift in generation. In Hindu epics, exiles in forests are usually associated with learning and change of mindsets.

Rules and Organization

Rules and organization were needed for the twelve tribes to survive forty years in the desert.

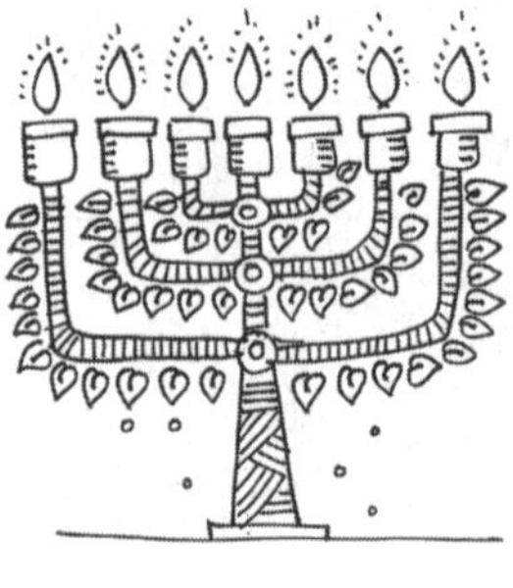

The tribes would follow the pillar of cloud and fire. They would camp when the pillar was still, move when it was on the move. The Ark of the Covenant would be carried in a palanquin leading the tribes.

Moses counted the Israelites and divided them into twelve groups: twelve tribes that claimed descent from the twelve sons of Jacob. When the ark was stationary, in the tabernacle,

the twelve tribes would set up their tents around it, three to the north, three to the south, three to the east and three to the west. When the ark was on the move, the twelve tribes would move behind in a predetermined sequence.

Strict rules of sacredness were explained—how to engage with the holiness manifest in the Ark of the Covenant, who could enter the tabernacle and how, and who could not. There were rules for priestly purity and food laws for all. There were rituals of purification when dealing with contamination that followed childbirth or contact with death. There were details enumerated of sacrifices to be offered to God, rituals to be followed, every day, every week, every month, every year, every seven years. There were rituals to express gratitude and rituals for atonement.

Every year two goats would be offered in sacrifice. One would be killed and the second—the scapegoat—would be released in the wilderness, carrying with it all the sins of the people.

Aaron was appointed chief priest. But many argued against it. So, Moses took the rods of all those who felt they were as worthy as Aaron if not more, and placed them in the tabernacle. The next day, only Aaron's rod had sprouted flowers and fruit and it was clear God had chosen Aaron as the chief priest.

- The five books of Moses (Genesis, Exodus, Leviticus, Numbers and Deuteronomy) are collectively known as the Torah in Jewish traditions and Pentateuch in Christian traditions.
- Leviticus introduces us to the idea of purity. Concepts such as holiness, sacredness, profanity, abomination and taboo are found in all tribes and cultures. It is associated with space, time and people. Some spaces are purer. Some time periods are holier. Some people, some food, some vocations are holier than others.
- Numbers is the Christian name for the Jewish Book of Wilderness, which is a travelogue of the wanderings over forty years.
- Deuteronomy or the repeat sermon has the final sermons and speeches of Moses before the wandering people enter the Promised Land at last, without Moses.

Struggles in the Desert

Life in the desert was not easy. There was no fertile ground to sow seeds and harvest crops. Yet, every morning, with the dew, the ground would be covered with manna that God asked the Israelites to collect and use as bread. It tasted like wafer made with honey. They were told to collect only a day's share and no more. Those who did not trust God did collect more, just to be safe, and the extra manna would turn into maggots the next day.

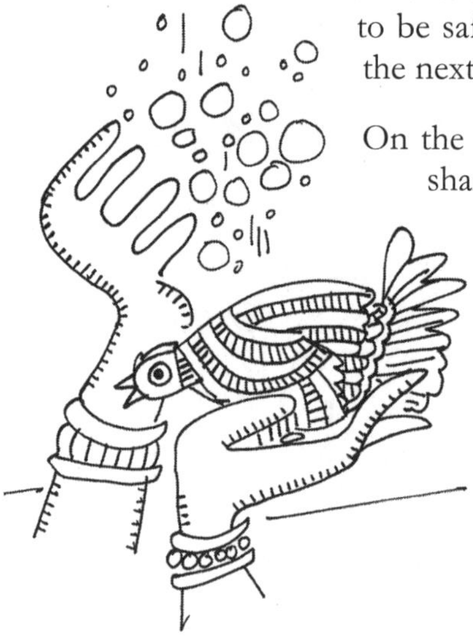

On the day before rest, everyone was told to collect two shares. The extra collected for the day of rest would not turn into maggots.

When people grew tired of eating manna and complained, God caused flocks of quails to fly into the camps, so people could catch them and get a reprieve from the diet of manna. No one ever went hungry on the days of wandering.

To cope with thirst, there was the well of

Miriam that accompanied her wherever she went. To cope with heat, there was the cloud of Aaron that sheltered the tribes wherever they went. At one point, venomous serpents attacked the Israelites. God told Moses to cast a serpent of bronze and hold it aloft. All those who saw this bronze serpent were saved from the effects of the poison.

Sometimes, the Israelites were attacked by hostile tribes who feared this migrating nation. Moses noticed that when he raised his hand, there was victory and when he lowered his hand there was defeat. He made men hold up both his tired arms, so that his people always won battles and were never afraid to fight.

At one point, men such as Korah, Dathan and Abiram murmured against the leadership of the Israelites. Korah told the following tale to incite people against Moses and Aaron: 'Moses did not allow a widow to plough her field with an ox and a mule. She was not allowed to plant mixed seeds nor was she allowed to pick up the fallen grain. The widow had to give away a part of the harvested grain. When she sold the land and got two sheep, she had to give away one of the sheep to the priests and the first fleece of the second sheep. When she killed the sheep, she had to give a portion of the meat to the priest; and when she, in protest, gave the meat to God, Aaron, as priest, claimed all the meat.'

In response to such false propaganda, God caused the earth to open and swallow these rebel leaders. Korah was burnt and buried alive, and all that he possessed was also pulled underground. His followers too were consumed by fire and buried alive.

There was also a time when people were drawn to idolatry. Those who led this practice were hanged and their followers killed by the plague.

Sometimes Moses's brother and sister, Miriam and Aaron, argued with him and threatened rebellion. At one point, Miriam was punished with leprosy until she atoned. Aaron was spared the same punishment as he was the high priest.

- In Jewish rituals commemorating the wanderings in the wilderness, a plate is laid out with fish, meat and egg, representing water, earth and air, symbolizing at one level Miriam, Moses and Aaron, who brought water, manna and quails to the hungry Israelites during the wandering, and at another level representing the three gigantic creatures of creation: Leviathan that swims in the sea, Behemoth that walks on land and Ziz that flies in the air.
- Korah rebelled against Moses and Aaron because he resented the rules he had to follow and the share he had to give to priests. He embodies the rich man who refuses to pay taxes and follow regulations and complains about the greed of priests. Korah is known as Qarun in Islam and he believes that he alone is the creator of his wealth and he owes nothing to Allah.
- Miriam and Aaron, sister and brother, often argue with Moses, and God intervenes to show that Moses is the chosen one, even though he is the youngest of the three.
- Monotheistic religions demand submission to the word and so its counter, dissent and rebellion, remains a consistent theme in Abrahamic lore. The obedient sheep is venerated, not the disobedient goat.
- Monotheistic religions do speak of equality. Yet, we find priests being treated differently, reminding us of the human love for special status despite the theoretical appeals against hierarchy.
- The widespread appeal of idolatry, frowned upon by monotheistic religions, reveals the human comfort with the tangible over the intangible. We prefer the literal over the metaphorical, an object over an idea. Tensions between Catholic and Protestant divisions of Christianity, and between Shia and Sunni divisions of Islam are often based on what constitutes idolatry.

Khidr, the Evergreen Prophet

During the wanderings, many people heard the long sermons of Moses. On a day, when his mind was full of doubt on the many years of wandering, a man asked, 'Is there anyone more knowledgeable than you?' And Moses replied he did not think so. So, God told Moses to take a dead fish and walk into the desert. At one point the dead fish would come to life, and that he should follow this fish to the sea, where he would meet a prophet who is more knowledgeable than he.

Moses did as he was told and encountered an old man with a long, white beard and green robes, who could travel in the sea on a fish as men in deserts do on camels. His name was Khidr. He knew Abraham and was so impressed by his words that he had submitted to the wisdom of the one true god. As he was curious, he had been educated by Gabriel himself.

Moses spent a lot of time with Khidr. Khidr had only one condition, 'Never question my actions. If you do so, we will part and you will never see me again.'

The two once took a ride on a ship. After alighting, Khidr took an axe and made a hole so that water entered the ship and it sank. While passing through a village, Khidr caught a child playing on the street and broke his neck. Then, in a village whose residents were rude and offered them no food, Khidr repaired the wall of a house. Unable to contain his curiosity, Moses finally demanded an explanation for Khidr's strange behaviour.

Khidr replied, 'By destroying the ship I saved the life of the sailors, for without a ship they would not be recruited by a king who was on his way to a great naval battle, where he would surely face defeat. By killing the child, who would grow up to be disobedient and horrible, I reduced the pain of his parents, who are good people and will soon be blessed with another child who will be obedient and nice. By repairing the wall, I have ensured the treasure in the wall is not claimed by the village but by the orphans who live in the house, a few years later, when they grow up. You see, I can see the future, which you cannot. But now since you broke your word and questioned by actions, we have to part ways.'

So, Moses returned to the desert a humbled man, enlightened in the ways of trust.

- This story is found in the Quran though the wise man whom Moses and his servant meet is not named.
- The man whom Moses meets is later identified as Khidr. In later literature, he is associated with water, the colour green, fish and immortality. He is considered immortal and wise.
- The story is popular in Persia and amongst seafaring merchants, and in the Muslim community of Sri Lanka. In Sindh, Khidr was linked to a local holy man, Jhulelal, who rides a fish upstream.
- This story is about realizing that even the greatest of men do not know everything.

Death of Miriam and Aaron

As the years passed, children were born and grew up and the older generation began to die. Miriam died. Without Miriam there was no water. The thirst became unbearable. God told Moses to strike a rock with his rod. But there was so much murmuring and rebellion that Moses impatiently struck his rod on a rock not once but twice. Water gushed out and turned into twelve streams to quench the thirst of all twelve tribes, but since Moses had lost his faith momentarily, and used God's name in vain, he was told that he, too, would not enter the Promised Land.

Aaron died too. No one except Moses was present when he died. People who loved Aaron felt Moses had killed him, as Aaron was loved more by the people. Moses, the leader, was not as loved, as he was firm and inflexible and distant, refusing to make room for human frailties, always condemning the tribes for their weakness and disobedience. With the death of Miriam and Aaron, the twelve tribes felt they had lost their mother and father.

Moses sang songs of mourning as he was now alone without sister or brother, and his songs revealed his pain, innocence and loneliness to all.

- Miriam is one of the few female prophets in Abrahamic lore. She is associated with song and dance, and water. She was the only woman allowed to enter the tabernacle.
- Aaron's personality is contrasted with Moses. He is soft and accommodating while Moses is stern and rigid.
- Aaron is called Harun in Islam.

Balaam

After forty years of wandering, the Israelites finally reached and camped in Moab, the edge of the Promised Land. The older generation who left Egypt had all died or were too old to travel to the new land. Even Moses would not—a punishment for having used God's name in vain. As God had decreed, a new generation, born in hardship, with no memory of Egypt, its idolatry and its luxury, would enter and finally claim the land of milk and honey.

As the assembled people were being counted, leaders chosen and everyone reminded of the rituals to follow to maintain their fidelity to God's law, Balak, who was the king of Moab, summoned a sorcerer called Balaam and ordered him to curse these assembled wild people who threatened the stability of his kingdom by their invasion.

Balaam rode a donkey to a mountaintop from where he could see the Israelites and curse them. But as he approached the mountaintop, the donkey would not proceed. So Balaam beat the donkey and to his shock the donkey spoke, 'Why do you hit me? Can't you see there is an angel not letting us go ahead?' And Balaam saw the angel, who told him that he would speak only what God would place on his tongue, nothing else.

From atop the hill, three times did Balaam try to curse the Israelites. Three times God caused blessings to pour out of his mouth. All his curses travelled in the reverse direction towards his own people.

The third time, Balaam opened his mouth, he said that from this tribe of wandering people would come the king who would establish the kingdom of God on earth and help the return of humanity to Eden.

- Balaam advises King Balak to corrupt the Israelites with sexual favours and food offered to idols. Those who are thus corrupted are brutally punished by Moses in the heresy of Peor.
- In Islamic retellings, Balaam embodies a person with magical powers, who helps the enemy for money. He creates obstacles to progress.

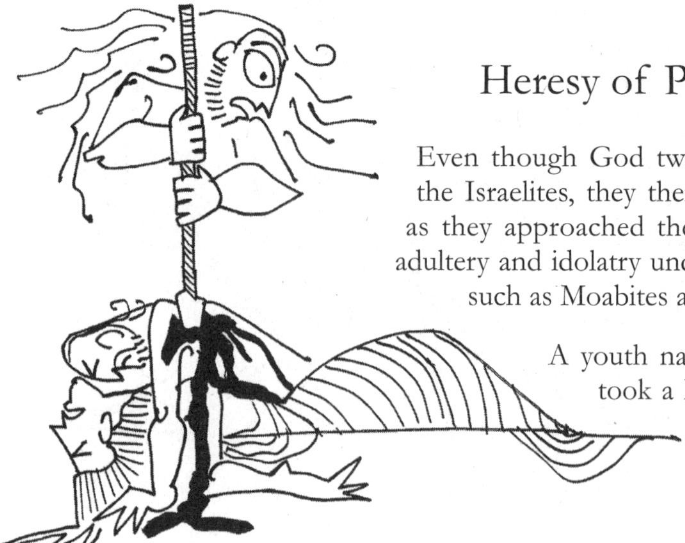

Heresy of Peor

Even though God twisted Balaam's tongue to bless the Israelites, they themselves kept disregarding God as they approached the Promised Land, indulging in adultery and idolatry under the influence of neighbours such as Moabites and Midianites.

A youth named Zimri, rather audaciously, took a Midianite woman named Cozbi into his tent right in front of Moses. Disgusted by this behaviour, Phineas, a grandson of Aaron, rushed into the tent, raised his spear and impaled Zimri and Cozbi even as they lay in each other's arms.

Moses then ordered the hanging of all those ungrateful Israelites who chose to worship false gods despite all the generosity bestowed upon them by God. This is known as the heresy of Peor.

- This story comes from the Hebrew Bible.
- The Hebrew expression 'One who acts like Zimri and asks for a reward as if he were Phineas' refers to hypocrites who ask for undeserved rewards and honours.
- God speaks directly to man before the Flood, but after the Flood, we find God talking to man through prophets. Until Abraham, God punishes transgressors directly, but later, that too happens through prophets.
- Forty is a recurring number in Abrahamic lore. God floods the earth by causing it to rain for forty days and forty nights. Moses goes up the mountain and returns with the commandments after forty days and forty nights. The spies sent to Canaan return with news after forty days and forty nights. The Israelites were doomed to wander in the wilderness for forty years.

The Death of Moses

When the angel of death came to Moses, Moses struck him in the eye. So, the angel went to Allah and said that Moses was not willing to die. Allah asked the angel to tell Moses to pull a fistful of hair from the back of a cow. He would live as many years as the hairs he pulls out.

When this was conveyed to Moses, he realized that there was no escaping death. So he told the angel to come to him that very same year, the fortieth year of exile, after he came in sight of the Promised Land.

So, Moses gathered his people and gave his last sermon and told them how to make the most of the Promised Land, always obeying God's law and trusting God's love. He made Joshua the leader of his people and prepared to die.

Moses then climbed a mountain from where he could see Canaan at a distance, the home of Abraham, Isaac and Jacob, and allowed death to come to him. No one was allowed to see where he was buried. And so many believed he rose to Heaven as Enoch before him.

- Moses's death is a mystery. It is not clear why he resists death or why his burial site is not known. There are stories of Michael fighting the Devil over his dead body.
- The psychoanalyst Freud in his work *Moses and Monotheism,* written in 1939, mentioned his belief that Moses was killed by his followers during the wanderings. The guilt of killing the father figure gave rise to monotheism, based on submission to a male authority figure and yearnings for a messiah who would save them.
- In Islamic retellings, Joshua is present at the time of Moses's death.
- In Islamic commentaries, Moses is considered a martyr even though he does not die in battle. The word used is *shaheed*, which means one who witnesses the truth, and lives and dies by the truth. Becoming a martyr does not need a violent end but an unquestioning resolve to align with God's law.

BOOK SIX

Settlement in Canaan

Joshua, the New Commander

Moses was dead. He had seen the Promised Land but had not entered it, like most of those who had left Egypt. Only two of that generation would enter the Promised Land. One of them was Joshua. The other was Caleb.

Joshua and Caleb were two of the twelve spies sent by Moses from Sinai to Canaan. While the rest of the spies demoralized the people who had escaped from Egypt, saying that it was not worth the effort to go to Canaan—which had mighty kings who would not share their rich and fertile land—Joshua and Caleb had given the people hope, saying that Canaan was indeed the Promised Land, a place they could call home, and that they had the strength to make a home for themselves there.

Joshua had been a young man when he left Egypt. He had been by Moses's side all through the wanderings over forty years. He was full of faith and hope. So, he was the chosen leader of the younger generation, which had never known the luxuries of Egypt, just the hardship of the wilderness. He was over eighty years of age when they reached what would be home.

- Joshua represents the transition between the old generation of Israelites and the new. He embodies both faith and hope.
- In medieval Europe, Joshua was one of the nine worthies, the others being two other Jews (King David and Judas Maccabees, who restored the worship of Jehovah in the Second Temple), three pagans (Hector of Troy, Julius Caesar and Alexander the Great) and three Christians (King Arthur of the Round Table, King Charlemagne, who united Christian Europe and drove out the Muslims, and Godfrey of Bouillon, who led the First Crusade).

Rahab

Like Moses, who had sent spies from the wilderness to Canaan, Joshua sent two spies to check the city of Jericho. The two put up at an inn owned by a woman called Rahab. She figured out that they were spies of the tribes who had escaped from Egypt and who kept wandering in the desert. She decided to help them as their ways, faithful to one true god, were much better than the ways of Jericho, full of wickedness, adultery and many gods.

She hid the spies under a pile of straw on her roof when the king's guards arrived, and helped them escape from the window of her house on the condition that when the Israelites attacked the city, they would spare her family. The spies agreed and told her to mark her house by tying a red cord at the door.

- In all probability, Rahab was a prostitute.
- In Jewish retellings, she marries Joshua. Her son is Boaz, who marries Ruth. So, she is the ancestor of King David and Jesus.
- Tamar (Judah's daughter-in-law), Rahab (the prostitute of Jericho who marries Joshua and is the mother of Boaz), Ruth (the daughter-in-law of Naomi and wife of Boaz), Bathsheba (wife of Uriah whom David gets killed so that he can make her his queen) and Mary (the virgin mother of Jesus) are considered the five most important women in the family tree of Jesus in the Christian tradition.

The Walls of Jericho

Joshua ordered his army to march towards Jericho. As soon as the priests carrying the Ark of the Covenant stepped into River Jordan, the waters parted as the sea had parted for Moses, reminding all that God watched over his people.

Across the river, Joshua met a mysterious soldier, who revealed that he was a captain of God's army. He told Joshua that instead of attacking the city, he should take a procession around the city carrying the Ark of the Covenant once a day for six days. On the seventh day, he should do the same seven times while blowing a ram's horn simultaneously.

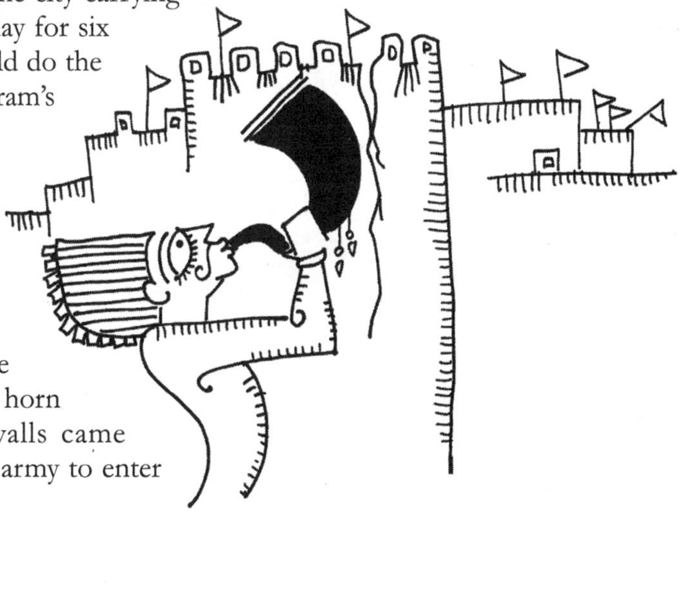

Not fight? Joshua realized this was a test of his people's faith in God, and so did as he was told. The parades took place once every day for six days. On the seventh day, they circled the city seven times, blowing a ram's horn simultaneously, until the city walls came tumbling down, allowing Joshua's army to enter the city and conquer it.

Every man, woman, child and animal in the city was killed. Joshua told his people to not take any of the treasures of the city for themselves; it was all for Jehovah, God, who had granted them victory.

- The brutality of the conquest can be disconcerting to the modern mind. It reveals the transition of the luxury-remembering ex-slaves of one generation into battle-hardened, freedom-loving wanderers of the next generation, who were determined to settle down.
- Rationalists argue that the method of pulling down the walls of Jericho is based on sonic wave resonance. Others argue it was an earthquake that brought down the walls.

Defeat at Ai

The victory at Jericho was followed by defeat at Ai. The Israelites were driven away by the city-dwellers rather easily. Joshua, humbled in defeat, wondered why. Had he or his people broken God's commandments? On enquiry, he learned that one of his soldiers, Achan, had taken some of the plundered gold and silver from Jericho for himself and not given it to Jehovah as everyone had been ordered.

Furious at this transgression that had resulted in defeat, Joshua ordered Achan be stoned to death as a warning to people to always follow God's law to display their love for God. Joshua then launched a second attack on Ai. This time there was success.

- Victory following obedience and defeat following disobedience are consistent themes in Abrahamic lore.
- The violence of the Old Testament (Hebrew Bible) is counterbalanced by the non-violence and pacificism of the New Testament (Christian Bible). This is how, at least initially, Christianity broke away from Judaism. Later, after being adopted by Roman emperors, even Christianity took on a military form, especially during the Crusades and at the time of imperial expansion to the Americas, Africa and Asia. The transition from non-violent dissent when in opposition to the use of violence when in power is a recurring theme in human history.

Treaty with Gibeonites

Joshua was met by a group of strangers wearing old, torn and dusty clothes, who claimed to be ambassadors from a distant city. They had heard how the Israelites had destroyed Jericho and Ai, and wanted to make a peace treaty with them, so as to live under their protection. Without consulting God, Joshua made an agreement with the strangers.

But, then he realized that these people were from the city of Gibeon, barely three days away from where the Israelites had encamped themselves. They had been tricked. Joshua had no choice and had make peace rather than war, as God willed it, with these residents of Canaan. But he enslaved the Gibeonites, and they were made water carriers and woodcutters who would serve Jehovah.

- 'Gibeonite deception' is often used as a phrase warning one to avoid taking hasty decisions out of pity without consulting God.
- It is ironical that those liberated from slavery in Egypt end up enslaving Gibeonites.
- These stories reveal how uncomfortable human negotiations and compromises are rationalized as God's will when chronicled by later generations.

Conquest of Canaan

The Amorite king created a confederacy of five Canaanite kings and attacked the city of Gibeon that had allied with the invading Israelites. In the war that followed, God helped Joshua's armies by causing hailstones to fall and by even stopping the movement of the sun and the moon to enable the victory of Joshua over the Amorites.

Victory followed victory. As the Israelites marched, many cities fell to them. Under Joshua's command all of Canaan fell to the children of the twelve tribes that had wandered in the wilderness for forty years. Finally, Joshua divided the land amongst the twelve tribes to the satisfaction of all.

Joshua, now over a hundred, told his people to always love God and obey his commandments if they wished peace and prosperity, and warned them of the misfortune that would follow disobedience. Then, he died, the only man to see the slavery in Egypt, the wanderings in the desert, and finally find residence in the Promised Land.

- Joshua is not referred to in the Quran, but he is revered in the wider Islamic tradition as Yusha. He was considered exceptional amongst Israelites as he followed Allah.
- Nabi Yusha or Prophet Joshua's tomb has been identified in various local traditions in Lebanon, Syria, Turkey and Iraq.
- Mormon pioneers in the United States first referred to the 'Spanish Dagger' tree as the 'Joshua' tree because its spread-out branches reminded them of Joshua stretching his arms upward in supplication, as he did to ensure victory in Canaan, guiding the travellers westward.

Judges

Joshua was gone. The land of Canaan was divided among the twelve tribes of Israel. But they had no king.

In the absence of a real leader, as the Israelites mingled with the neighbouring people—the Canaanites, the Philistines—they gradually gave up their old ways and began following new ways, which essentially meant disobeying God's commandments. They worshipped gods other than the one true god. They worshipped idols. They did not follow dietary laws and ate impure food. Neither did they rest on the Sabbath. They indulged in adultery, theft, lying and coveting. So, they lost God's love and became subject to the tyranny of local kings.

And when the people cried out, God heard them and sent amongst them military leaders known as Judges, who granted them deliverance. Unfortunately, the people slipped back into their old ways, and the cycle of transgression, oppression and deliverance by the Judges continued for a long time.

The first of the Judges was Othniel, who united the tribes and led in a victorious war against their oppressors, resulting in forty years of peace.

Another was Ehud, who came bearing gifts for the tyrant king Eglon of the Moabites. He sought a private audience with the king and when the latter's guards went away, he pulled out his sword, murdered the king, locked the doors and ran away. Ehud was long gone by the time the guards discovered their king had been assassinated.

Another Judge was Shamgar, who repelled the Philistine incursions into Israelite territory by smashing the heads of 600 invaders with his ox goad.

- The term 'Judges' is a literal translation of the original Hebrew term *shoftim*. These are not judges as in the legal system. They were elected non-hereditary military leaders, most probably tribal in nature.
- The period of the Judges is calculated to be between 1300 BCE and 1000 BCE. But such chronologies are speculative despite persistent attempts to locate biblical narratives through archaeology.
- In the Jewish tradition, as per the Talmud, Othniel was Caleb's brother and son-in-law.

Deborah, a Woman Judge

A woman called Deborah stood under a palm tree and revealed the messages of God. She motivated Barak to raise an army and fight Sisera, the general of the Canaanites, who had 900 iron chariots. Barak obeyed without question because he knew Deborah was a prophet and through her God spoke.

In the war that followed, Sisera's army was defeated but Sisera escaped. He ran from the battlefield and found refuge in the tent of a woman named Jael, who recognized him as the feared oppressor of her people. She offered him food and a place to rest and while he was sleeping, she hammered a tent peg into his head.

- This was a rare and unique war as it was initiated as well as concluded by women, a reminder that God saw women as defenders, leaders and Judges of Israel.
- The *Song of Deborah* is a victory hymn celebrating the triumph over the Canaanites. A line from the song states, 'The mountains flowed before the Lord' and so physicists designated the number used to indicate the flowing state of matter as the Deborah number.

Gideon, the One Who Doubted

Once again, the tribes transgressed. Midianites soldiers destroyed fields, stole crops and cattle, forcing Israelites to seek refuge in the mountain. So, the people of Israel begged for a leader. And God chose Gideon, who had little faith in God.

Gideon asked God to prove his identity: 'I will believe it is you if you make the woollen fleece I put on the floor wet with dew in the morning but not the floor below it.' God did this. Then Gideon said the next day, 'I will believe it is indeed you God, the one true god, if you keep the fleece I put on the floor dry in the morning but wet the floor beneath it.' God did this. Convinced it was indeed God directing him, Gideon raised an army of 32,000 people.

God told him he needed a much smaller army and to get rid of all those who are afraid. Gideon did so and was left with 10,000 who were not afraid.

'Get them to drink water from the river Jordan,' said God. About 300 soldiers bent their necks and licked the water like animals, unafraid of being ambushed, while the rest took water in the cup of their palms and drank, while keeping an eye on the surroundings. God told Gideon to attack the vast Midianite army with only the 300 bold men.

Gideon was not sure. So, God told Gideon to spy on the enemy army and eavesdrop on their conversations. Gideon heard them speak of a dream where a loaf of bread would roll over the entire Midianite army. Gideon realized the enemy was more frightened of the Israelites than the other way round.

On God's orders Gideon attacked the enemy at night, armed with only bugles and torches hidden in jars. The soldiers blew the bugles and created a racket and smashed the jars exposing the torches. The Midianites panicked fearing a vast ambush and ran in every direction, leaving their leaders exposed to be killed by Gideon.

Gideon's victory prompted calls that he should be king. He refused. Instead, he asked people to give him a piece of gold that they had acquired in raids and used it to build an idol that was worshipped in thanks for victory.

- Gideon's victory is often used as an example of a smaller army winning over a larger one using smart strategy.
- In Islamic traditions, a similar story is told with reference to Talut (King Saul). God asks Talut to tell his soldiers not to drink water from the river they encounter next. However, most men do so. So, God tells Talut to proceed with a smaller army of only those who faithfully obeyed God's words. Despite having a much smaller army, Talut succeeds just like Gideon.
- The character Gideon refers to one who doubts. This inspired the name of an international evangelical Christian association (the Gideons) famous for distributing free Bibles to hotels and motels to help travellers burdened by doubt. It was started in late nineteenth century by two travelling American salesmen.

Jephthah's Daughter

When he was young, Jephthah's half-brothers drove him out of the house because his mother was a prostitute. So, he grew up amongst outlaws and became their feared leader. When the people of Israel sought his help to defeat the Ammonites, Jephthah agreed.

In the course of the war, Jephthah told God, 'If I win, the first creature I see when I return home I will sacrifice to you.'

The Ammonites were defeated. When Jephthah returned home, his daughter ran out in joy playing cymbals to greet him. Jephthah had to keep his word and sacrifice his own daughter. He had no choice.

God, who had granted him victory, had simultaneously punished him for taking God's name in vain.

- This story of human sacrifice stands in stark contrast to Isaac's sacrifice that God prevents.
- In Jewish tradition, Jephthah had not read the laws, otherwise, he would not have made such a rash promise to God. For this crime, he lost his limbs slowly and each time a limb sloughed off, it was buried, which is why he ended up having many tombs.
- Greek mythology tells the story of Idomeneus, king of Crete, who while returning home from the Trojan war encounters a terrible storm and promises to offer the gods the first being he encounters on landing on shore. That being turns out to be his own son.

Samson and Timnah

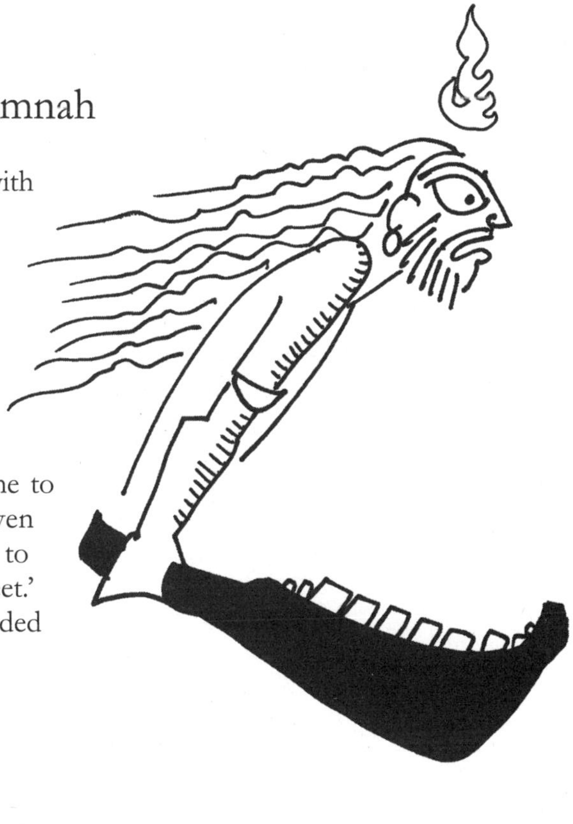

Samson was a strong and handsome man with lovely long hair, which his parents had never cut since his birth. He had a fondness for women, especially Philistine women, much to the irritation of his parents, who were Israelites from the tribe of Dan. He even decided to marry a Philistine woman called Timnah.

Samson challenged the guests who had come to the wedding to answer a riddle within seven days: 'What eater itself gave out something to eat? From the strong, what came forth sweet.' The answer was a dead lion whose corpse ended up providing shelter to a beehive, a secret that Samson knew since it was he who had killed the lion. If they lost, each of the thirty guests would have to give Samson a robe as gift.

Determined not to let this cocky Israelite dishonour the Philistines, the guests forced Samson's wife to glean the secret out of her husband and share it with them. Timnah, more true to her people than to her husband, did as told. Samson thus lost the bet. Instead of getting thirty robes, he had to give each of the thirty guests a robe.

Samson was told by his father-in-law to leave and not return till he got the robes for the wedding guests. So, Samson raided a nearby city and obtained the robes. When he returned to Timnah's house, he was horrified to learn that his father-in-law, not expecting him back, had got her married to someone else. A furious Samson caught three hundred foxes and tied torches to their tails, terrifying them and causing them to run amok and set fire to all the fields and vineyards of the Philistines.

In retaliation, the Philistines burnt the house of Timnah. Samson then attacked and burnt many Philistine houses and retreated to the land of his people. The Philistines then threatened Israelites with dire consequences. Things were escalating out of control.

To save his people, Samson told them to tie him with thick ropes and give him up to the Philistines. They did as advised. When he was in the middle of his captors, he stretched out his hands and tore the thick ropes as if they were thin threads, and picking up the jaw bone of an ass, beat a thousand Philistines to death.

- In the Jewish tradition, Samson is said to be so strong that he could lift mountains as if they were lumps of clay.
- The idea of a strong man with great passion and volatile impulses is found in Hindu mythology too. The epic hero Bhima of the Mahabharata has similar traits.

Samson and Delilah

But Samson had not learned his lesson about how untrustworthy the Philistines were. He married another Philistine woman, Delilah. Spellbound by her beauty, he told her that the secret of his great strength was his hair, a secret she shared with her people, in exchange for silver. For even more silver, she let them enter her house while Samson was sleeping, cut his long, beautiful locks, and shave his head.

When Samson woke up, he suddenly found himself surrounded by Philistine soldiers. He tried to fight them, but he no longer had his divine strength. They overpowered him easily, put him in chains, gouged out his eyes, and made him grind corn in a public mill like a domesticated animal, so that everyone could jeer at this Israelite who dared see himself as an equal to Philistines.

During a festival of their god Dagon, all Philistines gathered in the temple. As part of entertainment and display of power, they decided to present Samson to the crowds that had gathered. Everyone could see how the once mighty warrior had been subdued.

His heart broken, his trust betrayed, his pride crushed, Samson, whose hair had started to grow back, begged God to give him back his strength, so that he could take revenge against the cheering crowds of Philistines and redeem himself.

When Samson felt that God had heard his prayers, he begged his captors to let him lean against two pillars, as he was too weak to stand. When this was allowed, Samson used all his strength to crack the pillars, causing the roof of the temple to collapse and crush the thousands of Philistines who stood beneath. Samson died too, but he had the last laugh for in his death he had killed more people than he had in his life.

- Dagon is a fertility god of Mesopotamian mythology and is associated with grain. However, in the nineteenth century, many scholars linked Dagon with fish and assumed he was the 'merman' god of Babylonian art.
- In Jewish commentaries, Samson's eyes were cut out as punishment as he was obsessed with women and so pursued them to his downfall.
- In Christian commentaries, there is much in common between Samson and Jesus. Both their births were foretold. Samson's mother was a barren woman; Jesus's mother was a virgin. Samson killed a lion; Jesus overpowered the Devil. Samson was betrayed by Delilah while Jesus was betrayed by Judas; both of whom were bribed with silver.
- This is a classic 'femme fatale' story—a powerful man falling in love with a beautiful, sexy woman, revealing his vulnerabilities to her, and she betraying and destroying the man. Stories such as these that paint beautiful women as dangerous, evil temptations are male mechanisms to cope with rejection by beautiful and intelligent women.

Micah's Idol

Micah's mother feared that she had lost a thousand pieces of silver only to realize that her son had stolen them. When he returned the coins, she made him melt 200 of them and turn it into an idol. She then encouraged him to find a priest for the idol. He found a homeless Levite, whom he offered shelter and food in exchange for serving as priest.

Sometime later, a group of soldiers from the landless tribe of Dan took refuge in Micah's house, where they saw the idol and the priest. They were blessed by the Levite priest who wished them success in their mission. The mission—raiding of a fertile farm nearby—was a success.

The landless tribe suddenly had access to a rich land. The soldiers attributed their success to Micah's idol; so, they stole it from Micah's house for the tribe and asked the Levite to be the priest for the entire tribe. Thus, idolatry became a way of life for the tribe of Dan, and eventually the other tribes of Israel.

- In Jewish retellings, sometimes, Micah is identified as the son of Delilah. As he offered shelter to the Levite priest and later the soldiers of the Dan tribe, he is not seen in a negative light despite being an idolater. In one retelling, God stops an angel from punishing the idol-worshipping Micah.
- In some retellings, Micah was the one who brought idols with him out of Egypt. In one retelling, it was he who crafted the image of the golden calf. Thus, Micah is continuously linked to idolatry.
- Micah means 'the crushed one'. This has led to a Jewish retelling of a boy who was cast by his parents into clay to make brick during the days of Egyptian slavery. The Israelites had to finish making bricks but had no time to find straw and so put a child in it. Moses saved the child and breathed life into him. He came to be known as Micah.

The Levite's Concubine

A Levite had a concubine who had a fight with him and went to her father's house. The Levite followed her, made peace with her and together they returned home. On the way, they stopped in the city of Gibeah, in the land of the Benjamin tribe, where a stranger gave them shelter.

That night, the people of Gibeah knocked on their host's door and demanded access to the Levite so that they could know him better. The host refused to give the people access to his guest and offered his daughter instead. But the crowd of people kept insisting on getting access to the Levite. Finally, to be rid of them, the Levite shoved his concubine out of the door and she was brutally ravaged by them all night. The next day, the Levite found her at the door of the house, barely alive.

By the time the Levite returned home, the concubine was dead. Angry, the Levite cut her body into twelve pieces and sent each piece to the twelve tribes of Israel, seeking justice. And so a great war followed between the confederation of tribes on the one hand and the tribe of Benjamin on the other, who refused to hand over the men who had abused the Levite's concubine.

In that war, the Benjamin tribe was completely destroyed by the confederacy, all but 600, who survived by hiding in a cave for four months. It was then decided by the confederacy of tribes that no one would give their daughter to the tribe of Benjamin, which had not only abused the Levite's concubine but sheltered the perpetrators of the crime.

Later, the confederacy of tribes realized they had caused the destruction of one of their own. A tribe would die, and that was not acceptable, the fault of the Benjaminites notwithstanding. So, they decided to give them new wives.

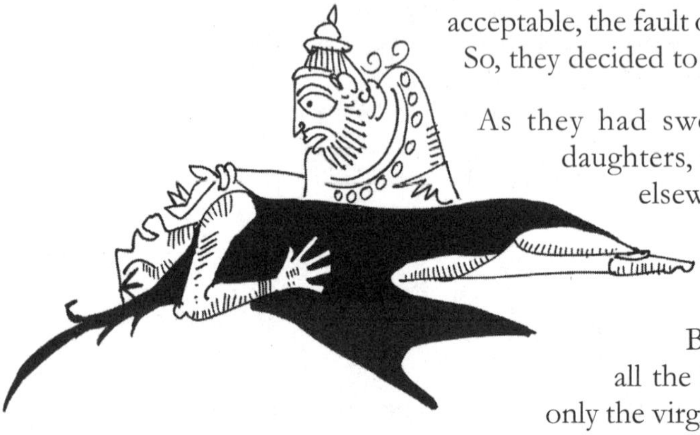

As they had sworn not to give them their own daughters, they needed to find women from elsewhere. So, the confederacy attacked a nearby town whose residents expressed no remorse at the tragedy that had befallen the Benjaminites. The confederacy killed all the town's men and women and spared only the virgins, whom they gave to the surviving men of the tribe of Benjamin.

But there were not enough virgins for all the men. So, the elders advised the 200 men without wives to abduct virgins from another town when they stepped out for a festival in the gardens outside the city. Thus was the Benjaminite tribe saved from extinction.

- This violent story is very similar to the story of Sodom. The people of the city of Gibeah instead of offering shelter to a stranger want to 'know him'—a metaphor for sex.
- The story is said to reveal a time when there was no king, hence, no order or morality. It is similar to the Hindu concept of *arajakta* (mayhem) that follows when a land has no raja (king).
- Feminists have argued that this is a classical patriarchal narrative, where women are raped and abducted, and have no agency nor a voice. The story is all about men's feelings and men's needs. It is a reminder that these stories were written in times where history was about men.

Loyal Ruth

In these early years in the Promised Land, life was tough. Once, there was a famine, so bad that Naomi, her husband and two sons had to migrate as refugees to the enemy territory of Moab. Here Naomi's sons got married to Moabite women and tried to settle down. But tragedy struck, and Naomi lost her husband and her two sons.

Naomi decided to return to her people, and told her widowed daughters-in-law to go their way as Moabites would not be safe in Israel. Of the two girls, the one called Oprah decided to return to her family while the other, Ruth, decided to stay with Naomi, declaring her loyalty with the words, 'Your god will be my god, your people will be my people. I always go where you go.'

When Naomi returned home to Bethlehem, the barley harvest was over. But the poor were allowed to glean leftover grain from the field.

Ruth gleaned to find food for herself and Naomi in the field of Boaz, a generous landowner.

Boaz treated Ruth kindly for he realized that she was a Moabite who had stayed loyal to her Jewish mother-in-law even after her husband died. He told her to work with the women, told the men not to bother her and offered her food and water.

Naomi realized that Boaz was related to her late husband. So, she told Ruth to give up her widow's attire, wear bridal finery, go to Boaz's field at night and lay at his feet, covering her head with the edge of his cloak, indicating to him that she sought his guardianship.

Boaz could not refuse but he had to first check if there was any other male relative who was closer to Naomi's husband who had first right over Ruth. There was one, but he did not want to offer guardianship to a Moabite. So, Boaz agreed to be Ruth's guardian. He married her and they had a son. And people called the newborn, the son of Naomi.

In this family would be born the future kings of the land, the temporal king David and the spiritual king Jesus.

- In Jewish retellings, Ruth is the granddaughter of King Balak, who sent the sorcerer Balaam to curse the Israelites when they entered the Promised Land. Though a princess, she had fallen on bad times, and was forced to do a lowly job to survive, which she carried out with dignity.
- The poor were allowed to glean leftover rice from the fields after the harvest as an act of charity.
- If the story of Samson is often used to caution people against marrying foreigners, the story of Ruth is used to state the very opposite. She is foreign but faithful.
- Many scholars of queer theory see in this story a homoerotic, perhaps even a lesbian, relationship between Ruth and Naomi. In keeping with the times, they needed male protection, but Ruth's child was called the son of Naomi, indicative of the comfort of the unconventional intimate relationship of two women.

BOOK SEVEN

A Kingdom, Finally

Saul, the First King

The people had no king to lead them. They did what they felt was right in their own eyes. They did not listen to prophets. Even the Judges broke laws and indulged in idolatry. Finally, the people united under a man called Saul, who was identified by the prophet Samuel as being fit to be king.

Saul was looking for his father's lost donkeys when he encountered the Ammonites laying siege to a city, demanding the right eye of every man as tribute in exchange for their life. Saul raised an army, defeated the Ammonites, and was deemed a worthy leader.

Unfortunately, Saul was not the most obedient of people. Once, he did not wait for Samuel to arrive and impatiently made offerings to God. Another time, despite express instructions to kill all Amalekites, even their livestock, he spared the king and the good livestock, angering Samuel, who killed the enemy king with his bare hands and told Saul that God had rejected him and chosen another king instead.

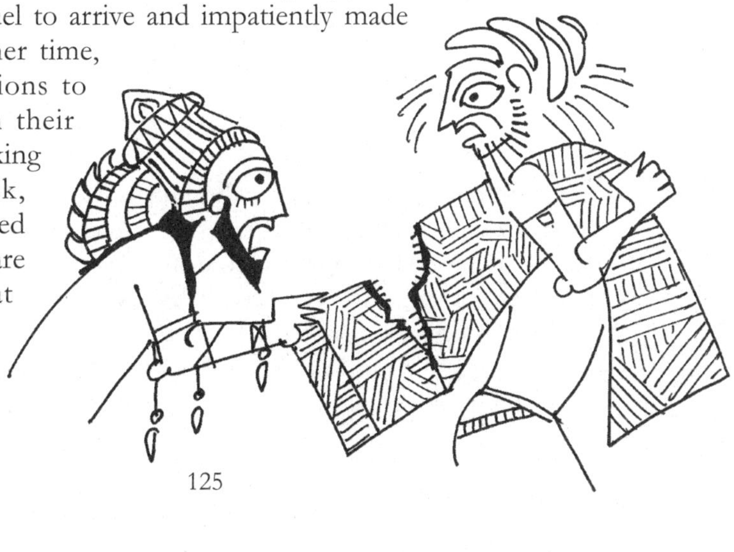

As Samuel turned away from Saul and prepared to leave, Saul grabbed his robe and ended up tearing it. 'As you have torn my robe from my body, the kingdom shall be torn away from you,' said Samuel.

- The selection of Saul perhaps took place using Urim and Thummim, two objects used by Jewish high priests to determine the will of God. When a question was clearly asked, Urim flashed light to indicate approval while Thummim flashed light when it was disapproved. Similar divination was practised in pre-Islamic Arabia, where two arrow shafts in the temple of Hubal were used to indicate approval (arrowhead in same direction) and disapproval (arrowhead in different directions).
- The selection and then rejection of Saul has been argued as an example of a mistake that even God can make.
- In Islamic retellings, Saul is called Talut, which means tall. They speak of how his selection is not accepted by many Israelites as he is not rich enough. While God chooses him as king, he is not a messenger, as in the case of David (Dawood) and Solomon (Suleiman), who are both kings and messengers.
- The prophet Samuel's mother, Hannah, was childless for a long time. Her husband's second wife bore many children. In sorrow, she prayed to God and declared that if she gave birth, that child would forever serve God. The child she conceived following this declaration was Samuel, who was dedicated since birth to God. This idea of a child dedicated to God starts appearing repeatedly after the exodus.

Death of Goliath

After Samuel's departure, Saul became restless. Denied access to the prophet, he consulted witches to foretell the future, even though this was forbidden by God's law. These witches told him that he and his sons would soon die, and that he would be replaced by a man, more worthy, more mighty, more talented—one who would be loved by his son and who would marry his daughter. Saul found no comfort in these words and he became more and more paranoid.

To soothe his nerves, he asked for a squire who could sing and make music. This is how David came into his life—to sing for him, and to make music with his harp. Little did Saul know that this David had been chosen by God, and identified by prophets, as the king who would replace him.

David was a good shepherd and was chosen over his brothers to protect his father's sheep. He was good with his slings and shot stones to keep wolves and lions at bay. He served Saul, took care of his armour, sang songs to comfort him, and watched the nervous restless king fight his nightmares all night and his enemies all day.

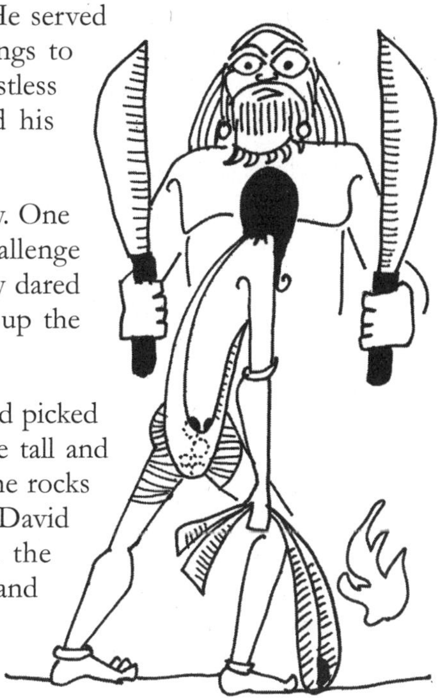

The Philistines attacked Israel relentlessly. One day, they sent their giant Goliath to challenge Israelites to a duel. No one in Saul's army dared to rise to the challenge. So, David took up the challenge.

Though much smaller, and younger, David picked up stones and used his sling to strike the tall and mighty Goliath. To everyone's surprise, the rocks cracked the giant's skull and Goliath fell. David then picked up a sword and beheaded the giant, striking fear among the Philistines and earning the admiration of the Israelites.

The incident made Saul nervous.

- As per the Dead Sea Scrolls, dated from 300 BCE to 100 BCE, Goliath was nearly seven feet tall. But in later Masoretic texts, dated to 1000 CE, he is said to be ten feet tall. This suggests that the giant's height kept increasing over time as the story was transmitted orally.
- The Book of Psalms is attributed to David, who played the lyre, and was thus a musician and a warrior, sensitive yet strong, hence, having the ideal qualities of a good king.
- The story is meant to show that David is more worthy to be king than Saul. Saul

is tall (Talut of Islamic tales) but Goliath is a giant. Saul cowers in fear despite having an armour. David walks to face the giant without armour, just as he fought lions and bears to save his father's sheep.

- In Jewish retellings, Ruth and Oprah were sisters. Ruth is faithful to her Israelite mother-in-law Naomi and marries an Israelite Boaz, and David is her great grandson. Oprah, who abandons Naomi, is the mother of Goliath, who is born from the sperm of a hundred Philistines.
- In Islamic tradition, Goliath is called Jalut. Victory of David (Dawood in Islam) over Jalut is used as a prefiguration of the victory of Prophet Muhammad over his formidable opponents at the battle of Badr.
- This biblical tale is similar to the Greek tale of Nestor fighting the giant Ereuthalion.
- The story is now used to describe confrontations between unequal rivals.

Love of Jonathan

David became a soldier in Saul's army. He led forces into battle and killed many enemy soldiers, much more than Saul or his sons. The soldiers said, 'Saul kills thousands, David kills tens of thousands.'

David became best friends with Saul's son, Jonathan. Saul had promised his daughter to a soldier who secured a 100 enemy foreskins; David procured 200 and became the king's son-in-law. The prophecy was coming true and Saul became even more nervous.

As David's popularity grew, Saul became increasingly hostile once even hurling a spear at him in a drunken state. Fearing for David's life, Jonathan advised him to escape, even if this meant risking the wrath of his royal father. But Jonathan loved David and knew his father was wrong.

David escaped and became an outlaw. Soon, he became the leader of outlaws. Saul sought to hunt him down, killing everyone, even priests, who dared shelter David. But David always outsmarted him.

Once, David entered Saul's tent while Saul was asleep, cut a piece of Saul's royal robe, and replaced Saul's spear with his own. The message was clear: David could have killed Saul if he wanted to but he respected Saul too much to kill him. And so, Saul made his peace with David, and let him be.

David lived in exile until the day Saul was defeated in a battle. That battle witnessed the death of all of Saul's sons, including his beloved Jonathan. A heartbroken Saul killed himself by throwing himself on his sword to avoid capture.

With Saul gone, the people turned to David and asked him to be king. David conquered Jerusalem and entered the city with the Ark of the Covenant, shedding his royal robes and dancing naked before it.

- Saul gives his daughter Michal to David, and then when David becomes an outlaw gives her to another man. When David becomes king, he reclaims Michal. She mocks him for dancing naked like a madman and commoner before the Ark of the Covenant as it enters the city.
- David's nakedness before the Ark of the Covenant refers to shedding of royal robes, and not being fully unclothed, as the latter would be considered disrespectful to God. He sees his act as a demonstration of faith while his wife, who berates him, sees it as unbecoming of his royal status.
- Queer theorists see the relationship between David and Jonathan in homoerotic terms. When Jonathan meets David for the first time, following the defeat of Goliath, he gives David his robes, armour and sword, and says that he loves David as he loves himself. When David hears of Jonathan's death, he says: 'Your love for me was more wonderful than the love of women.' People debate on whether these statements are platonic or romantic.
- In Jewish retellings, there is no idolatry or famine during the reign of Saul. Saul is told that when he dies he will reside in the afterlife Sheol along with Samuel, indicating he is eventually forgiven by God.
- As per the Quran, Allah gave Dawood power over iron to make it soft (wrought iron) and make chain-mail of it, which enabled him to overpower his opponents, who used bronze and the more brittle cast iron.

- In Islamic retellings, David's singing could captivate man and animal, thus connecting him with the Greek musician, Orpheus. Though king, he spent a lot of time in prayer and fasting.

The Beautiful Bathsheba

David was a great king. He led Israelites to many victorious battles against Philistines, Moabites, Edomites, Amalekites and Ammonites, after which they became his tributaries. He married many women and had many concubines and had many children with them. Wealth flowed into Israel and he wished to build a temple for the God of Abraham, where the Ark of the Covenant could be housed.

Then, David fell in love with a beautiful woman called Bathsheba. But she was already married to Uriah, the Hittite, a soldier in his army. David had Uriah sent to battle and ordered that he fight in the frontlines, thus ensuring his death, and enabling his widow to remarry.

But David's cleverness did not fool God, who communicated his displeasure through Prophet Nathan.

Nathan approached David and sought justice for a poor man who had been wronged by a rich man. Rather than taking one from his own flocks to feed a traveller, the rich man claimed the one lamb that the poor neighbour dearly loved. David was understandably upset when he heard the complaint. He decreed that the rich man should die. No sooner did he take this decision than Nathan revealed that the rich man in his story was none other than David himself, a king with many wives. The poor neighbour was the Hittite, Uriah, with whose only wife, Bathsheba, the king had had an adulterous affair. By using the parable, Nathan had tricked the king into judging himself. He had made the king realize his own hypocrisy: quick to judge others but not himself.

For this crime, Nathan foretold that David would never be able to build the temple, and he would lose many of his sons, including the first son that Bathsheba would bear him.

- In some Jewish retellings, when Bathsheba was bathing behind a screen, Satan took the form of a bird and got David to strike him. In the process the screen shattered and David saw Bathsheba.
- Uriah was summoned back from war so that he may be with his wife and so that his wife's child by the king could be passed off as his own. But Uriah stays in the palace with soldiers and not in his house with his wife, in keeping with warrior's code of not being with the wife during periods of war, thus frustrating David's plan.
- Feminists wonder whether David and Bathsheba's relationship was about love or about power. No woman in Bathsheba's position could defy the king's desire. David was thus abusing his royal authority.
- Following the arrival of Bathsheba, David is no longer in control of the situation as heroes are supposed to be; he is instead at the mercy of circumstances.
- The Islamic tradition rejects the story of Bathsheba entirely.

Absalom

David had many children by his many wives and concubines. His firstborn, Amnon, raped his half-sister Tamar. Tamar's brother Absalom, the handsome, talented and much-admired third son of David avenged her abuse by murdering Amnon.

Absalom then escaped from Jerusalem. David should have had the killer of his firstborn pursued and killed as per law but he loved Absalom too much. So, he forgave his son after Absalom had spent a few years in exile.

Absalom returned an ambitious man. He made himself popular with the people and slowly challenged David's authority, before declaring an open revolt, raising an army. He claimed his father's cities, and even slept with his father's concubines. Though this infuriated David, he still could not bring himself to strike down this errant son. Soldiers sent to quell the rebellion were expressly told not to hurt the rebel leader.

Joab, a general in David's army, defeated Absalom in a battle. After his forces were routed, Absalom escaped on his mule. Joab chased him. During the chase, Absalom's hair got entangled in the branches of an oak tree, and was pulled off his mule. Joab found the rebel prince helplessly hanging by his hair from a tree. Overriding the king's express orders, he severed Absalom's head.

David mourned his son for many days until Joab told his king to stop this extravagance of grief that was unbecoming of a king.

- Absalom is famous for his beauty, especially his hair, that is ultimately the cause of his death.
- Absalom has come to embody unfilial conduct, ambition and vainglory.
- In Jewish retellings, Absalom suffers in Gehenna at the hands of angels though God reminds them to spare him, on grounds that he is the son of David.

Solomon's wives

Solomon was not the oldest son of David but the wisest, shrewdest and smartest. And he was chosen king over his brothers. He consolidated his father's kingdom, turning it into an empire by establishing relationships with neighbouring kings. He married their daughters and had children by them.

Solomon ended up with 700 wives and 300 concubines, amongst them the pharaoh's daughter and women from the Moab, Ammon, Edom and Sidon as well as Hittites. But the arrival of foreign women to Solomon's palace meant that it was filled with foreign customs and rituals and images of foreign gods, which the people of Israel did not like.

So great was Solomon's fame that the Queen of Sheba, Bilqis, paid him a visit to test his intelligence. She came with a large retinue bearing many gifts and asked the king many riddles. She was impressed by his answers. She was also awed by his buildings where polished marble appeared like water, and his ability to teleport things, such as her throne, to his palace. She became a worshipper of the one true god, and became his wife. And their children went on to be kings of Ethiopia.

- Scholars cannot agree about where Sheba was located. There are inscriptions suggesting that Arabia had queens in ancient times. Others believe she came from Africa. Most believe that Sheba refers to Saba, in Yemen.
- *Kebra Nagast* (glory of kings) is the national Ethiopian book that was translated in the fourteenth century. It tells the story of how Menelik, the son of Solomon and the Queen of Sheba, came back to Ethiopia from Jerusalem with the Ark of the Covenant and converted the people who worshipped the sun and the moon to the worshippers of the one true god.
- The Quran speaks of a bird who informs Solomon of the Queen of Sheba, who worships the sun instead of Allah. Sheba visits Solomon and mistakes the polished floor for a pool of water. She realizes that he has managed to teleport her throne to his palace. This convinces her to convert to Islam.
- In Islamic retellings, the Queen of Sheba is often addressed as Bilqis and considered to be the daughter of a djinn.
- The Yoruba clan of Nigeria claims the Queen of Sheba to be a rich Yoruba noblewoman called Oloye Bilikisu Sungbo, who built palaces whose walls are still standing.

Solomon's Judgement

Solomon was famous for his intelligence and judgement.

A vineyard owner wanted compensation from a shepherd whose sheep had destroyed his grapevines. Solomon told the shepherd to take care of the vineyard till all damages had been repaired and it had been restored to its former condition. Until then, said Solomon, his sheep would belong to the vineyard owner, who would benefit from the wool of the sheep.

Two women approached Solomon, each claiming the same baby as her own. So, Solomon asked that the baby be cut in two and one half given to either. One of the women opposed this barbaric solution, and Solomon declared that she who cared for the child, rather than her victory, was the true mother.

At another time, a man with two heads, the son of a demon father, demanded double his share of property as he had two heads. But Solomon argued that he would get only one share as he had one stomach despite having two heads.

When God offered him boons, Solomon did not seek wealth and power but knowledge. And so, he was able to speak to animals, control the elements and demons, and make djinns work for him. Since he understood the language of animals, he was able to take his armies on paths that did not destroy the kingdom of ants, earning for himself much fame in the animal kingdom.

- The story of the two-headed man comes from Jewish legends; the story of the baby and two mothers is popular in Christian traditions; and the story of the vineyard comes from the Quran itself. All three establish Solomon as the wise king.
- In the Quran, Solomon is referred to as Suleiman. He is considered both a prophet (nabi) and king (malik). His father David (Dawood) was malik, nabi as well as rasul, and he was linked with a book called *Psalms*. Suleiman could speak to

animals and control djinns. He also had control over the winds and could cause metal to melt and flow. In other words, he was linked to magic. Saul (Talut) was malik (king) but not (nabi) or prophet. Following him came David (Dawood), who was malik and nabi as well as rasul (messenger). David's son Solomon (Suleiman) was malik and nabi, not rasul.

- Suleiman could speak to animals and control djinns. He also had control over the winds and could cause metal to melt and flow. In other words, he was linked to magic.

Solomon's Magic

Solomon was deeply immersed in occult sciences as he wanted to build the most fabulous city around the most fabulous temple dedicated to the one true god. He managed to build a flying chariot using eagles and travelled to paradise, where he found the fallen angels Uzza and Azazel chained to a rock.

Solomon used his magical ring to force them to reveal all their secrets, including the trick by which to overpower a magical rooster who caught the ancient worm that could cut rocks with the precision of an artisan. The rocks, thus cut, flew by themselves and stacked themselves next to each other to build the massive walls of Solomon's many royal buildings, including the temple where he would house the Ark of the Covenant.

During Solomon's reign, many sorcerers came to Jerusalem and brought with them witchcraft from Babylon. This dented Solomon's reputation, for people believed that he had turned away from the one true god. Solomon wrote many books on the secret arts and occult knowledge but hid them under his throne to prevent them from falling into the hands of sorcerers who did not believe in Allah and who arrogantly believed that they could change the fate of man.

God made djinns serve Solomon. They would bring to Jerusalem gems for his palace, water for his plants and food for his wives and concubines. The markets overflowed with exotic fabrics and carpets and attracted traders from around the world.

- Jewish legends and Kabbalah are full of stories about how Solomon recruits angels, demons and djinns to build his fabulous temple.
- The 'Seal of Solomon' is sometimes equated with the 'Star of David'. But this sign became a popular Jewish symbol only 1,000 years ago during the Crusades, when it came to be known as the 'Shield of David'. Before that the pentagram was the more common sign of the Jewish people.
- In the Quran, there is the story of Harut and Marut, two angels who descend to earth, where they are tricked by a woman to consume alcohol. So they get stuck on earth and are punished by Allah. They hang upside down in the towers of Babylon. They teach sorcery to people who come to them but warn them about how sorcery can ruin their lives. Sorcerers trained by Harut and Marut prosper in Suleiman's time. Suleiman knew magic but he followed Allah while the sorcerers trained by Harut and Marut did not follow the one true god.
- In the famous collection of folktales *One Thousand and One Nights*, there are tales of djinns being locked in bottles and thrown into the sea by Suleiman.

Solomon's Buildings

Solomon built the temple to the one true god, and established its ceremonies and rituals; he enshrined the Ark of the Covenant there.

But more impressive, felt many visitors, was Solomon's throne, which was located atop a flight of stairs. The stairs had images of mechanical toys that looked like hawks, doves, peacocks, lions and serpents that would move and make sounds as soon as Solomon ascended the throne, which impressed all those who came to visit the king.

People came to Jerusalem to visit God's temples, and stayed to see Solomon's throne; they were also spellbound by Solomon's many buildings, built so quickly during his reign that most visitors were convinced that the king was being helped by supernatural beings, the djinns. They had all heard stories of how Solomon had even secured the help of Asmodeus, the king of demons, who he released from Hell and brought to his city. There was also the story of djinns who served him at night and sorcerers who wandered in the shadows, discussing unholy spells.

As great wealth poured into the land, the people of Israel began withdrawing from this powerful king, who seemed to value outsiders as much as insiders.

- Solomon's temple, the First Temple, is dated to 1000 BCE.
- As per legend, builders of Solomon's temple organized themselves and established the secretive Freemason society.
- Middle Eastern legends are full of stories of the fabulous adventures of Solomon linked to the djinn and to a magical throne. These stories perhaps originated in India and travelled to the Middle East via Arab traders, as they have many parallels in the twenty-four stories of Raja Vikramaditya and the ghost (*vetal*, in Sanskrit) and in the thirty-two stories of Raja Bhoja and the throne. The word 'djinn' gave rise to the word 'genie' in Western literature.
- As per court chroniclers, when Firoz Shah Tuglaq and later Aurangzeb encountered the mysterious rust-free iron pillar of Delhi and the abandoned Hindu cave temples of Ellora, they were convinced that these were built by djinns in India's pre-Islamic period.

Death of Solomon

Allah had created djinns, just as he created humans. This race of beings could hear the whispers of angels and so assumed they knew the future. This made them arrogant. To teach them a lesson, God made them slaves of Solomon, forced to do his bidding.

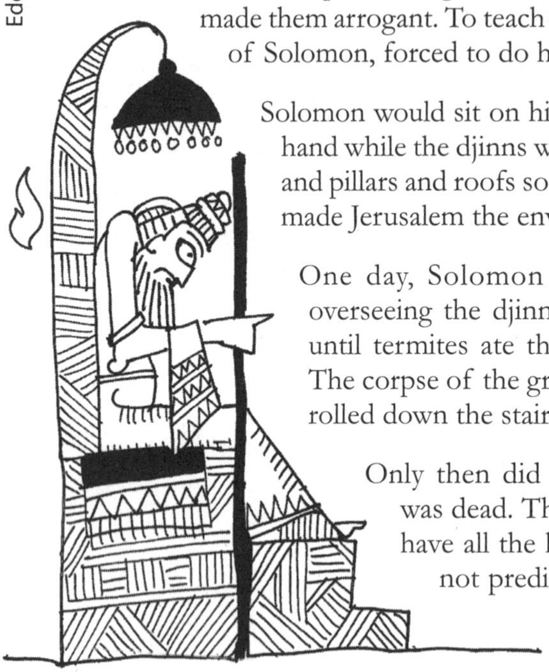

Solomon would sit on his fabulous throne and hold a staff in hand while the djinns worked, using their magic to raise walls and pillars and roofs so as to build spectacular structures that made Jerusalem the envy of the world.

One day, Solomon died while he sat on the throne overseeing the djinns. But no one realized he was dead until termites ate the staff he held, causing it to break. The corpse of the great king then fell from his throne and rolled down the stairs.

Only then did the djinns realize that their master was dead. They learnt the lesson that they did not have all the knowledge of the future. They could not predict this incident and so were enslaved much longer. Thus humbled, they apologized to Allah.

- The story of Solomon's death on his throne comes from the Quran and the Islamic retellings of this incident.
- The Quran refers to the djinn several times. Allah sent prophets and messengers to both humans and djinns. In Islamic tradition, they are considered to be of equal status to humans, not superior, and so not worthy of veneration. Worshipping them as gods was a mistake made in pre-Islamic Arabia, which was rectified by Prophet Muhammad.
- Islamic communities are divided over whether the belief in djinns is an essential component of the faith. There are numerous traditions about them. In one Hadith, they are classified as appearing in human form, in the form of animals like dogs and serpents, and depicted as flying through the air. Some believe

that djinns are formless, created of smokeless fire before Adam. Some of them acquire form. The ones with form who have faith become angels and those with form who have no faith become demons. There are some who believe they look just like humans but are stronger and faster, and have children, and seek direction from prophets. In another tradition, djinns think they are superior to humans as they were created before Adam, and so need to learn humility as all are equal before God.

Song of Solomon

Like his father David, who had composed and sung many psalms, Solomon composed many works of literature. He wrote books to educate his children, born of his many foreign wives, about the one true god. He wrote proverbs that explained how orderly and fair the world is. He also speculated on how random and unfair the world seemed in his ecclesiastical books.

Finally, Solomon composed the Song of Songs, full of love and longing, of a man for a woman and a woman for a man. They yearn, they meet, they separate, they yearn again. She searches for him in the streets of the city. He finds her in gardens amongst lilies. They unite in orchards and by streams. People witness their grand wedding. Everyone is invited to find their lover, but only when they are ready.

These songs of union and separation are at once literal, about a beloved and his or her lover, and metaphorical, of humanity and wisdom, of humanity and God, each one seeking the other in search of fulfilment. This mysticism and romance was what Solomon left behind for his children and his people, along with his laws, spells, speculations, parables, and great wealth, fame and power.

- The Song of Songs comes from the final section of the *Tanakh* or Jewish Bible and introduces love for the first time in a narrative focused on law and transgressions.
- Some Christians saw in the song an esoteric explanation of the relationship between Church and God. Others saw the bride as the Virgin Mary.
- Muslims believe that Muhammad is mentioned in the Song of Solomon, though the Hebrew word *mahamaddim* is believed to be a common noun, meaning 'delightful'.
- Prophet Iddo is said to have written a book detailing the life and works of Solomon known as the *Acts of Solomon*, which is now lost.

BOOK EIGHT

Exiled to Babylon

Two Kingdoms

Solomon ruled the twelve tribes of Israel, but after his death all but two tribes swore allegiance to the House of David. The rest split away to form the northern kingdom of Israel with its capital in Samaria. The House of David was left with two tribes in the southern kingdom of Judea, with its capital in Jerusalem.

As time passed, both king and people lost faith in God and in God's commandments. And this manifested in the worship of false gods, indulgence in idolatry and even child sacrifice.

Worse, people lost their sense of responsibility and focussed on their own dreams and desires without any thought for the poor and the needy, exploiting widows and orphans against God's commandment.

While the kingdom of Israel grew more and more weak, and split into two, to the east rose the empire of Assyria and later, the empire of Babylon. Eventually, these powerful empires conquered Israel and Judea, destroyed the city of Jerusalem and its temple, enslaving and deporting the Chosen People of the God of Abraham. This happened slowly over a long period of about five centuries during which

there were many prophets who tried to warn people of God's wrath, of the transgressions of people, while giving hope of God's love if people returned to the way of God's law and love.

- Unification is followed by division, followed by unification. Enslavement is followed by liberation, followed by enslavement. These are recurring themes in Abrahamic mythology. Thus, there is the loss of Eden and the quest to return; exile in Egypt and return to Canaan; and exile in Babylon and return to Jerusalem.
- Eventually, the northern kingdom of Israel is captured by Assyrians, who deport all the ten tribes of Israel to various locations. These become the 'lost tribes of Israel'.
- The southern kingdom is captured later by Babylonians, who deport all residents to Babylon—a single location, where the Jewish heritage was preserved, even enriched, by local Persian beliefs, until its return to build the Second Temple.
- Assyrians, who settled in the capital city of Samar after deporting local Hebrew folk, slowly adopt the worship of the one true god, Yahweh. But since they were of non-Israelite origin, they are seen as inferior during the time of Jesus. They were called Samaritans and deemed half-breeds, a mix of native tribes and foreigners. Such discomfort with mixed groups is found even in Manusmriti, a Hindu text. In the former case, the group is tribe. In the latter, the group is caste.

Bravery of Judith

A warlord called Holofernes, sent by his Assyrian masters, attacked Israel and brutalized its people. People felt they were without hope. But, one woman called Judith gave them the strength to fight back.

Judith's husband had been killed by this warlord, but she did not lose her faith. She entered the enemy camp wearing jewels, painting her face and draping herself in fine scented robes. She seduced the general, gained access to his tent, beheaded him while he was sleeping and emerged with his head.

The vision of Judith with the enemy's head in her hand motivated the people of Israel to fight back.

- The story of Judith is part of 'apocrypha', meaning Abrahamic lore that is not part of the mainstream or official version.
- The story has become famous as it inspired many artworks, including those by Caravaggio and Klimt. The idea of a woman killing the enemy by using her charms fascinated the ancient and medieval world. Here is a rare story where a woman's sexuality is weaponized for, not against, Jewish folk.
- The femme fatale Delilah uses her charms against her own husband, Samson, hence against God, while Judith, a chaste married woman, uses her charms against those who attack the People of God.

Compassion of Hosea

Hosea's wife Gomer had been unfaithful. Still God commanded Hosea to forgive her, pay all that she owed her lovers, treat her with respect and bring her back home as his wife and his children's mother.

Hosea learned from this experience that though Israel had abandoned God, just like his adulterous wife had abandoned him, God still loved his people and was willing to forgive them.

Hosea was amongst the first of the prophets who wrote down his prophecies. He saw the relationship between God and his people in human terms. He saw God as the loving father who is angry at being betrayed by his son, but willing to forgive him. He foresaw the destruction of Babylon, and the exile and the eventual return of the people. He foresaw the rise of a new leader and a new kingdom on earth.

- Hosea belongs to the time when kings failed the people and prophets warned of impending doom, but gave hope of eventual reconciliation with God.
- Hosea is one of the twelve minor prophets, others being Joel, Amos, Obadiah, Jonah, Micah, Nahum, Habakkuk, Zephaniah, Haggai, Zechariah and Malachi.
- Islamic scholars believe Hosea is one of the many unnamed prophets in the Quran.

Rise of Jezebel

Zimri, the commander of royal chariots, killed Elah, king of Israel, who lay drunk in his palace. Zimri then declared himself king and ruled for barely seven days, when he learned that the army had chosen Omri, the army general, his former master, to replace him as king. Refusing to give up his crown, Zimri decided to die a king: he burnt the palace down and himself with it.

As king, Omri established his power by building temples of many gods popular amongst people and in neighbouring kingdoms. He got his son, Ahab, married to Jezebel, the princess of Phoenicia.

Jezebel ignored the worship of the God of Abraham. Temples of Jehovah made way for temples of Baal and Asherah; the priests of Jehovah were killed and replaced by priests of Baal and Asherah. The prophet Elijah alone rose to openly challenge this idolatry.

- Jezebel has been linked in Jewish and Christian lore to idolatry and the subsequent opposition to Jewish patriarchs and prophets who promoted montheism. She has become symbolic of dangerous feminine seductive energies that can distract the faithful from God.
- Jezebel applied make-up before her death and so became the symbol of female vanity, vulgarity and promiscuity.
- The idea of Jezebel is similar to the seductive damsels known as apsaras in Hindu lore who distract ascetics from the spiritual path.
- Marriage is a key part of political alliances. But it also brings in change in the culture of the royal household. As in the case of Solomon, we find marriages ushering in idolatry and new gods to Israel.

Cycle of Baal and Asherah

Jezebel had many gods, like many Phoenicians, Philistines and other Syrian communities who sailed the sea. One of them, El, the father god, lived atop a hill in the desert.

The bards narrated El's story, how he found two women at sea and asked them if they wished to address him as husband or father. One, Asherah, chose to be his wife, the other, Anath, his daughter. By his wife, El fathered many children, who in turn had many children. Yam became the god of sea, Mot became the god of death, and Baal, son of Dagon, grandson of El, wanted to be the god of land.

Yam hated Baal and they fought until Baal defeated Yam and became the lord of the shores. He built for himself a palace, with the permission of the wise El and the support of the talented Kothar-wa-Khasis, the god of crafts. His sister Anath sat beside him.

Angry at not being invited to the house-warming party, Mot killed Baal. Anath searched the world and the underworld for her beloved. She smote Mot as women thresh grain on the threshing floor. She finally found Baal's corpse and revived him. Baal was then restored to power and Asherah sat beside him, only to be challenged by Mot once again a few months later.

When Mot rose, Baal fell. When Mot was defeated by Anath, Baal rose. This repetition of triumph and tragedy created the cycle of seasons, enabling sowing and harvesting. When Asherah sat with Baal, there was sowing. When Anath overpowered Mot, there was harvest.

- The wise god El, of the desert, respected by all, is seen as Elohim, the one true god of the Israelites, also called Allah, Yahweh and Jehovah. Temples to him, built away from the sea, at first included his wives and children. But later, Jewish elders saw this was polytheism and the cause of Jerusalem's fall. So, later temples only had God without a family.
- In nineteenth-century Trinidad, indentured labourers from India and Africa worked in plantations owned by Christians. In local newspapers, journalists spoke of the cosmic battle between three gods: Jehovah of Christians, Mahad (Mahadev) of Hindus and Baal of Africans. In a rather racist vein, the colonial writers equated Baal not only with a biblical 'false-god' but also with Ravana, the demon-king of Hindu epics. The burning of the Ravana effigy during Ramlila was described in the local newspapers as the burning of the Negro false-god, Baal.

Aggression of Elijah

King Ahab worshipped Baal and Asherah, local gods associated with rain and fertility. Elijah said that their worship would only cause drought. This upset the king. To escape royal wrath, Elijah had to hide in the wilderness and survive by eating what the ravens fed him.

Elijah challenged the priests of Asherah to a contest of death. He asked them to build an altar on top of a hill and get the goddess to light the fire. He would do the same and ask Jehovah to light the fire. All the prayers, and rituals, and offerings of priests of Asherah failed to get the fire lit but Elijah succeeded. The people of Israel rose up and killed the priests of the false god, angering Jezebel. She threatened to kill Elijah, once again forcing him to flee to the wilderness.

Next to Ahab's palace was a vineyard that belonged to Naboth. Ahab wanted it but Naboth refused to part with it. Jezebel could not understand what law was greater than a king's desire. But Ahab was wary of people's wrath if he went against God's commandments that said even a king should not covet another man's property. But Jezebel was determined to have her way. She spread rumours that Naboth had blasphemed against Jehovah and so had to be stoned to death. When this was done, Ahab was able to claim Naboth's vineyard. Elijah declared that just as dogs licked the blood of Naboth, so would dogs lick the blood of the unjust king and the queen.

And so it came to pass that Ahab was killed in a battle by a rebel called Jehu, who then threw Jezebel out of the palace window. Both their bodies were eaten by dogs, even pigs. As for Elijah, he rose to the sky in a chariot of fire, witnessed by his student, Elisha. Many were convinced he was not human, for his parents were not known; he was perhaps an angel.

- Elijah is also referred to as Elias in European cultures and as Ilyas in Arabic cultures.
- Jewish folklore is full of references to Elijah, who is believed to be supernatural, perhaps becoming the four-winged angel Sandalphon, as he was taken to Heaven instead of dying as humans do.
- During the circumcision ritual, many Jewish communities place an empty chair in honour of Elijah. It is similar to the North Indian Hindu custom of keeping an empty seat for Hanuman every time the Ramayana is narrated.
- When Jewish rabbis disagree on a topic, they often postpone matters by saying 'until Elijah arrives', as Elijah's arrival in folklore marks the end of time, and a time of reconciliation.
- Christians equate Elijah with John the Baptist. Both are 'prophets of the desert'.

- In the New Testament, during the incident known as Transfiguration, an incident witnessed by Jesus's disciples atop a mount, Jesus's face shone, and he was seen flanked by Moses and Elijah, when God declared Jesus to be his 'beloved Son'. Jesus mentioned Elijah as one of those many prophets who are rejected in the land of their origin.
- In the Quran, Elijah is referred to as a prophet who speaks against idolatry.
- In Islamic folklore, he is linked to Khidr, the green prophet, who is sometimes identified as his brother. Both have consumed waters of the 'fountain of life'. Both meet every year in Jerusalem and travel to Mecca. He frequently appears as a character in the collection of tales known as *Hamzanama*, which describes the adventures of Hamza, uncle of Prophet Muhammad.

Miracles of Elisha

Elisha was Elijah's student. He never left his master's side. He was the only prophet to witness Elijah rise to the Heavens in a windswept chariot of fire. And since he accompanied Elijah everywhere and witnessed his miraculous departure, he was given double the power of Elijah, so that he could perform double the number of miracles that Elijah performed.

Like Elijah, Elisha was able to part the waters of River Jordan, ensure that the oil jars in the house of a widow who took care of him were always full, bless a childless woman that she would bear a son and resurrect that woman's son when he met an untimely death.

A woodcutter's axe, borrowed

from a friend, fell in the river. Elisha managed to cause it to float rather than sink. Elisha prophesized the invasion by a Syrian army, struck the invaders blind and eventually restored their sight. During a famine, he turned poisonous food into a nourishing stew that everyone could eat. He fed thousands with a few loaves of bread.

A group of youths mocked his baldness and were ripped to shreds by she-bears who appeared from nowhere. Naman, a soldier, had leprosy. Elisha told him to take a dip in River Jordan seven times and he was cured of the dreadful disease.

So great was Elisha's power that a corpse placed on his burial mound was restored to life.

- Elisha is known in Islam as al-Yasa and is venerated as a prophet.
- In Christian traditions, Elisha is known as a wonder-worker and saint.
- Elisha was known to be bald while Elijah was hairy. Elisha came from a wealthy family while Elijah was of unknown mysterious origin. Elisha was taller than Elijah. Elisha performed more miracles than Elijah and died a natural death, his tomb becoming a spot for many miracles even after his death.
- Elijah, Elisha and Hosea witness the fall of the northern kingdom of Israel to the Assyrians, who controlled northern Mesopotamia. Jeremiah, Daniel and Ezekiel witness the fall of the southern kingdom of Judah, and the breaking of the Temple by the Babylonians, who controlled southern Mesopotamia. Both Assyria and Babylon eventually fall to the Persians, who allow the rebuilding of the Temple.

Reluctance of Jonah

Jonah was chosen to be a prophet and convey God's message to the city of Ninevah, which was full of wickedness, that in forty days it would be overthrown. Jonah did not want to convey the bad news and so ran in the opposite direction towards the sea and jumped into a boat going west.

God caused a storm and the sailors who grappled with the sail and their oars realized it was no ordinary storm. Some god, or goddess, was clearly upset. Jonah told the sailors that Jehovah was angry with him, and if they threw him overboard, all would be well. The sailors did not want to do such a terrible thing, but eventually Jonah, and the storm, convinced the sailors to do it.

When Jonah was cast overboard, he was swallowed by a gigantic fish, a whale. He did not die. He survived in the whale's belly, and realized God was not planning to kill him, or let him escape. After three days and three nights of being trapped, an exasperated Jonah agreed to go to Ninevah. Instantly, the big fish spat him on to the shore and Jonah went eastwards to the wicked city of Ninevah to convey the bad news.

Standing in the centre of the city, after mustering great courage, he shouted, 'In forty days this city will be overthrown'. A short prophecy of just a few words in Hebrew. He feared he would be jeered by the crowd, or even beaten up by the king. But none of that happened. The king heard him and fell to his knees and repented, and promised to fast and pray for mercy, and so did the people, and even the animals of Ninevah, much to Jonah's surprise.

He stormed out of the city angry at this turn of events. He went to a hill overlooking the city waiting for the people to go back to their wicked ways and for God to destroy the city as he had Sodom and Gomorrah.

As Jonah waited, God caused a tree to sprout behind him and give him shade. And then, God caused a worm to eat the roots of this tree and caused it to die. This made Jonah even more angry.

And God said, 'You are angry with what has happened to the tree even though you never contributed to its life or death. You are also angry with what has not happened to Ninevah, even though that city has done nothing to hurt you. Why will you not let me forgive those who wish to be forgiven? Why are you so angry? Is it because the world does not function as per your assumptions?'

- In Jewish retellings, Jonah is the dead son of the widow resurrected by Elisha. Jonah's mother always gave Elisha shelter. She had faith but Jonah had doubt.
- In Jewish retellings, the whale that swallowed Jonah feared that the even bigger fish Leviathan would eat it; but the Leviathan saw that Jonah, inside the whale's belly, was circumcised and thus dear to God, and so, it left Jonah's whale alone.
- In Christian tradition, Jesus came back from the dead after three days and three nights. This was prefigured by Jonah, who came out of the belly of the whale after three days and three nights.
- Jonah is called Yunus in Islamic retellings. The Quran refers to him many times. His father's name, Amittai, which means truth, comes from the wider Islamic tradition. Amittai was an old man when he died and he left his wife only a wooden spoon that would miraculously produce food when placed next to Jonah's lips; still Jonah doubted his own role as a prophet. In Islamic folklore, the fish that had swallowed Jonah made its body transparent so that Jonah could see the wonders of the deep sea. He saw fishes chanting, 'Allah'.
- The phrase 'to be a Jonah' means to be a passenger on a ship who brings bad luck.

Death of Zedekiah

When Zedekiah, king of Judea, revolted against Babylon with the support of Hoprah, the pharaoh of Egypt, Nebuchadnezzar, the king of Babylon, invaded and laid siege to Jerusalem.

It was a horrible time when food and water were in short supply, and people were consumed by ailment and depression. After thirty months of the siege, the Babylonians destroyed the city of Jerusalem, enslaved its people and deported them to live in Babylon.

Thus began the Babylonian exile.

King Zedekiah's children were killed before his eyes.

It was the last sight he saw. For then, his eyes were gouged out, he was put in chains and taken as prisoner to Babylon, where he died.

- Judah was caught in the triangular conflict between the Assyrians, Babylonians and Egyptians.
- Jerusalem was finally captured in 600 BCE, marking the end of the kingdom of Israel and Judah.
- As per the Book of Mormon, the Church of Latter Day Saints, established in America in the nineteenth century by Joseph Smith, Zedekiah's son Mulek escaped to the Americas in the sixth century CE, following the fall of Jerusalem, and established the nation of the Mulekites that lived by the law of Moses in America, long before its discovery by Columbus, a thousand years later.

Lamentations of Jeremiah

Jeremiah was born in Jerusalem before its fall. He had lamented the rejection of God and God's commandments by the people of Israel on the streets of Jerusalem, equating the behaviour of the people to adultery.

He roamed the streets with a wooden yoke around the neck to constantly remind all those who saw him of God's wrath, which would manifest in the form of an attack on the city, its destruction and their enslavement. Irritated by his relentless lamentations and criticism, people broke the yoke that the prophet carried around. In response, Jeremiah said, 'You have broken the yoke of wood but you cannot escape the yoke of iron that is being forged by Babylon.'

When Jerusalem finally fell, and Zedekiah was taken prisoner, Jeremiah changed his tunes. Now, he gave people hope.

Jeremiah told the people of Jerusalem that eventually Babylon would be punished for its crimes, people would return, Jerusalem would riseand the message of God would once again be told not in stone but in the hearts of men, through a prophet who would rise in the House of David. He was prophesizing the arrival of Jesus. Unfortunately, that would happen after 600 years.

Jeremiah was taken against his will by those who opposed the Babylonians to Egypt, where he wrote songs of hope for the heartbroken exiled people of Israel before he died.

- In Christian traditions, Jeremiah is often called the 'weeping prophet'.
- In Islamic traditions, Jeremiah is referred to as Urmiya in Arabic.
- Jeremiah's tribe, irritated with his words, threw him in a cistern but he was saved by a slave. This has led to Jeremiah often being compared to Moses, who was thrown in water and saved by a slave of the Pharaoh's household. Both Jeremiah and Moses were prophets for forty long years. Both reprimanded their people for transgressions and were often rejected by them.

Hope for Ezekiel

Ezekiel was born in Jerusalem but was exiled to Babylon, where he lived in exile for years hoping to one day return home. In his thirtieth year, the year he would have become priest in the Temple, he sat mourning by a river, thinking of home, when he saw a grand vision.

He saw strange creatures with many heads and many wings riding on wheels and carrying on their outstretched wings a dazzling throne on which he saw what he realized was the personification of God's glory. What was God doing so far from Jerusalem, he wondered. And then, he heard the news that Jerusalem had been sacked and its Temple destroyed.

A devastated Ezekiel had another vision. He saw a valley filled with dry bones. Then a soft breeze blew through the valley and he felt the spirit of God animating the bones, covering them with breath and sinews and flesh and blood and skin and organs and wrapping them in skin till all humanity came alive.

He saw the vast barbaric armies of Gog, king of Magog, threatening the world with their violence, and God destroying them with earthquake and fire and causing their bodies to lie unattended in the open field eaten by dogs and vultures.

And then, he saw a temple, grander than the one in Jerusalem, complete with incense stands and lamps and curtains and vessels and musical instruments and priests and rituals and ceremonies and altars. There was a river running out of it and flowing to the Dead Sea, bringing life wherever if flowed: all kinds of plants with flowers and fruits, and animals and birds and fishes. This was Eden, where God lived, and humanity would return.

- If Jeremiah filled those who listened to him with despair, Ezekiel gave hope. Both came from the family tree that originated with Joshua, the Israelite commander, and Rahab, the prostitute of Jericho. In some Jewish traditions, Ezekiel is the son of Jeremiah.
- Though not mentioned in the Quran, Islamic tradition identifies Ezekiel as a prophet and sometimes identifies him with Zul-Kifl or Dhul-Kifl.

Visions of Daniel

Nebuchadnezzar, who destroyed Jerusalem and sacked the First Temple, took many slaves back to Babylon. Amongst them was Daniel and his three friends, all educated men of Jewish nobility. They were taken to the king's palace to serve as the king's courtiers as they were well groomed and good-looking and learned in the ways of administration as well as magic.

But Daniel and his friends, displaced from home, refused to give up their Jewish ways, respecting the rules of food, work and rest. This annoyed the king's staff, who tried their very best to get rid of them. Once, they managed to get the king to decree that the men should be thrown in a furnace of fire, but the fire did not harm them. Another time, Daniel was thrown into a pit full of hungry lions, but the animals did not hurt him, indicating he had God's grace. This won him the affection of the king.

The king revealed to Daniel his dreams. Of a statue whose head was made of gold, trunk of silver, arms of copper, legs of iron and feet of clay. A stone hit the feet and the mighty statue came crumbling down. Daniel interpreted the dream as the eventual replacement of the Babylonian Empire with that of the Persians, who would then be overthrown by Greeks, who in turn would be overthrown by Romans.

In another dream, Nebuchadnezzar saw a giant tree that sheltered the world, which was cut down by mysterious hands but the stump was left behind. Daniel interpreted this as the temporary end of the king's rule due to the loss of his sanity. His sanity would be restored eventually if he accepted the greatness of God and the limitations of human kings. The king did go mad for seven years, behaving like a beast, before his sanity returned, and the restored king did acknowledge the supreme greatness of Jehovah.

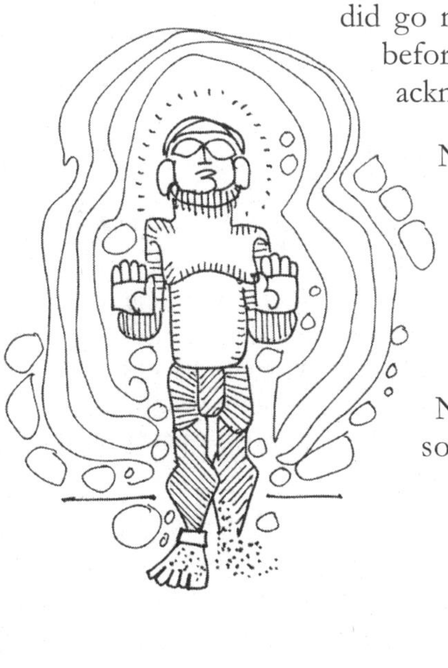

Nebuchadnezzar in his deathbed wanted to bequeath property to Daniel, who he had grown fond of. But Daniel refused the honour saying all his inheritance was in Israel and he wanted nothing from the uncircumcised.

Not long after Nebuchadnezzar's demise, his son, Belshazzar, threw a feast during which a mysterious hand appeared and wrote something on a wall. Only Daniel could read it. It foretold the downfall of the king and his city. That night, Belshazzar died and the kingdom was overrun by the Persians.

Daniel himself had many dreams. Of beasts rising from waters and sprouting many horns. And he realized that these were images of kings who would rise on earth by the grace of God but who would forget God in their success and so lose their power to other kings, until the kingdom of God eventually arrived. But when would that be? He thought it would be seventy years, but dreams revealed that since the Israelites, despite exile, had not learned their lesson, the kingdom of God would come only after seven times seventy years, meaning after five centuries.

- Daniel though popular was not a prophet.
- Daniel is known as Danyal in Arabic literature. He is not mentioned in the Quran but is part of wider Islamic literature.
- There are many more tales of Daniel. How he saved a chaste girl, who was wrongfully accused of being unchaste by two lecherous Jewish men. This is a unique tale as the villains are Jewish, and not foreigners. It speaks of men who abuse power bestowed upon them by God. In another tale he unmasks priests who eat food offered to an idol and claim it was eaten by the idol. He also kills a great beast, assumed to be a serpent, and is imprisoned and given no food, but he miraculously survives as a prophet appears out of thin air and feeds him.
- Daniel in all probability was a eunuch in Babylon as he never married and he once showed his mutilated body to the king to prove that he had never been unchaste. He appears after the last of the prophets, Malachi.
- Though known for their brutality, the Assyrians were also the first empire builders. They used deportation of the elite to minimize rebellion. This practice was later followed by Babylonians and Persians.
- In popular Christian art, angels are depicted as innocent children (cherubim) and pale-skinned musicians (seraphim), but the descriptions of angels in the Bible are rather abstract and fearsome: human-lion-ox-eagle hybrids to floating wheels with eyes to having six wings that covered their bodies and faces as they served in the presence of God. Biblical angels struck fear into the hearts of anyone who witnessed them. Over time, angels came to have a mythology of their own. Sandalphon was referred to as the archangel of music. Some holy

men were raised to the status of angels, similar to the Chinese idea of great men becoming gods and being allowed to eat the peaches of immortality on orders of the Jade Emperor of Heaven.

Patience of Job

Job lived the good life. He had health, wealth and a happy family. But then, one day, all that he had and all that he liked went away. He became sick, poor and lost his family. Misfortune followed misfortune. Calamity followed calamity.

Job's friends wondered if Job had done something wrong to upset God, if he had brought this upon himself. Job did not understand. But his faith in God was unshakeable. There were a few moments when he wondered what was going on. Why did bad things happen to good people?

Then, one day, God spoke to him and showed him the infinite universe: billions of stars and planets, billions of animals and birds and insects and fishes and reptiles and humans and cities and villages and tribes. He saw life and death, predators and prey, enemies and friends. He saw gigantic and terrifying beasts like the Leviathan and the Behemoth. Job realized eventually that though he feared these beasts, they were not frightening. They were all part of an ecosystem, a food chain, a pecking order, a circle of life. Infinite systems, intertwined and codependent. He saw infinity beyond planets and infinity between atoms. In this vast universe, his world was but a tiny fraction. The disorder in his life existed within a vast cosmic order. Not everything could possibly make sense to him.

And so, Job calmed down. He realized that good things happen, and bad things happen, for no apparent reason. Faith in God helps you to not be arrogant in good times and depressed in bad times. Faith gives you humility in fortune and hope in misfortune.

As time passed, health, wealth and family returned to Job's life. All was well, even better. But still, he did not have all the answers. He just had to trust that God was just, and the universe fair.

- In Jewish tradition, Job was punished with misfortune as he refused to comment one way or another when the pharaoh of Egypt sought his advice on whether he should allow the killing of Israelite newborns every alternate year to control their rising population.
- The Quran refers to Job as Ayyub, who never loses faith in Allah and despite his misery is never bitter or doubtful of God's mercy. At the end of his ordeal, Allah asks Ayyub to strike his foot against the ground and water springs out, ending his misfortune.

Rescue by Esther

In a drunken stupor, during a banquet, the king of Persia wanted to show the beauty of his queen to his guests. She refused to indulge him. So, the king decided to hold a beauty contest and choose another queen. He chose a beautiful girl called Esther.

Esther was Jewish. She descended from the families that had been exiled to Babylon. She hid her Jewish identity by not following the various rules related to food, work and rest, shared by prophets over the centuries.

Haman, the king's advisor, held a grouse against Jews as their leader did not bow to him. So, he cunningly got the king to sign a decree to kill all the Jewish people.

To save her people, Esther took

the risk of approaching the king unannounced and invited him to a banquet at her palace. The king accepted the invitation and during the grand feast offered to fulfil any of her desires.

'Spare me and my people,' she said, revealing her Jewish identity. The king did not understand. When told of what was happening in his name, he had Haman killed. But the royal decree against Jewish people had already been announced and the king could not go against his own word. So the king of Persia wrote another decree giving the Jewish people the right to carry weapons and defend themselves.

- The Jewish people celebrate the festival of Purim in memory of this incident. Purim comes from the word *pur* which means lots or dice that were used by Haman to determine the date on which all Jewish people in the Persian Empire would be killed.
- On Purim, triangular sweets resembling the hat of Haman are eaten. And when the story of Esther is narrated, they stamp their feet so that the name of Haman is not heard.

Cyrus and the Second Temple

The Assyrian Empire was absorbed into the Babylonian Empire, which eventually made way for the Persian Empire. Persia extended to the east of Mesopotamia.

During the reign of the Persian monarch, Cyrus the Great, the exiled Jews were allowed to return home. As soon as they returned, the Jewish people built the Second Temple. It took twenty years to build, and though grand, it was not as grand as Solomon's. There was no Ark of the Covenant and no doors of gold. There were lamps, incense stands and curtains instead.

The people who returned from Babylon were a rather

different people, exposed to the Persian ways. Ezra was the first amongst them. He was related to the last priest of the First Temple and also to the first priest of the Second Temple. He alone remembered where the holy books and the holy temples were hidden. He played a key role in reintroducing the Jewish ways in Jerusalem, and in documenting the memories of the Jewish people, the stories, the songs, the laws of God.

Nehemiah had served in the royal courts as a cup-bearer and had been exposed to the Persian ways, and their stories. He was appointed by the Persian Emperor Artaxerxes as governor of Judah, and he secured orders to build the Second Temple, and establish the rituals with the help of Ezra. Defying all enemies, he built the walls in fifty-two days.

- In Islamic lore, Uzair or Ezra wondered how the resurrection will take place on the Day of Judgement. So, Allah caused his death and had him brought back to life after a 100 years, during which time Solomon's temple was broken. He rode on his revived donkey and entered his native place. No one recognized him, except an old maid, who was now an old, blind woman. He prayed to God to cure her blindness and she could see again. His son, now older than he was, recognized him by a mole between his shoulders. He then led people to locate the only surviving copy of the holy books. This story is often connected with Ezekiel's vision of dry bones.
- The Book of Nehemiah describes the rebuilding of the temple.
- Nehemiah is associated with the structure of the temple and Ezra with the rituals.
- Like Danyal, Nehemiah was probably also a eunuch as he was allowed in the presence of the queen.

The Path of Zarathustra

Unlike the polytheistic Assyrians and Babylonians, the Persians believed in one God, who they called Ahura Mazda. They believed Ahura Mazda was in constant conflict with a negative force, Angra Mainyu, the evil one, and the only way to combat the latter was to think good thoughts, speak good words and do good deeds. And, this was the role of the king on earth.

To do good to all people and keep Angra Mainyu at bay, Ahura Mazda had angels who assisted him, the Amesha Spenta, and there were guardian spirits for every individual, the bird-like Fravashi. The Persians believed in judgement after death, which involved passing over a bridge that would widen for the good and lead them to Heaven, and narrowed for the bad and caused them to fall into Hell.

Zarathustra was the prophet who had introduced the Persians to Ahura Mazda, represented as fire, and had helped people give away their old gods.

Ahura Mazda was not a jealous God who demanded obedience and punished transgression. He was a kind and loving God who expected his followers to do good to all people, not just those who obeyed him. That is why the Persian Empire was vast and successful in ruling different nations, without expecting anyone to give up their religious beliefs. This policy of not imposing religion on conquered people is why the Persian emperor allowed the Jewish people to rebuild their Second Temple, a lesson few remember today.

- The Egyptian Empire started to wane from around 1,000 BCE. The Assyrians controlled Northern Mesopotamia, where the Tigris and Euphrates originated, and the Babylonians controlled Southern Mesopotamia that contained the delta. The Persian Empire overthrew the Assyrians and Babylonians around 550 BCE.
- The Second Temple survived for 420 years. It was repaired and made grand by King Herod; during his reign, Jesus was born. Shortly thereafter, the Romans destroyed the temple in 70 CE, while crushing a local rebellion. In the centuries that followed, the Jewish way was consolidated in writing, and Rabbinic Judaism arose based on the synagogue, where God's laws were discussed and elaborated and interpreted, and the Jewish way of life sustained while everyone waited for the Third Temple.
- Today, all that remains of the Second Temple is the Temple Mount marked by the Wailing Wall of the Jewish people and the Dome of the Rock and the Al Aqsa Mosque, which is said to be the spot where the temple was once located and from where Prophet Muhammad made his journey to Heaven. This spot

is popular amongst Christians too as the Second Temple was visited by Jesus many times.

- The impact of Zoroastrian mythology on later Judaism and then Christianity cannot be overstressed. Ideas such as of the Devil, archangels, Heaven, Hell and Day of Judgement come from Persia.
- In early Abrahamic lore, God speaks directly (to Abraham, Noah, Moses). Later, he speaks through prophets (Elijah, Jeremiah), and even later, he is silent (Esther, Jesus), indicating a drifting away from humanity or God expressing His majesty, as Persian emperors did, through distance.
- Persian emperors called themselves Aryas. Aryas refer to the eastern branch of the Indo-European tribes that migrated out of Eurasia with their horse and spoked-wheel chariots around 2000 BCE. The western arm, which spread to Anatolia and Europe, gave rise to the Mittani people, whose inscriptions in 1300 BCE reveal knowledge of Vedic gods such as Indra and Varuna. They came into contact with the Hittites and Egyptians and passed on horse-driven chariot technology. The eastern arm, meanwhile, split into the Iranian arm and the Indian arm around 2000 BCE, making their presence felt in the Iranian plateau and the Gangetic plains by 1500 BCE, where they gave rise to the Avesta and the Veda, respectively. We find the word Arya or noble people in both scriptures, and many other common ideas like *soma/hoama* (stimulant herb, ephedra) and *yagna/yasna* (a ceremony). But the word for demon (asura) in Hinduism becomes the word for God (Ahura) in Zoroastrianism, and the word for god (deva) in Hinduism refers to demons (div) in Zoroastrianism. Most significantly, the Iranian arm turned away from polytheism towards monotheism, anchored on Ahura Mazda. For the Iranians, following monotheism is what made a person Arya or civilized. From Arya came the word 'Iran', another name for Persia, which was formalized in the early twentieth century. These migratory patterns have been affirmed by linguistic and literary evidence, archaeology, and now, genetics.

BOOK NINE

Son of God

Zachariah and Elizabeth

Five hundred years passed after the building of the Second Temple. No prophet was heard. The Persian Empire waned. The Roman Empire rose.

An elderly man, Zachariah, and his wife, Elizabeth, went to the temple at Jerusalem regularly and tended to the incense there. During one such visit, they saw the archangel Gabriel, who declared that Elizabeth would bear a child, who would announce the arrival of a prophet, who would, in fact, be the Son of God, who would save all of humanity by sacrificing himself.

Zachariah did not believe the angel, just like Abraham did not believe the angel long ago, as his wife was too old to bear a child. So, he was struck dumb.

Nine months later, Elizabeth, who was over sixty years old, did deliver a son. As soon as Zachariah wrote on a tablet that his son's name should be John, his speech was restored.

John grew up an unusual child, with a deep understanding of God's will. He chose to live in the wilderness, and grow his hair long, and wear animal skin. He wandered from settlement to settlement, speaking of God and his message, reminding people of Abraham and his covenant with God. He reminded people of stories they had forgotten: of Noah and Moses, of David and Solomon, of those who obeyed God's will and those who did not. He immersed people in the waters of River Jordan to baptise them, bring them closer to God, to make them repent for their sins, and await the arrival of the Son of God. That is why he became popularly known as John the Baptist.

- The sources of the story of Jesus are primarily the four Gospels. These were written in Greek many decades after the crucifixion of Jesus and were later attributed to Mathew, Mark, Luke and John.
- The authors of the four Gospels are visualized as a winged man or angel (Matthew), winged lion (Mark), winged ox (Luke) and rising eagle (John).
- The Christian Bible has two parts: the Old and the New Testaments. Testament refers to 'witnessing the contract between the one true god, and his people'. The Old Testament, known as Tanakh in Hebrew, emerged over 1,000 years. The New Testament was compiled in the century following the death and resurrection of Jesus Christ, and contains the writings of first-generation Christians.
- The story of Jesus makes up the New Testament. This division of old and new is to express the Christian belief that the Old Testament simply prepares the ground for Jesus. In commentaries, Christian theologians show repeatedly how events in the Old Testament prefigure and foreshadow the arrival of Jesus, who is not just a prophet, but also the Son of God. In other words, the Old Testament or Jewish bible is simply the background while the New Testament or Christian bible is the climax. Jewish people reject this idea, a rejection that informs anti-Semitism that was, and is, widely prevalent in Christian communities.
- The New Testament was first written in Greek and all its books came together as a unit in the fourth century CE. It comprises the four Gospels, which detail the birth, life, death and resurrection of Jesus by Matthew, Mark, Luke and John. It also contains the Acts, which describes how the first converts, the Apostles, were appointed to take Christian ideas to Rome, explaining how a Jewish teacher's ideas spread amongst non-Jewish people after it was rejected by the Jewish establishment. Then, there are the Letters of early converts, especially Paul. Finally, there is the Revelation of St John, which explains the end of the world, and details ideas of the Rapture, the Second Coming, the Apocalypse and the Day of Judgement.

- The theme of a disbelieving old man and his old wife, Zachariah and Elizabeth, bearing a child re-establishes the connection with Abraham of the Old Testament.
- John announces the arrival of Jesus, just as a herald announces the arrival of a king. Even this herald's birth is referred to in the last book of the Old Testament, the Book of Malachi.
- In Islam, John the Baptist is called Yahya. He and his parents are considered the humble servants of Allah.
- Baptism means immersion in water. It was a ritual act to spiritually cleanse a person and transform him. Amongst Hindus, this act meant wiping out all karmic debts. Amongst ancient Egyptians, this act ensured death would be followed by an afterlife. Amongst ancient Mesopotamians, it provided the grace of the water-god Enki. The Jewish people used immersion in water as a ritual act of purification. John used this ritual to reaffirm the covenant with God. Jesus made this the primary ritual to enter his ministry, replacing the old Jewish practice of circumcision. Baptism became the ritual that makes one a Christian, one who believes Jesus is the saviour.

Joachim and Anna

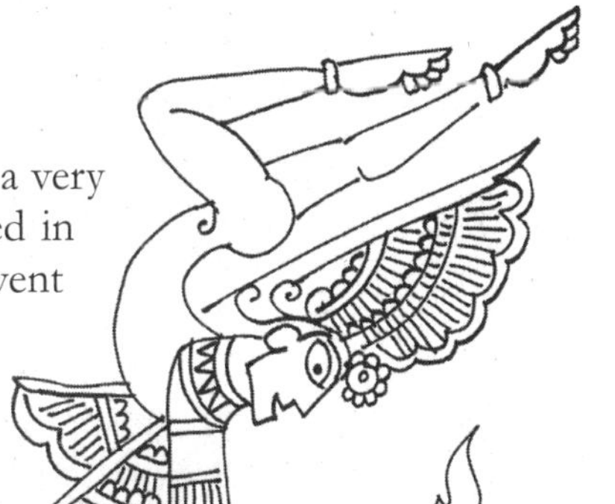

Elizabeth had a cousin called Anna. She was the wife of a very rich man called Joachim. His offerings were not accepted in the temple as he had borne no children. Humiliated, he went to the desert to pray.

Fearing for his life and mourning her barren status, his wife prayed in the temple. In answer to her prayers, she was visited by an angel, who said she would bear a child, a daughter, despite her advanced years. As she rushed out of Jerusalem, at the gates of the city, she met her husband who hugged her and informed her that while he was in the desert he had been visited by an angel who had said that his wife, though of advanced years, would bear a child, a special child. Both had received the good news at the same time. Both had trusted the angel's words.

Anna conceived her child immaculately, and when she gave birth to a daughter, she named her Mary and dedicated her to the service of the temple so that she lived a pious life. Her uncle Zachariah was her guardian and would often visit her in the sacred sanctuary, and find that she was always surrounded by food. 'Where does this food come from?' he asked. She replied, from God.

Then one day, in the temple, Mary was visited by an angel, who told her that she would soon be mother of a child who would save the world. How could that be, Mary wondered. For she was not married. The angel said that anything is possible if God wills it.

Mary visited Elizabeth, who had given birth to a child, though advanced in years, and so understood miracles. On seeing her, Elizabeth knew at once that Mary was the chosen vessel through whom the Son of God would appear on earth and save all humankind.

- The story of Mary's immaculate conception is not part of the New Testament, but part of apocrypha accepted by many Catholic communities.
- The Quran states that Imran's wife prayed to Allah for a child and promised to dedicate the child to God. When she bore a daughter, Mary, she gave the child to the service of God. She was pure, untouched by Satan. This tale from Islam mirrors the tale of Hannah and Samuel found in the Hebrew Bible.
- In Islamic tradition, in the Shia Hadith, Elizabeth (Ishba) and Anna (Hannah) are considered sisters. Anna's husband, Joachim, is identified as Imran, a prophet. Elizabeth's husband is appointed the guardian of Mary. Like Imran, Zachariah is also a prophet.
- The Quran has many female characters but none are referred to by name, except Mary, mother of Jesus. The Quran states that of all creatures born, only Mary and Jesus were pure, untouched by Satan.

Virgin Birth

Mary was engaged to marry Joseph, a carpenter from Nazareth. At first, Joseph was not pleased to learn that the woman he was to marry was already pregnant. However, Gabriel helped him accept the will of God.

The marriage took place and the couple awaited the arrival of their special child, when the Roman Empire decided to conduct a census, registering people in order to collect taxes more efficiently. This meant men had to go with their families to their ancestral villages to which they were attached. Joseph had to move to Bethlehem, the village of King David, as Joseph descended from the family of David.

So the couple travelled on a donkey. On the way, whenever Mary felt tired, the child in her womb would speak soothing words to her. Once, in hunger and thirst, she leaned against a date palm tree, and to her delight, the tree shed dates so that she could eat to her heart's content and a stream of water came from under the ground to quench her thirst.

The couple reached Bethlehem on a cold winter's night and sought shelter. All they managed to get was a barn. There, Mary gave birth to her special child,

the Son of God. This was Jesus. There was no place to keep the child warm except in a manger, the trough meant to feed farm animals, filled with straw. Was this worthy of the Son of God? God did not mind: high and low are words that matter little to those with faith.

Shepherds came to see this child for an angel told them to be witness to the birth of the special child. And then, three kings, the wise magi from the East, who were following a bright star, came to see the child, bearing gifts of gold, frankincense and myrrh. Yes, the king was born.

- The story of Jesus comes from four biographies written by Matthew, Mark, Luke and John. There are differences among them in terms of details, content, style and approach. Matthew and John were among the twelve apostles. Mark was a student of the apostle, Peter. Luke was a student of Paul, who converted to Christianity and became an evangelist (bearer of the good news) when he had a vision of a resurrected Jesus.
- The story of Jesus speaking to Mary from her womb and of Mary being refreshed by date palms and fresh running water emerging from the ground comes from Islamic tradition.
- It is not clear exactly when Jesus was born. Some have argued that since sheep were out in the pasture at night, it couldn't have been in winter. Others believe it is simply an exact calculation of nine months from the Spring Equinox, when Jesus is said to have been conceived, the same day as his resurrection—based on an old fertility myth of a God who rises on the same day as he was conceived. Others have argued that the date 25 December, traditionally associated with the birth of Jesus, indicates an old pagan practice linked to the Winter Solstice, the longest night of the year. Since the Eastern Orthodox Church uses the older Julian calendar, instead of the Gregorian, they celebrate Christmas on 7 January.
- The Nativity (birth of Jesus Christ) is either re-enacted during Christmas or its model recreated at homes. This practice was started in the thirteenth century by St Francis of Assisi in Italy to popularize the worship of Christ. Some believe the barn in which Jesus was born was actually a cave. In the barn, one finds, besides sheep, a donkey, a bullock and camels.
- Snow, the Christmas tree, mistletoes and Santa Claus, all integral to Christmas celebrations today, have roots in pagan customs of Scandinavia that reached America by the eighteenth century.

- The Gospels do not mention animals at the time of Jesus's birth, yet the Nativity scene always has sheep, camels, a donkey and a bull. The presence of sheep and camels are understandable as shepherds and magi witnessed the arrival of Christ. The donkey could be the one on which Mary travelled to Bethlehem. But the bull? Its presence is symbolic. Bull, an animal of sacrifice, traditionally represented the high-born, and the donkey, which was not an animal of sacrifice, the low-born. Thus, everyone is called to witness the birth of Jesus.
- The Arabian Peninsula was famous for its incense. There was great demand for frankincense and myrrh, which were dried resins of locally grown and intensely fragrant flowering trees. These were offered in temples and churches as part of sacrifice, offerings and even funerals. The kings who visited Jesus were clearly traders as well as wise men who knew how to read the stars.
- There is reference to brothers and sisters of Jesus. The brothers James and Jude are most prominent as their letters are included in the New Testament. Another brother is Simon. This is variously interpreted as his cousins or Joseph's children from a previous marriage.
- The veneration of Mary as 'Mother of God' is a Catholic idea that is not accepted by many Protestants, a faction that split from the Church during its Reformation in the sixteenth century.

Escape to Egypt

When the wise men from the East had left, Joseph went to sleep and in a dream heard God tell him to go to Egypt and not return until Herod had died.

Herod, king of Judea, had heard that the wise magi, guided by a star, had come to Judea seeking a child in Bethlehem who was prophesized to be the messiah and king of the Jews. Terrified that his rule would come to an end, he had ordered that every infant in and around the village should be killed. By the time his soldiers arrived, Joseph and Mary had taken Jesus to faraway Egypt.

- For Matthew, Jesus is the king of the Jews. For Mark, he is the servant of God. For Luke, he is human, the merciful healer. For John, he is the Son of God.
- Escaping to Egypt is a recurring theme in Abrahamic lore. Abraham travels there during famine. Joseph is sold there in slavery and provides a home for his brothers in times of famine.
- In mythologies around the world, when a hero is born, his prophesized arrival threatens a king who goes about killing babies in order to eliminate the threat to his life. Babies are killed at the time of Moses's birth. Greek myths are full of tales of kings (Laius, Acrisius, Pelias) trying to kill babies (Oedipus, Perseus, Jason) who are a threat to their lives as per oracles. In Hindu lore, babies are killed by Kansa with the help of Putana, who fills her breast with poison, when he learns of Krishna's birth.

Teachers in the Temple

When Herod died, the Roman emperor divided his kingdom between his sons to ensure none was too powerful to revolt against Rome. It was now safe for Joseph and Mary to return home to Nazareth.

Every year, the couple would go with Jesus to Jerusalem to light incense in the temple. There their baby was seen by many sages and seers, who knew this was no ordinary child.

When Jesus was twelve, Joseph and Mary lost sight of him. After much searching for three days, they found him at the hall of teachers, scholars and lawyers, engaged in deep conversation on God's message. Everyone assembled there was impressed by the child's curiosity and depth of knowledge. When his worried parents tried admonishing him, Jesus said, 'But why were you worried? Where else would I be except in the house of my father?'

- Losing and finding their son after three days is a foreshadowing of how Jesus will die and resurrect himself in three days.
- Jesus is born and raised Jewish. He was known as a Jewish rabbi in his lifetime. This is a detail that many Christians have never liked as they indulged in anti-Semitism or institutionalized hatred of Jewish people.
- There are many miracles associated with the Child Jesus that are not part of official Gospels. In what are called Infancy Gospels, dated to 200 years after the death of Jesus, are stories of miracles associated with his childhood. He is said to have modelled birds using clay and breathed life into them, stretched a board of wood that fell short during carpentry, cured his brother of a viper's bite, brought back to life a playmate and a teacher who he struck accidentally, held water in his cloak and harvested a hundred bushels of wheat from a single seed.

John Baptises Jesus

When Jesus was thirty, he met John the Baptist. From John, he learned more about God and God's message and the coming of the messiah. He heard how God does not differentiate between the rich and the poor, the powerful and the powerless, the educated and the uneducated. He was impressed by John's words and sought to be baptised by John in the River Jordan.

John hesitated for he recognized Jesus for who he was. 'You should be baptising me,' he said.

Jesus replied, 'Let us just do what we are supposed to do.' And so John baptised him in the river.

The heavens opened up and the spirit of God came upon Jesus's shoulder in the form of a dove and God declared, 'This is my beloved son in whom I delight.'

- The baptism of Jesus by John marks the official start of his ministry. He now became preacher, teacher, healer, miracle worker, and gathered around him disciples and followers.
- White doves were associated in ancient Mesopotamia with Ishtar, goddess of fertility. In Greece, doves were associated with Aphrodite, goddess of love. In the Mesopotamian flood myth, Utnapishtim releases a dove to check if the flood has ended but it circles the world and comes back. A raven is then let loose and it does not return indicating flood waters were receding. In biblical mythology, Noah sends a dove and it returns with a fresh sprig of olive to indicate the end of the flood.
- Not much is known of the life of Jesus from the time of his visit to the temple when he was twelve to his baptism when he was thirty. What happened in the intervening eighteen years? Some say he travelled eastwards in search of knowledge and encountered Buddhist sages in India and/or Tibet who taught him yoga and tantra, which enabled him to perform miracles and healings.
- In medieval times, many believed that Jesus travelled to Britain after his father Joseph died and found shelter with a merchant known as Joseph of Arimathea, who played a key role in Arthurian legends of the Holy Grail.
- Christ means the anointed one, the messiah.

Beheading of John

King Herod's son Antipas, ruler of Galilee, had forced his brother Philip to divorce his beautiful wife, Herodias, so that he could marry her.

John accused Antipas of breaking God's law, much as Prophet Nathan had accused King David of breaking God's law when he married Bathsheba, the wife of a soldier. Angry, Antipas had John imprisoned. But John's words had a deep impact on the people of the kingdom; everyone frowned on the relationship forged between the king and his sister-in-law. Herodias decided to use her daughter, Salome, to wreak revenge on John.

Salome impressed the king with her dancing and as reward asked him to give her John's head on a plate. The king could not refuse her reward and so John was beheaded, an act that made the king even more unpopular.

- While divorce was practised in Jewish society, the idea of adultery was frowned upon.
- Herodias, which means princess of the Herod clan, seems more like a title. As wife of Herod Antipas and mother of Salome, she is sometimes considered a witch who ensnares men, and sometimes a proto-feminist, who slays men who abuse her.

Temptation in the Desert

After being baptised by John, Jesus went to the desert and fasted for forty days and nights in solitude. Here, over a period of forty days, he was tempted by the Devil three times.

The first time, when he was hungry, the Devil tempted Jesus to turn the stones to bread. Jesus refused, trusting God to provide for him as he had provided manna to those who followed Moses out of Egypt and had wandered in the desert seeking the Promised Land. 'We live not by bread alone, but by words of God too,' he told the Devil.

The second time, when he thought about being God's messenger and the chosen one, the Devil tempted him to jump from the highest point of the temple into the courtyard. God would save him, and the miracle would convince people that he was indeed the awaited messiah. But Jesus refused to listen to the Devil: people had to follow him of their free will, not drawn by magic. 'Those with faith have no doubt and so will not test God,' he told the Devil.

The third time, when he thought of the Kingdom of God, the Devil showed him all the kingdoms of the world stretching to the horizons, and offered them to him, provided he bowed to him. And Jesus refused, for he knew what was being offered was a world of violence and deceit and greed, not one of love and kindness and goodness. 'Only God shall be worshipped, no other,' he told the Devil.

The Devil failed and slunk away. Jesus was now ready to face the world and continue his ministry, and confront all the hardships that life had in store.

- The Devil does not play an important role in Jewish lore. It plays a very important role in Christian lore.
- The idea of evil first appears in Zoroastrian mythology of Persia that speaks of God (Ahura Mazda) in constant opposition to the Devil (Angra Mainyu) and how doing good deeds, having good thoughts and speaking good words were the only ways to defeat the Devil.
- Manichean mythology, which also emerged in the Middle East, saw the flesh as evil and the soul as good, and so valued celibacy, which would play a key role in the development of the Christian Church. Neither John nor Jesus are married. They are ascetics without wives or families, unlike earlier Jewish prophets.
- The fasting of Jesus for forty days has led to the Christian season of fasting known as Lent.
- Forty days of fasting alludes to the forty years of wandering of Moses in the wilderness in search of the Promised Land.
- There are claims that Jesus travelled to India during his wanderings and may have been exposed to Buddhist teachers, Buddhist Tantra and Buddhist community, which some argue explains his pacificism, his ability to survive crucifixion and the creation of the evangelical church. There is even the theory that he was buried in Kashmir as a holy man. He returned to Kashmir after his escape from the Roman authorities. In Islamic lore, Jesus did not die on the cross and so there is no truth in the story of his resurrection.
- In *Bhavishya Purana* are verses that claim how the Hindu king Shalivahana who drove out Sakas and other foreigners came upon a holy man beyond the Indus river, in the land of barbarians, who was probably Jesus (Isa). There are even verses telling stories of Adam and Eve (Adhama and Havyavati), Noah (Nyuha) and Moses (Musa). These verses are of dubious origin and believed to be nineteenth-century interpolations, probably made by Christian missionaries.

Jesus, the Provider

Jesus did not just speak. He also provided.

At a wedding in Cana, he got the servants to fill pots with water and serve it to the guests—it turned out to be wine!

At a gathering, he was able to feed a crowd of five thousand people with just two fishes and five loaves of bread.

On his advice, fishermen returning from a failed trip cast their net again and found it full of fish.

- The turning of water into wine at the wedding in Cana is the first miracle by Jesus. It was mentioned only in the Gospel of John, not the other Gospels.
- The idea of a bowl that serves more food than it can contain is a recurring theme in mythologies from around the world. Thus, we have the *akshaya patra* of Hindu mythology, and the 'cornucopeia' of Greek mythology.

Jesus, the Protector

Jesus provided not just food but also shelter, support and salvation.

He stood by a woman who was accused of adultery, daring those who wanted to stone her to death to cast the first stone only if they had never sinned.

He gave hope to prostitutes, who, overwhelmed by gratitude, washed his feet with their tears and wiped them dry with their hair.

People of Israel hated the tax collectors appointed by the king. But Jesus did not shun them. He invited them to join him, listen to him. For he knew they were lonely, torn between duty and popularity.

- Mary Magdalene, a female companion of Jesus, was the first to see the resurrected Jesus, but she was sidelined in later patriarchal traditions of the Church.
- Some scholars, and conspiracy theorists, argue that Mary was probably married to Jesus. This idea is heresy in the mainstream. Opponents call her a reformed prostitute.

Jesus, the Healer

People came from far and near to meet Jesus as he healed the sick, cured lepers, and enabled the cripple to walk, the dumb to speak and the deaf to hear. He stopped a woman's bleeding and cured a man of dropsy. Those cured said, 'This must be the Son of God, foretold to rise in the house of David.'

He drew and drove out demons from the bodies of those possessed. He said that this was possible if one believed in God. He did this in a synagogue. He did this in the field. Once, a legion of demons leapt out from the body of a man into the body of a pig, which, driven mad by demonic possession, jumped off a cliff.

He healed the son of a royal official and the servant of a Roman soldier. He helped those who came to him and even healed those afar. He helped heal a woman who had bled for twelve years. He raised people from the dead: a widow's son; a courtier's daughter; and Lazarus, brother of Mary and Martha, who had been his friend.

Jesus healed a man's withered hand so that it could function again. But he did this on a Sabbath, the traditional day of rest, declaring that helping others pleased God more than mere obedience, a declaration that annoyed many orthodox Jewish priests, who began seeing him as the enemy who had to be stopped.

- The signs of Jesus's divinity are many: he healed a royal official's son; by his blessing the blind could see and the paralysed could walk; he fed 5,000 people; he could walk on water; and he raised Lazarus from the dead. Curing people accounts for the largest number of miracles associated with Jesus.
- The major departure of Christianity from Judaism is the idea of God's love over God's law. Jesus demonstrates this when he heals the withered hand of a man on the Sabbath despite opposition of the orthodoxy.
- In the house of Lazarus, Mary heard Jesus speak while Martha was in the kitchen. This led to tension between the two sisters, with Jesus stating that what Mary was doing was more important as it grants eternal life to the spirit, and does not simply nourish the flesh like bread. This mirrors the Upanishadic value placed on knowledge over wealth. When Yagnavalkya offers the two to his wives, he appreciates Maitreyi over Katyayani for choosing knowledge over wealth.
- Demons in ancient scriptures probably referred to people who suffered from mental ailment. Exorcism was a kind of ritual that rebooted the brain like electroconvulsive therapy. But for the faithful, there are real demons and real miracles.

Jesus, the Teacher

Jesus gave a sermon on a mount like teachers and prophets before him. People came from all over to listen to him. He told people about God's Commandments, the Day of Judgement and the Kingdom of God that was to come. He told many parables using farming, herding, trading and feasting analogies and metaphors to make his message accessible to all.

He spoke of how his message was different from the messages received earlier, like new wine (*love*) that leaks out if poured in old wineskin (*law*). His message was like the pearl (*spiritual knowledge*), to buy which a merchant sold all he possessed (*material possessions*). Those who know of its value will behave like the peasant who sold all that he possessed (*material benefits*) to buy the field where he had found a treasure (*God's love*).

He spoke of how his ministry will grow from a mustard seed (*small beginnings*) to a mustard tree (*huge impact*), and how like yeast (*insignificant now*) will cause dough to swell (*significant eventually*).

He told people how when seeds are cast not all sprout and grow in the same way (*God's message is received differently by different people*). Seeds that fall on a road are eaten by birds (*some don't understand*). Seeds that fall on rocky soil do not grow long roots (*some give up when the going gets tough*). Seeds that fall next to thorny bushes are choked (*some get distracted by materialism*). The rest grow to their full potential (*some learn and keep gaining more and more knowledge*).

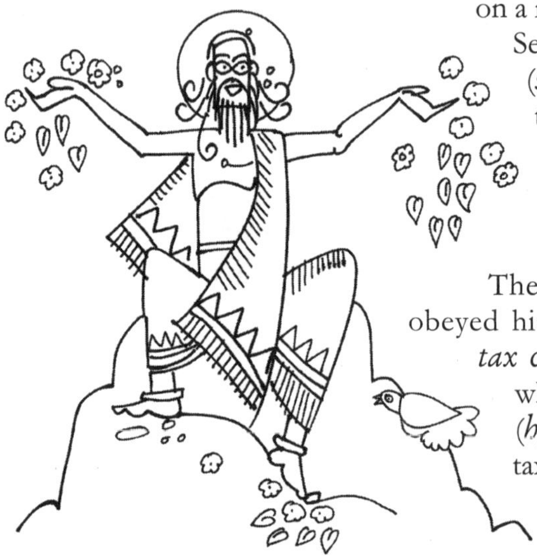

The son who disobeyed his father in word but obeyed his father in action (*repentant prostitutes and tax collectors*) mattered much more than the son who obeyed his father in word but not in action (*hypocritical religious leaders*). God preferred the tax collector who admitted his crimes in the temple to the rich man who flaunted his piety.

Jesus spoke of God's fairness and the world's diversity. He spoke of how a landowner paid the same wages to the labourer hired at dawn as he did to the labourer hired at noon and the labourer hired at dusk, angering the first, who felt that he was being effectively paid less, until he was told he had been paid what he had agreed to, and that his anger had nothing to do with unfairness (*we get our due*), but everything to do with envy (*we compare and feel we got less*). He explained how forgiving a greater debt (*people with more sin*) brings greater joy than forgiving a lesser debt (*people with less sin*).

Jesus laid out the expectations of God. He pointed out how when our servants return from working in the field, we do not let them rest (*don't have unrealistic expectations*), we tell them to prepare the meal (*do your job*). He told people to not focus on the splinter in other people's eye (*don't see fault in others*) when there is a log of wood in your eye (*check fault in yourself*). He warned people not to be like the rich fool who stores his immense wealth to enjoy another day only to be struck by death the very same day (*one should not delay enjoying and sharing wealth*).

He said God wants humans to be like the traveller (*those who care*) who helped the man who had been robbed on the road (*those less fortunate*), expecting nothing in return, and not like those passers-by who simply ignored (*those who are indifferent*) the man as he was a stranger. He told the story of the king (*God*) who forgave a servant's massive debt (*bestowed fortune on a sinner*) and punished the same servant on learning that he was not forgiving the tiny debt owed to him (*the fortunate who do not help the less fortunate*).

Jesus spoke of how we must live our life. He spoke of a master, who before going on a journey gave five bags of money to one servant, two to another and one to a third (*God gives different talents and fortunes to different people*) and was pleased with those who invested and doubled his wealth while he was away (*one who uses his talent and fortune for benefit of society*) and displeased with the one who simply saved and returned the same amount to him on his return (*one who did not use his talent and fortune for the benefit of society*). He told people to be like a lamp that is not hidden in a bowl (*goodness must not be hidden*) but displayed on a stand (*goodness must be displayed*).

Jesus told parables related to the Day of Judgement and the coming of God's kingdom. He spoke of how the rich man who never cared for the poor went to Hell after death and the poor man who suffered all his life went to Heaven after death, and how God told the rich that even the warnings of the dead will not make the living change their ways if they do not listen to the words of the prophet already available to all. Heaven is like a net that catches all kinds of fish, and fishermen (*angels*) choose the good fish (*those without sin*) and throw out the bad (*those with sin*). In a field (*world*), a farmer (*God*) sows seeds that grow into crops (*good people*) and his enemy (*Devil*) sows seeds that grow into weeds (*bad people*). One cannot remove weeds without destroying crops (*the good have to learn to live with the bad*) until the final harvest (*Day of Judgement*). He described how sheep (*those who follow God's law and feed the hungry and clothe the naked*) are kept on the right hand of God (*raised up to Heaven*) while goats (*who follow their own way and ignore the hungry and the naked*) are kept on the left (*cast down to Hell*).

To secure a place in Heaven, Jesus advised people to be like the man who invited to his banquet not just the rich who could return the favour, but also the poor who could not. And, when invited to a banquet, he told people to always choose the lowliest seat rather than the loftiest and wait for the host to give them a better place. He told the story of a steward who feared he would lose his job as his master had found him cheating (*one who thinks only of himself risks losing God's kingdom*) and so proceeded to cheat his master even more, only this time to reduce the debt of his master's debtors in the hope that they would treat him well when he is jobless (*one who thinks of others, prepares for a better afterlife*).

Jesus spoke of God's demands. A fig tree that does not bear fruit (*one who does not help others*) will be cut down (*will not enter God's kingdom*). The king invites all to his son's wedding (*Heaven is for everyone*) but many do not come as they are busy (*many are indifferent to God*) and many come out of compulsion (*some are forcibly brought to the presence of God*); but only those who are properly dressed (*those who choose the way of Jesus*) enjoy the banquet (*experience Heaven*). He spoke of the value of being ever vigilant of God's way. Of the ten bridesmaids who wait with torches for the groom to arrive (*those who await the second coming of Jesus*), only the five who carried extra oil (*those who are always prepared*) meet him, while the five who run home to fetch oil (*those not prepared*) miss him.

He told people never to lose hope and to keep praying. He told the parables of the uncaring judge who refused to entertain the poor widow but finally gave judgement to be rid of her, since she persisted, and that of the uncaring neighbour who finally helped his stubborn neighbour at midnight so that he could go to sleep.

Jesus reminded everyone of God's kindness. How the shepherd (*the messiah*) who had ninety-nine sheep (*the faithful*) still went in search of the lost sheep (*the faithless*), refusing to abandon it. How the woman (*messiah*) searched her house for the one lost coin (*the faithless*) even though she had nine in hand (*the faithful*). How the father (*the messiah*) threw a banquet to welcome the lost son (*the faithless*) who had returned home after squandering his inheritance, and assured his other son, who was always by his side (*the faithful*), that he had his inheritance and his father's company, and so should learn to be more gracious and generous.

- The Gospel of Matthew is meant for educated Jews and Matthew views Jesus as a king, the descendant of Abraham, who teaches about the Kingdom of God that is to come. The Gospel of Mark is for Romans, and Mark sees Jesus as the suffering servant of God, who does what he says, who performs miracles, and is the sacrifice. The Gospel of Luke is meant for Greeks and Luke sees Jesus as human and divine, the descendant of Adam, and he who heals suffering and is the saviour. The Gospel of John is for the Churches of the world and it is different from the other three as it focuses, less on what Jesus does and more on who Jesus is, the Son of God.
- A parable is instructive. Unlike a myth, it does not create a world view but assumes a world view. Unlike a legend, it is does not seek to valorize a historical figure using supernatural means.
- Parables of Jesus are considered to be the most authentic accounts of the teachings of the historical Jesus, as per scholars.
- The use of parables was well known in the time of Jesus, with Greeks and Romans as well as Israelites using them. The most famous biblical parable is the one told by Nathan to Solomon to condemn his relationship with Bathsheba.
- For Christians, 'an eye for an eye' was an Old Testament idea based on retaliation, while the New Testament said 'turn the other cheek', which was a milder, gentler and conciliatory idea proposed by Jesus.
- Buddhist monks were amongst the first people to use parables to communicate ideas and spread Buddhism. The Jataka tales instruct people about the benefits of generosity and compassion to realize the Buddha nature.
- The teacher who sits atop a mountain is a recurring idea in mythology around the world. Rishabha, the Tirthankara, sits atop Mount Kailasa and explains the Jain doctrine to the world. Moses descends from Mount Sinai.

Miracles of Jesus

Amongst Jesus's disciples were fishermen and tax collectors, even zealots who felt that Jesus was the military leader they hoped would lead them in a war against the Romans. They saw him calm a storm in the sea. They saw him walk on water.

Three of them saw a vision on a mountain which revealed that Jesus was no ordinary rabbi or even prophet. He was special. They saw him suddenly rise to the sky and glow like the sun, his clothes white, flanked by the prophets Elijah and Moses to whom he spoke.

- For many Jews, the saviour and the king would be a warrior, but Jesus was a teacher. He spoke less of retribution and the material world, and more about love and the spiritual world.
- The Jewish faithful congregated in temples, and after the temples were destroyed in synagogues. Christian congregations were known as churches.
- In the early days, Jesus was represented as a fish as he was closely associated with fishermen and he called his apostles, those who spread his word, as fishers amongst men.
- The acronym based on the Greek translation of 'Jesus Christ, Son of God, Our Savior' is ICHTHYS, which also means fish. Hence, the fish is a common symbol in Christianity.
- The vision of Jesus in the sky with Moses and Elijah is called Transfiguration. The mountain where this vision was seen has not been identified but is traditionally believed to be Mount Tabor in Israel.

Entry into Jerusalem

Jesus always knew he would face great hardship and meet death in violence. He did not resist the inevitable.

When Jesus went to Jerusalem with his disciples and followers, seated on a donkey, he was given a hero's welcome. People who had heard of him thought he would be the future king, one who would overthrow the Romans and restore God's law in the land. They waved palm leaves to cheer him, making the Jewish elders nervous and the Roman rulers suspicious. They did not know that the way of Jesus was different from the old ways: not violent, not legal, not established by war or argument, not settled in battlefields and courtrooms, but one based on love.

Jesus entered the Temple and found there a market. People were exchanging Roman coins for local coins so that they could buy sacrificial animals. Jesus picked up a whip and drove everyone away, shouting angrily that they disrespect the Temple, the house of his father. His behaviour annoyed the Jewish priests and made the Romans even more suspicious of his motives.

- Jesus entered Jerusalem on a Sunday, the day after he raised Lazarus, and was welcomed by the residents, who waved palm leaves as they believed he was the messiah. This is celebrated as Palm Sunday, a week before Easter Sunday.
- Jesus entered on a donkey with a colt. In Jewish tradition, the final messiah would come on a donkey. The phrase 'messiah's donkey' refers to one who does all the dirty work.
- The triumphant entry of Jesus into Jerusalem mirrors the triumphant entry of Krishna into Mathura. Jesus is anointed with oil by a woman and people spread their cloaks before him. Krishna is offered flowers and sandalwood paste.

Last Supper

It was at Passover time, in spring, that the Jewish people reminded themselves of the journey from slavery in Egypt to freedom in the Promised Land. Jesus gathered his disciples around him for the evening meal, washed their feet, and offered them bread and wine, stating that those were his flesh and blood.

Jesus spoke of being betrayed by one of them. He spoke of being denied by another out of fear. He spoke of dying and resurrecting himself. He told those gathered to love all as he loved them, and to share the good news about God's Kingdom and salvation from the Original Sin.

His disciples were suddenly filled with a sense of foreboding.

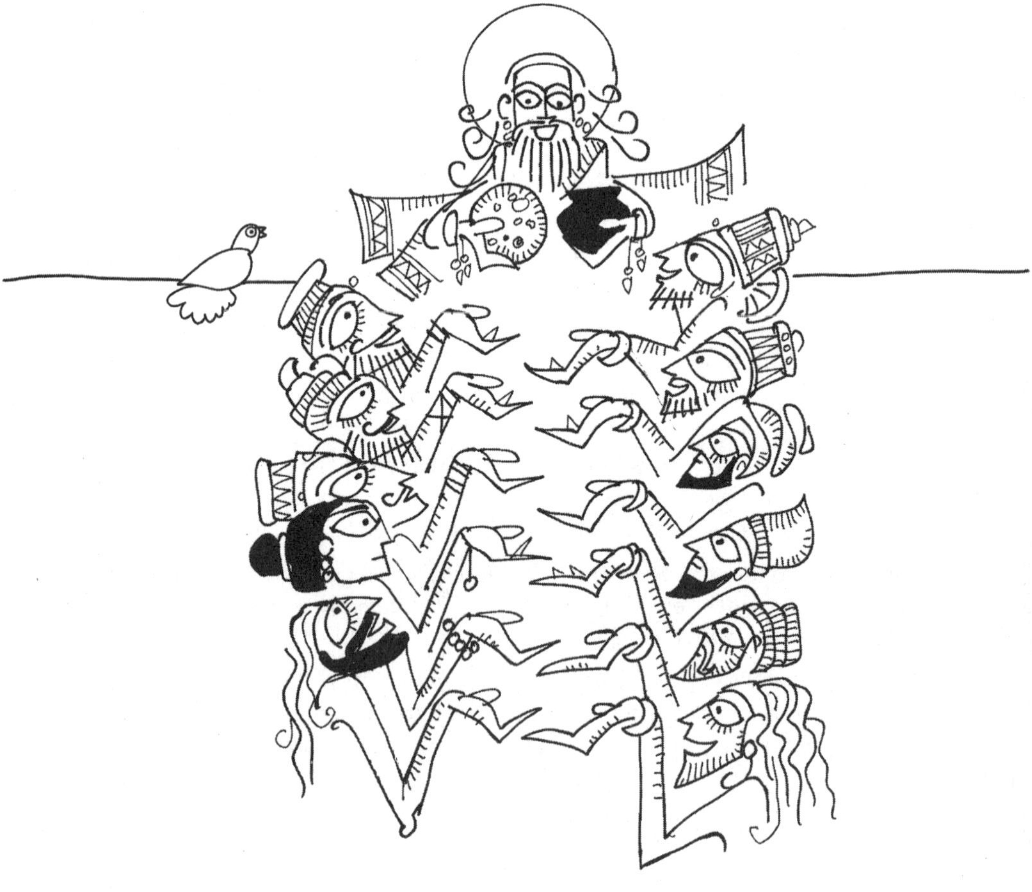

- The phrase 'Last Supper' is not found in the New Testament but is a popular phrase. The Protestants prefer the phrase 'Lord's Supper' and the Orthodox prefer 'Mystical Supper'.
- This event happens on Thursday, between Palm Sunday and Easter Sunday, and is known as Maundy Thursday from the Latin word for commandment, *mandatum*.
- Judas is the one who betrays Jesus and Peter is the one who denies knowing him.
- The Quran refers to a table sent down by Allah so that Isa (Jesus) can have a meal with his apostles (Hawariyyin). It does not speak of the Last Supper explicitly though.

Betrayal and Arrest

That night, Jesus went to a garden, atop a mountain, and prayed to God to prepare for what was to come. As he was leaving, a group of soldiers from the Temple gathered around him. Judas kissed Jesus's cheek, thus identifying the man who claimed to be the king of Jews.

Most disciples ran away. Peter picked a sword and cut the ear of one of the servants of the high priest. Jesus intervened, fixed the ear back in place and declared, 'Those who live by the sword, die by the sword.' He offered no resistance and identified himself as Jesus of Nazareth.

Judas had betrayed Jesus for thirty pieces of silver. Filled with guilt, he tried returning the money but as it was blood money, the Temple refused to accept it. Judas then used the silver to buy land, where he hanged himself to death. His body fell from the tree where it was hanging and fell on rocks that cracked open his skull and tore out his guts. The field became a burial ground.

- The Gnostic Gospel of Judas claims that Judas was the truest disciple of Jesus, who was told by Jesus himself to betray him to the authorities. The play-acting by Judas mirrors the Hindu concept of *leela*, where God play-acts to get an idea across to humanity.
- In art, Judas is often depicted as red-haired, seen as a negative trait in medieval times, when Jews were also depicted so. He is sometimes shown without a halo or with a black halo to distinguish him from the other followers of Jesus.

Trial

Jesus was accused of sedition and blasphemy, of sorcery, of engaging with demons, of working on the Day of Rest, of threatening to destroy the Temple and of claiming to be the messiah, the Son of God, and the king of the Jews. Jesus did not defend his case. For he knew the decision had already been taken by those who accused him. The trial was a sham. When they asked him if he was the messiah, he said without hesitation, knowing it would be the death of him, 'You say I am.'

The priests of Jerusalem sentenced Jesus to death on grounds of treason against the Roman emperor for declaring himself the king of Jews and for blaspheming against Jewish law. But they could not kill him. So, they took him to the Roman governor, Pontius Pilate, who said the decision should be made by the local leader, Herod Antipas of Galilee, as Jesus was from Galilee.

Herod, who had heard of Jesus, hoped that Jesus would perform miracles for him. But Jesus performed no miracles and did not argue his case, and so Herod simply mocked him and sent him back to the Roman governor for his decision. The priests were getting impatient. They told Pilate, 'If you let Jesus go, you are no friend of Caesar.'

Pilate did not want to kill an innocent man. His wife begged him not to. He sought a way out. During Passover, it was traditional to set one criminal free. Pilate asked the crowds who they wanted to set free: a thief and murderer called Barabbas or Jesus, who had hurt no one. The crowds shouted they wanted Barabbas to be set free and Jesus to be crucified.

Pilate then washed his hands in public. Thus symbolically stating that he had nothing to do with the death of Jesus. It was the decision of the priests and mobs of Jerusalem.

- Pilate's reluctance to condemn Jesus is seen as a later development to show Romans as more merciful than Jewish people. In earlier works, Pilate agrees with the Jewish elders to crucify Jesus.
- Narratives emerged in later traditions that Pilate lost his high position after ordering the crucifixion of Jesus. Disgraced, he committed suicide.
- Pilate was perceived in negative light in Roman and Byzantine Churches but as positive in Egypt and Ethiopian churches. Pilate became a positive figure as Romans gradually accepted Christianity. There are even tales of Pilate becoming Christian and eventually being martyred for his faith.
- The selection of Barabbas over Jesus, a bandit over a prophet, by the Jewish crowd, is often viewed as a way of reinforcing anti-Semitism.

Crucifixion

Roman soldiers whipped Jesus and abused him. They covered him with a scarlet robe and placed a crown of thorns on his head to mock him for claiming he was the 'king of Jews'. Then they made him carry his own cross through the streets of Jerusalem to where he would be crucified between two thieves.

Nails were hammered through his wrists and ankles. A board declaring the charge against him, that he claimed to be 'king of Jews', was nailed above his head. The cross was raised and, in the hours before he died, he was subjected to constant abuse by soldiers and to the jeers of the people.

When he died, the sky turned dark, the earth shook and the Temple curtain tore. A soldier drove his spear into Jesus's side to confirm he was dead, and water came out along with blood.

- In Islamic traditions, Jesus did not die on the cross. He was taken by God to Heaven and will descend before Judgement Day, when the world comes to an end, to kill the Devil. His place on the cross was taken up by Simon of Cyrene, who looked just like him, and who, as per Christian tradition, was asked by Roman soldiers to carry the cross when the burden became too much for Jesus.

- The crucifix became a symbol of Christianity by the second century CE. Catholics generally prefer the image of Jesus on the crucifix while Protestants generally avoid human representation. In the Byzantine Eastern Orthodox Church, the icons of Jesus as king are more popular.
- In medieval Europe, the pelican became a symbol of Jesus as it is believed that a pelican feeds its own blood to its young when food is in short supply. Jesus was also linked to the mythical unicorn, that was drawn to virgins. Ancient Greeks believed that a peacock's flesh does not rot and so the peacock was a symbol of Jesus.
- Good Friday each year marks the day Jesus was crucified.
- Although the crucified were stripped of clothes, Jesus is always shown covered with a loin cloth, perhaps to avoid showing he was circumcised, hence Jewish.
- Popularly, the nails used to crucify Jesus are shown as going through his palms but it is more likely that they were driven through his wrists. The hands were also probably bound to the crucifix to avoid the body from tearing itself on the nails as a result of its own weight when the crucifix was lifted and planted on the ground.
- Few in academia refer to the veneration of the crucifix as being the veneration of a torture instrument; yet, many in academia insist on pointing out that the worship of the Shiva linga is essentially a phallic symbol, despite devotees insisting it is not so. Such bias stems from a deep-seated colonial prejudice that non-monotheistic faiths are pagan, polytheistic, idolatrous, and therefore, do not deserve the same respect as monotheistic religions.
- The Crusades, wars between European Christians and Middle Eastern Muslims for control over Jerusalem, between 1000 CE and 1300 CE, gave rise to many legends of knights in shining armour, who maintained the vow of chastity and fought for their ladies. These were metaphors for the Church and Mother Mary respectively.
- The Crusades gave rise to the Arthurian legends in Britain, of a king chosen by God, whose knights sit around a round table, a reminder of the Last Supper. And the purest of them, Perceval, eventually goes on the greatest quest—fetch the Holy Grail from the wounded Fisher King, whose kingdom turns into wilderness when he gives away faith, chastity and charity. The Holy Grail is said to be the vessel in which the blood of Jesus Christ was collected and brought to Avalon (ancient name for British Isles) by Joseph of Arimathea.
- In post-Gospel literature, the centurion who pierced Jesus with his lance came

to be known as Longinus. There were many places in the Christian world that claimed to have the Lance of Longinus, or parts of it.

- The Shroud of Turin, a linen cloth with a negative image of a man on it, first spoken of in the fourteenth century, is believed to be the shroud of Jesus Christ.

Resurrection

The body of Jesus was brought down from the cross, anointed with oil and placed in a tomb.

Three days later, when women went to anoint the corpse as was custom, they found that the stone door at the gate had been rolled away, and the tomb was empty. They saw an angel, who announced that Jesus who was Christ had risen from the dead and would return to save all humanity.

The women then saw Jesus himself and he told them to inform his twelve followers that he would appear before them too and guide them. The women communicated it to the men, and as foretold, Jesus appeared to many of his followers, at different times, and commanded them to spread the good news of God's Son who had been sacrificed to save humanity from its Original Sin, and of the Kingdom of God where everyone would be welcome.

Thomas doubted if the person speaking to him was indeed Jesus. He saw the wounds, and touched the wounds, and was convinced it was indeed Jesus resurrected.

- Three Marys (Jesus's mother, Mary Magdalene and Lazarus's sister Mary) saw Christ crucified. Mary Magdalene was the first to see his empty tomb and his resurrected form. Yet, women do not play a dominant role in churches around the world. This is changing only in recent times.
- Easter Sunday is the day of the resurrection of Jesus Christ. In pre-Christian times It was a festival associated with the Spring Equinox and fertility—hence the symbolic value given even today to hares and eggs during its celebration. Easter comes from Eostre, an ancient goddess of spring.
- During the Age of Crusades, many European Christians believed that beyond the Muslim worlds, was a vast Christian kingdom ruled by Prester John. Many European explorers who travelled to Africa, India and China in the fifteenth century hoped to encounter Prester John.
- The phrase 'Doubting Thomas' comes from the story of Thomas doubting the resurrection of Jesus.

Ascension and Pentecost

After his resurrection, Jesus appeared to his followers for forty days and then rose skywards, and was finally covered by a cloud. Many concluded that the cloud was a symbol of God and that Jesus had gone back to his father's house.

Ten days after his ascension, fifty days after the resurrection, on the feast of the Pentecost, which marks the harvest as well as the giving of the law by God to Moses on Mount Sinai, when all the followers of Jesus had gathered at a single location, the Holy Spirit descended upon them, sounding like wind and appearing like tongues of fire.

All were able to speak in all the languages of the world, so that they could unite the people divided by language at the Tower of Babel. They all had access to the common message of redemption conveyed by God through the Son of God about the Second Coming and the eventual return of all of Adam's descendants to God's Heaven.

So, the apostles travelled in every direction to spread the good word. They were known as the Evangelists, bearers of the good word.

- Pentecost is an ancient Jewish harvest festival celebrated fifty days after Passover. Christians refer to it as White Sunday. It is the seventh Sunday after Easter, when children are dressed in white and baptised in many Christian denominations.
- There are people who have argued that the Rig Veda of the Hindus has verses that allude to the sacrifice and resurrection of Jesus. Verse 10.90.7, they claim, refers to the sacrifice of man on a wooden stake conducted by kings. However, such liberal translations have not received academic approval. The complex metaphorical verse deals with the dismemberment of the cosmic man (purusha) in the creation of the world, and the word 'sacrifice' or 'yagna' means exchange.

BOOK TEN

Martyrs and Saints

Zeus and Dionysus

Christianity began as a Jewish sect. But its message was based more on love than on law. This message was taken by the apostles to different parts of the world. Peter and Paul took it to Rome.

The Romans on hearing of a son of god, born of a virgin, who could turn water into wine, thought of Bacchus, son of Jupiter. Roman mythology was influenced by Greek mythology, and many Greek gods acquired Roman names. Jupiter was Zeus and Bacchus was Dionysus.

Zeus was known to have loved many mortal women who had borne him sons, the heroes of Greek mythology. Once, Zeus approached Semele but Semele, tricked by Zeus' wife Hera, asked to see his divine form before letting him touch her. Zeus revealed his divine form, and it was so bright and radiant that Semele conceived a child in her womb but also died instantly. This child was raised by nymphs in the forests and became the god of wine and mysteries, much loved by women as he liberated them from the drudgery of life.

For Romans, Jesus was an eastern god, just like Bacchus-Dionysus, whose mystery involved the partaking of wine. His father in Heaven was like Jupiter-Zeus, almighty and all-powerful, keeper of order. His mother, a mortal virgin. His followers, mostly women, who were drawn into his ecstatic mysteries.

Romans converted rapidly to Christianity. First, the women, then the slaves, and finally, the aristocrats; and then, the Roman emperor himself.

In the old days, the Roman Empire tolerated all faiths, provided veneration was offered to the Roman emperor. However, when the Roman emperor converted to Christianity, he insisted that all subjects accept the new faith. Old temples of Zeus, Mithra and Isis were torn down. Such intolerance was new. Even the Persian Empire, which was based on Zoroastrian monotheism, had been tolerant of other faiths. This marked the beginning of the end of the pagan world. Many gods gave way to one true god.

- Early Christians depicted Jesus symbolically as a fish or a peacock, a pelican (as per folklore, the pelican pierced its own heart to feed its child its own blood), and an anchor.
- Images of Jesus were rare as Jewish commandments prohibited any depictions of God. Also, early Christians who faced Roman persecution avoided any visual depictions of their faith. Instead of images, people used the alphabet, like alpha and omega, meaning the first and last, or the letter T to represent the cross. The crucifix became popular as a symbol of Christianity only after the conversion of the Roman emperor, who banned crucifixion as punishment.
- The earliest images of Jesus showed him as a beardless youth with sheep. Later he was shown holding a staff, like a magician. Then he was shown seated on a throne, like the Greek god Zeus. Only from 500 CE do we find images of a suffering Christ. East European (Byzantine, Orthodox) churches shunned the realistic art that was favoured by West European churches (Roman).
- To save himself from the attack of barbarian hordes, the Roman emperor moved east to Byzantium. Here, in the fourth century, Constantine declared himself Christian, hoping to use the concept of 'one God' to consolidate his divided empire. His sons ordered the purging of pagan faiths from the army, the aristocracy and the empire in general. These events from the fourth century CE mark the rise of religion as a political lever.
- The kingdom of Armenia was the first to declare itself Christian.

- Members of the mystery cults of the Roman empire, associated with Cybele, Mithra, Osiris and Adonis, indulged in consumption of alcohol and other narcotics to enter altered states of consciousness, where they could experience death like Greek heroes and return to the land of the living enlightened by this spiritual journey. They claimed, 'If you die, before you die, you will not die, when you die.' Later, as Christianity gained ground, and ceremonies became more public, the rites became more symbolic: the idea of baptism became the rite of symbolic death and symbolic resurrection.

Enduring Persecution

The Romans respected Jewish practices, despite their defiance of Roman emperors, as they saw Judaism as an old faith. However, they were suspicious of Christian faith as it was new, and it lacked legitimacy in their eyes. As the word of Christ spread across the Roman empire, those who spread and accepted the good word, and rejected the pagan ways, faced persecution. Many were killed and they came to be known as martyrs.

Martyrs were venerated. Their bones were considered sacred relics that had healing powers. This cult of the martyr was an extension of the old Graeco-Roman cult of the hero, with one crucial difference. The Graeco-Romans saw death and tombs as inauspicious. But for early Christians, tombs were sanctuaries to meet in secret, away from prying Roman eyes. And so, over time, the bones of martyrs came to be linked with power and protection.

Martyrs included Peter, who was crucified, and Paul, who was beheaded. They also included soldiers who refused to fight and prostitutes who changed their ways. The Church venerated the martyrs and many became saints. Many old pagan gods became Christian saints too.

The story of St George, who defeats a dragon, is inspired by the killing of the sea-monster by Perseus, who tries to save Andromeda, a damsel in distress, or that of Tiamat, the monster of chaos, overpowered by Marduk, the Mesopotamian hero-god.

St Brigid of Ireland was linked to the Irish goddess Brigid, daughter of Dagda, goddess of healing and childbirth and inspiration; her festival continued to be held in February and so was associated with the arrival of spring.

King Abenner, who persecuted the Christian Church in his realm, was told by astrologers that his own son would someday become a Christian. The king kept the young prince in isolation, but unfortunately, the prince, Josaphat, met a sage called Barlaam, and under his influence converted, and eventually renounced the throne. This story is clearly influenced by the life of the Buddha, whose father tried to isolate him with luxuries to prevent him from becoming a hermit.

Many pagan festivals became part of the Christian world. The Spring Equinox was linked to Easter, the day when Jesus was conceived and resurrected. The Winter Solstice was linked to Christmas, the day Jesus was born. Mardi Gras, celebrated in spring with feasting, had its roots in the Roman spring festival of fertility known as Lupercalia.

The memories of old pagan gods and practices, thus, faded away. New ideas emerged and mingled with old ones until they were unrecognizable.

Jesus's father Joseph became St Joseph, patron saint of carpenters. Jesus's grandmother is revered as St Anna.

Different vocations had different patron gods in Roman times, and so in the Christian church, saints rose who were favoured by different groups.

St Barbara was linked to miners as she tried to hide in a mine to escape the wrath of her father who was opposed to her conversion.

St Dominic, who popularized the use of the rosary in the Christian church, was so named as his mother dreamt of a hound leaping from her womb with a torch that set the world on fire. His name means the hound (canis) of God (domini).

St Xavier was one of the first Jesuits to travel to South Asia, Southeast Asia and East Asia, and became the patron saint of Roman Catholic missions.

St Patrick of Ireland was sold into slavery and returned as a Christian to Ireland, where he drove away snakes and explained the idea of the trinity using a shamrock sprig. St Anthony of Portugal, who was called the 'hammer of heretics', was a popular speaker, and is remembered when something is lost. St Francis of Assisi, who once loved to party, became a hermit after an illness and after spending time in prison, and became the patron saint of animals. St Joan of France is remembered for her inspired march into battle on behalf of the French king against the English; she was declared a witch and burnt at the stake.

Though saints are not worshipped, many believed they spoke to God on behalf of those who venerated them.

- Sainthood is a Roman Catholic concept conferred on venerable beings, through a complex church process. In the Orthodox Church of East Europe, sainthood is determined by people's faith and not by the decree of authorities and so there is no official record of saints.
- Martyrs refer to those who have witnessed God, and so are willing to die for Him. Martyrs are of two types: red martyrs, who were persecuted and killed by Romans, and white martyrs, who surrendered to God totally and performed severe penance to express their faith.
- Two centuries after the conversion of the Roman Empire into Christianity, Islam arose in Arabia and became a mighty military force, claiming most of the Byzantine Empire and conquering Jerusalem. Egypt, which was Christian, became

an Islamic country, and the Byzantium Empire was surrounded by Muslim hordes. Islam spread along the southern shores of the Mediterranean along Africa and reached Europe via Spain, where it was pushed back at the Battle of Tours by Franks, led by Charles Martel, whose grandson, Charlemagne, was crowned emperor of the Holy Roman Empire.

- The Mediterranean region, long under Roman control, was split into the Muslim south and the Christian north, that is, Muslim Africa (Moors) and Christian Europe. The Pope inspired the Christians to fight the Muslims and reclaim Jerusalem from them. This led to centuries of holy wars known as Crusades. The fierce battle between Christians and Muslims continues even today in Africa.
- For Christians, Muslims were heretics, even Devil-worshippers, as they did not believe in Original Sin, and they did not accept Jesus as the Son of God. They saw Heaven as a place of sensual pleasures. Christianity meanwhile turned ascetic, valorizing a life of celibacy and poverty. As monastic orders took control of Christianity, women were gradually sidelined.
- Christian asceticism took three forms—the solitary monk, who lived in isolation like John the Baptist; the communities of monks, who lived and prayed together in cloistered groups; and the monks who served society and engaged in social matters. The third group became popular in Western Christianity, but also became associated with many controversial and corrupt practices, including living a materialistic life, indulging in power politics and sexual misdemeanour.
- Five hundred years ago, the Protestants challenged the might of the Roman Catholic Church, the value it placed on asceticism, and what it deemed were pagan practices: veneration of saints; veneration of relics; veneration of Mother Mary and veneration of the idea of the Trinity (Father, Son and Holy Spirit), which was seen as polytheism. Protestants sought direct access to God by reading the Bible, and not via middlemen, that is, priests. Many Christian groups, facing persecution in Europe, migrated to the Americas.
- North America is predominantly Protestant while South America is predominantly Catholic.
- In Kerala, the cult of St George has turned into veneration of Geevarghese Sahada, who cures snake bites and protects from malevolent spirits.

Blood Money

In Kerala, a Nair family gave shelter to a Jewish man who had travelled by sea and suffered from scurvy and sore throat. The man identified himself as Thomas.

The head of the family had been injured in battle and was cured by the prayers of Thomas. So, the Nair patriarch helped Thomas and gave him local treatment for his ailments based on the Indian gooseberry, long before Vitamin C was discovered in Europe.

In gratitude, Thomas gave his host four silver coins, issued by the Roman Emperor Tiberius, saying that his teacher, who was killed by his enemies, had resurrected himself three days after his death and had given thirty such coins to him stating that he had been killed for these pieces of silver. The man he was referring to was clearly Jesus Christ, which means that he was Thomas, the apostle.

The descendants of the family continue to worship a folk deity called Thondacchan, perhaps in memory of 'Thomacchan', whose name sounded like Thondacchan when he had sore throat. Thomacchan, or Thoma-acchan, means Father Thomas in Malayalam. The coins are called *rakta-velli* or blood money, as they are believed to have been paid to Judas to enable the killing of Jesus Christ.

- Christianity came to India in waves. Legend has it that St Thomas, one of the apostles of Christ, came to India and spread Christianity nearly 2,000 years ago. Christianity also came with merchants who traded at Indian sea ports of the western coast, and who were part of the lucrative spice trade. European Christianity came with the Portuguese in the sixteenth century to Goa. The British East India Company and the government maintained a distance from the missionaries as they were more focused on commercially exploiting the colony. American Protestant Christianity such as Baptists and Presbyterians arrived in the twentieth century and spread in tribal areas, especially in Northeast India.

- St Thomas, as per Christian legends, played a key role in spreading the Christian message to India and China. There is a legend in South India that he travelled through the Parthian kingdoms and met Gondophares; then, he travelled to Kerala, introduced Christianity and met a martyr's death at the hands of the local Brahmins at Mylapore. The story of his killing is probably a later invention by Portuguese missionaries to India, who tried to spread Christianity by force in the sixteenth and seventeenth centuries.
- The church established in India during the lifetime of Jesus Christ was probably established by a sect of Jewish sea merchants, and came to be known as Mar Thoma (Saint Thomas) or Nazarani (referring to Nazareth, home of Jesus).
- The Konkani translation of the New Testament known as *Krista Purana* was written in the sixteenth century by a Jesuit Priest, Father Thomas Joseph, when the Portuguese ruled Goa.
- In the eighteenth century, the Bible was translated into Tamil by a German missionary, Bartholomäus Ziengenbalg. Since he had no printing press initially (he imported it later), he had the Bible written on palm leaves with an iron stylus with the help of local scribes.

Prester John

During the days of the Crusades, Christian soldiers fought to reclaim the Holy Lands, especially Jerusalem, which had been under the control of Muslims since the eighth century. News came of a mysterious eastern ruler known as Prester John.

Prester John's empire stretched beyond Persia and Arabia across India. It extended from the Tower of Babel to the land of the rising sun. Seventy-two kings paid him tribute. His land was home to elephants, camels, crocodiles, wild asses, white and red lions, white bears, crickets, griffins, tigers, hyenas, wild horses, wild oxen and wild men—men with horns, men with eyes before and behind, centaurs, phoenixes, fauns, satyrs, pygmies, giants, cyclopes, Amazons and Brahmins.

There were letters doing the rounds of European courts with elaborate accounts of the marvels and riches of his great kingdom, and his declared intention of visiting Rome after defeating the enemies of Christ. Perhaps the most fantastic of all was his magical mirror that enabled him to see and control his vast empire from one place.

With an eastern Christian flank opening up, European monarchs, who were attacking Muslims from the west, hoped to trap and crush the Muslims once and for all. But sadly, this great Christian king and his army never appeared.

- The flourishing maritime culture of Europe from the fifteenth century was in many ways the direct result of the Crusades. Since land routes for trade with Asia were controlled by Muslims, the Christian kings, especially of Spain and Portugal, encouraged exploration of new sea routes. This led to the 'discovery' of America and sea routes to India. Vasco Da Gama hoped to meet Prester John in India.

Arthur of Avalon

In the British Isles, they spoke of a magician called Merlin, son of the Devil, born of a virgin, who enabled a knight called Uther to trick a chaste woman and make her pregnant. Thus was conceived Arthur. Merlin claimed Uther's child and raised him secretly.

Though just a boy, Arthur was able to do the impossible, such as pull out a sword embedded in a rock, thus identifying himself as the true king. Merlin served him and sought to establish a kingdom where the old pagan ways were abandoned and people accepted Jesus as their saviour. In other words, Merlin challenged his own origins and wanted to be purged of the Devil.

Arthur, with the help of Merlin, established the great kingdom of England with his capital at Camelot, where he set up a round table. There sat twelve knights, who fought witches and dragons, rescued damsels in distress, and who, through the practice of celibacy and chivalry, established a Christian kingdom.

Like Jesus, Arthur was betrayed by his most powerful knight, Lancelot, who broke the king's heart by falling in love with Arthur's wife, Queen Guinevere.

The knights went on many quests. The greatest of the quests was to find the Holy Grail, the cup that contained the blood of Jesus, and the lance that had pierced his side long ago. These were found by Knight Perceval, the pure one, but only after he showed compassion for the Fisher King, guardian of these relics, and restored the fertility of the wasteland that was his kingdom.

Eventually, Arthur was injured in battle by Mordred, his own son, born of incest, through his half-sister, Morgana. He was taken into a cave inside a hill, where he sleeps peacefully. He will rise once again, when England needs him, when the time is right for his second coming. As for Merlin, he was enchanted by Vivien, lady of the lake, who learnt all his magic and used it against him, entombing him alive under a mountain of crystal rocks.

- As Christianity spread across Europe, new stories emerged about Christian kings and monks of England, Ireland, Wales, France, Germany, Scandinavia and Spain.
- These stories reveal the tension in the Christian world between sensuality (love for women), asceticism (love for Christ) and the value placed on the warrior ideal as well as on pagan magic.
- Many people believed that the Holy Grail was actually a person: Mary Magdalene, the wife of Jesus Christ, who moved to Europe to bear her child. The male followers of Jesus wanted control of the Church and did not want a

woman, or her bloodline, to lead them. In French, *san greal*, which means holy grail, can also be read as a code for 'sang real' which means royal blood. This is the subject of the very popular 2003 novel *Da Vinci Code*.

Visions of the Mother

In south India, a cowherd was on his way to the market to sell milk when he stopped to drink water from a pond and rest under a banyan tree. A woman appeared before him holding a child and asked for some milk for her child. The boy gave her his pot of milk. After feeding her son, she returned the pot, thanked the cowherd, and disappeared. When the boy reached the market, his customers were upset because he was late. He apologized and told them of what he had encountered. Then, to everyone's astonishment, the pot started overflowing with milk. Upon hearing her description, local Catholics recognized her as the Virgin Mary. This happened in the sixteenth century.

A few years later, she appeared once again to a lame boy who was selling buttermilk on the roadside. She asked for some buttermilk to feed her child. After the child was fed, she asked the boy to deliver a message to a Catholic resident in the town, requesting him to build a church for her. But the boy pointed out that he was lame and would be unable to act as her messenger. The lady smiled and asked him to try to stand up. To the boy's surprise, not only could he stand, he could also walk and run to the town and deliver the message. The gentleman was in no doubt that Our Lady of Good Health, Mary, Mother of God, was responsible for this miracle.

Finally, a group of Portuguese sailors on their way from Macau, China, to Sri Lanka encountered a terrible storm in the Bay of Bengal and prayed to Mother Mary, promising to build a church for her if saved. They landed safely in the area associated with Our Lady of Good Health.

Similar stories of visions of Mary have been communicated from other parts of the world.

In the sixteenth century, in Mexico, Mary appeared to Juan Diego, and spoke to him in his native Nahuatl language (the language of the Aztec Empire). She identified herself as the Virgin Mary and asked for a shrine to be built at that site in her honour. No one believed Juan Diego and he kept getting visions of the lady, who insisted on a shrine in her honour. Then, when Juan Diego's uncle was dying and he made his way early in the morning to fetch the priest, she appeared again, blocking his path, gently chiding him with the words, 'Am I not here, I who am your mother?' She instructed him to gather flowers from the top of a hill, which was usually barren, especially in the cold of December. Juan followed her instructions and he found there roses that were not native to Mexico. Juan put the flowers under his cloak and when he revealed this to the local priest, they found in the cloak the image of the Virgin of Guadalupe. She was associated with many miracles, saving the wounded and healing the sick.

In the nineteenth century, a peasant girl collecting firewood had a vision of Mary in a grotto at Lourdes, France. She had numerous visions before people believed her. The lady with white veil, blue girdle and yellow roses at her feet asked that a chapel be built for her and that people drink water of the spring if they wished to be healed. Lourdes eventually became a place of Catholic pilgrimage and many people bathe and drink water at the spring of the grotto, hoping to be cured of ailments and be imbued with regenerated spiritually.

- The veneration of Mary by the Christian Church became officially recognized as part of Christian faith when the Roman Empire became Christian. It is argued that during the purging of pagan cults, the one cult that resisted extermination was that which venerated the mother goddess. The worship of the goddess and her child was widespread in the ancient world.
- Jesus was linked to Adonis, the god who dies and is resurrected by his mother

and lover, Artemis-Aphrodite-Cybele, the goddess of vegetation of Ephesus in Turkey, who was both virgin and mother. Priests of Cybele castrated themselves and served the goddess. This practice was frowned upon by the Jewish people, but Jesus said eunuchs were welcome in the kingdom of God.

- It was in Ephesus, the ancient centre of goddess worship, that Mary was declared Theokotos or God-bearer in the fifth century CE. This happened after the intervention of Pulcheria, the powerful sister of the Byzantine emperor, who ruled as regent in the fifth century.
- Early images of Mother Mary with Jesus in her arm mirrored images of Isis with Horus, popular in ancient Egypt. Alexandria, in Egypt, was a major centre of Christianity before the arrival of Islam.
- An unusual image of Devaki–Krishna found in Goa mirrors the image of Mary with Jesus, indicating the Catholic influence on local Hindu communities.

Mormon

Many people in America believe that when the Temple at Jerusalem was destroyed in 600 BCE, Lehi and his followers migrated westwards and reached America. Their descendants formed two groups: Lamanites and Nephites.

Lamanites forgot their beliefs and became the native American tribes. They attacked and destroyed the Nephites around 400 CE. But before this tragedy happened, Jesus had appeared to the Nephites and spoken the good word about God's kingdom.

Prophet Mormon wrote this in golden tablets and these were buried for 1,400 years before they were revealed to Joseph Smith in 1830, who translated the Book of Mormon, which is the holy book of the Church of the Latter Day Saints.

Mormon spoke of Elohim as God the Father, who once had a human body before he attained his exalted immortal divine status with a flesh-and-blood body. With this immortal body he made Mary pregnant and she gave birth to Jesus, who was known as Jehovah when he was just a spirit. Jesus attained divine status with an immortal flesh and blood body by living an exalted life and accepting the sins of the future generations. All humans lived as spirits before they obtained their physical body and they too can become gods by accepting the atonement of Jesus Christ.

In this world view, Elohim, Jehovah–Jesus and Holy Spirit are three distinct entities of which the first two have physical bodies. They made a plan to help all spirits become gods, but it was rejected by Satan and his followers, who tempt humanity away from this proposed plan. The Holy Spirit is spirit but not body and comforts humans in their struggle to eventually attain exaltation, and become gods like Jesus, live in the presence of God and continue as families.

- Mormonism is popular in North America. Its unique feature is that its doctrine evolves with new members. It uses modern scientific methods like genealogy to save souls of ancestors unfamiliar with Mormon doctrine.
- Mormons were accused of practising polygamy but are now known for puritanical beliefs and the value placed on family.
- Since the word 'Mormon' is often used derogatorily, members of this church prefer to refer to themselves as 'Latter Day Saints'.

BOOK ELEVEN

Final Messenger

Kabah in Mecca

Long ago, when Ishmael was dying of thirst in the desert, Hagar had run to the top of the hill of Safa, and then to the top of the hill of Marwa, hoping to find water. She did this seven times until the angel Gabriel revealed to her that water was located right below where Ishmael lay, between the two hills. This was Zamzam, a gift from Allah.

Next to Zamzam was the spot where stood the first house of worship, used by angels before creation, built by Adam after creation and rebuilt by Noah after the flood. It is here that Abraham and Ishmael built the Kabah.

Ishmael was given shelter and a wife by the Jurhum tribe, who eventually became guardians of Zamzam as well as Kabah. Mecca grew to be a pilgrim spot. People came to drink the water of Zamzam and circumambulate the Kabah in the anticlockwise direction. It also became a trading spot and thriving market, as it stood in the caravan route between Judea in the north and Yemen in the south.

Amongst the many traders and pilgrims who came to Mecca were Asaf and Naila, a couple, who finding themselves alone in Kabah decided to perform coitus there, an act of disrespect and desecration that turned them into stones. The stone images were removed from Kabah and separated. Asaf's idol was kept atop Safa and Naila's atop Marwa, so no one ever forgot their crime. Unfortunately, over time people forgot the stone image were symbols of punishment and assumed these were images of a god and a goddess to whom sacrifices had to be offered.

As the Jurhum did nothing to stop the growing idolatry, and even considered offerings at Kabah as their personal income, they lost their power over Mecca and were eventually driven out by the Khuza tribe. Before leaving, the Jurhum filled the Zamzam spring so that no one would ever get access to it.

- The sources of Islamic lore are the Quran (word of God revealed to the Prophet), the Sira (biographies of the Prophet) and the Hadith (traditions approved by the Prophet). These were all put down in writing after the lifetime of the Prophet. There is much disagreement in details and interpretation.
- In Islam, Mecca is the centre of the world, the direction that one has to face while praying. Mecca was a market that connected the markets of Syria in the north with the incense farms of Yemen in the south.
- Pre-Islamic Arabs of the North claimed descent from Adnan, grandson of Ishmail (Ishmael), son of Ibrahim (Abraham). The Arabs of the South considered themselves pure/original Arabs and claimed descent from Quhatan, from whom descended the Jurhum tribe that gave shelter to Ishmail.
- Hagar left her thirsty son between the two hills. While climbing the hills, she could see her son but between the hills she could not. So, during the Sai ritual of walking to and fro between the hills during the Hajj pilgrimage, men run between the hills and walk near them, reminding themselves of Hagar's anxiety about Ishmael's well-being.
- Historians have shown that many Islamic practices have pre-Islamic roots, including the pilgrimage to Mecca during a stipulated period of the year (Hajj), or during the rest of the year (Umrah), bathing and perfuming the body and wearing two pieces of unstitched cloth (Imrah), the counter-clockwise circumambulation of the Kabah (Tawaf), dressing the Kabah with cloth (Kiswah), walking to and fro between the hills of Safa and Marwa (Sai) and drinking of the water of Zamzam.

- The association of pre-Islamic Kabah with water and coitus indicates the presence of a fertility cult. Since pre-Islamic times, before entering the sanctuary of Kabah known as haram (the sacred, the forbidden, the taboo), body hair was removed and the body was perfumed. Wearing of clothes was voluntary in pre-Islamic pagan times but now is mandatory. But the clothes worn are a pair of unstitched cloths. Women cover their head but are asked to uncover their face and hands.
- The water of Zamzam is sacred in Islam as it saved Abraham's son from dying of thirst. The water of river Ganga is sacred in Hinduism as it ensured the rebirth of the dead sons of Sagara.

Idolatry at Mecca

A leader of the Khuza tribe travelled to Syria, where he heard of a god who would cure his skin ailment. He found an idol there and learnt how there were different idols to solve different problems. So, he brought images of gods and placed them inside the Kabah and around it—some who brought rain, some who gave children, some who helped solve disputes, some who granted victory in war, others who brought peace.

As the leader was quite respected, others imitated his practice. Viewing a leader's deed as precedent was an ancient Arab tribal practice. Mecca soon became a pagan pilgrimage attracting people from all around. It even became a centre for idol-making, supplying idols to other cities in Arabia.

The Khuza tribe was eventually replaced by the Quraysh, whose leader had married the daughter of the leader of the Khuza tribe. A resourceful and respected man, he earned the trust of his father-in-law, who gave him the keys to the Kabah. His brother-in-law did not appreciate this decision but gave up his claim in exchange for a camel and a skin of wine. This is how the shrine moved from the hands of the Khuza to the Quraysh.

- The Jurhum controlled Mecca for over a thousand years, and the Khuza for almost 500 years, while the Quraysh did so for nearly two centuries before the arrival of Prophet Muhammad.
- These stories aim to show that originally Kabah was monotheistic and it later became polytheistic. That monotheism was original and not a later invention. Paganism or polytheism is equated with loss of integrity and morality.
- In the nineteenth century, monotheism and rejection of idol worship were seen as the defining features of a true religion. Hence, many Hindu reform organizations such as the Brahmo Samaj founded by Raja Ram Mohan Roy and Arya Samaj founded by Dayanand Saraswati went out of their way to prove Hinduism was 'actually' monotheistic as indicated by the Upanishads, and that Hinduism was 'originally' not idolatrous as indicated by Vedic rituals.

Rediscovery of Zamzam

Centuries later, a pious man of the Banu Hashim clan of the Quraysh tribe, known as Abdul Muttalib, also known as Shaybah, or the ancient one because of the white streak in his black beard, had a mysterious dream that he would find the pure, the precious, the eternal spring of Zamzam between dung and blood, near a crow with white legs and an anthill.

During his visit to the Kabah the next day, Abdul Muttalib found camel dung and the blood of a slaughtered camel, near an anthill, not far from the Kabah, and a crow with white legs was cawing near it. He realized this was the spot the dream had revealed to him. So, he started digging there, accompanied by his only son, annoying the other members of his tribe, who tried to stop him. But he persisted, and to everyone's surprise found the Zamzam that had been lost for over generations.

The tribal leaders claimed the waters for all, but Abdul Muttalib insisted he was the owner. The quarrel became intense and would have resulted in war, but it was decided that a witch who had a connection with the spirit world would be consulted.

On the way to the witch's abode, the travellers got lost in the desert and would have died of thirst; but Abdul Muttalib dug again and found water, making all his companions realize he was indeed meant to be the guardian of Zamzam. So, they all gave up their claims to Zamzam and Abdul Muttalib gave the special water to all pilgrims who came to Mecca.

- Dreams revealing the location of sacred sites is a recurring theme in mythologies around the world. In Hindu mythology, one often hears of sacred images found near anthills, marked by hooded serpents or by cows voluntarily voiding their milk.
- Considering the Arabian Peninsula is a desert and nomadic life is tough, the value placed on the water of Zamzam is understandable. Later, Islamic descriptions of paradise reveal a fondness for fountains. Paradise mirrors the luxurious lifestyle in the distant well-watered plains of Mesopotamia: a courtyard full of trees bearing sweet fruits and fragrant flowers, running water fountains, clothes of silk, and the companionship of beautiful boys and girls who serve every whim. The word 'paradise' comes from *parIdaeza*, the Persian word for 'enclosed garden'.
- Without water there can be no culture. The acts of washing, bathing and drinking are central to most religious practices. There are washing and bathing rituals in Judaism. In Christianity, the ritual of baptism involves water. In Hinduism, a dip in a waterbody is seen as spiritually cleansing.

Sacrifice of Abdullah

While digging the well and facing opposition of other members of the tribe, Abdul Muttalib felt his problems emerged as he had fathered only one son. So, he made a declaration that should he father ten sons, he would sacrifice one of them to the idols enshrined in Kabah. Sure enough, he fathered ten sons, the youngest being Abdullah.

Now, Abdul Muttalib was bound by his promise to sacrifice Abdullah. He wrote the name of his sons on ten arrows and using traditional divination methods picked one. It had his youngest son's name on it.

But when Abdul Muttalib was about to sacrifice his tenth son, his other sons and his relatives tried to stop him, arguing that as he was a respected man, his action would set a precedent and more and more people would sacrifice their sons to the idols enshrined in Kabah. It was bad enough that people were sacrificing daughters, now it would also extend to sons.

Abdul Muttalib saw their point but he had made a promise and he wanted to keep his word. To find a way out, they decided to consult a witch who could speak to the spirit world of djinns. She said that the only way out was to pay the unseen forces of the cosmos blood money. Blood money was the traditional fine to be paid to the family of the deceased to atone for murder. That was the equivalent of ten camels. 'The spirits may want more. So, keep adding ten camels each time they refuse, till the time they agree.'

And so, divination was conducted. The arrows of Hubal were cast between Abdullah and ten camels. They turned towards Abdullah. So, ten more camels were added and the arrows were thrown again. Abdullah was chosen over the camels again, and again, until the number of camels became one hundred.

Abdul Muttalib was not convinced this was the way out of keeping his promise. He felt this was trickery. So, the exercise was repeated three times: each time the arrows pointed to the hundred camels instead of Abdullah and so Abdul Muttalib sacrificed the hundred camels instead of Abdullah.

The meat of the camels was distributed to pilgrims, and to the tribe, and even to the birds in the sky, for Abdul Muttalib claimed none of it. Thus, Abdul Muttalib became famous for his generosity, he who gave water and food to everyone who came to Mecca. He would be the grandfather of the final prophet, Muhammad.

- Abdul Muttalib's sacrifice of his son and replacing him with camels mirror the story of Abraham sacrificing his son and replacing him at the last minute with a ram. The horns of this ram were once said to be located inside Kabah. The story also points to the practice of human sacrifice in pre-Islamic Arabia.
- Abdul Muttalib's camel sacrifice created a precedent. Blood money was now hundred camels, ten times more than the older rate of ten. The high price contributed to reducing violence.
- The quality of generosity is highly regarded in Islam. For it indicates rejection of ownership ('this is mine alone'), a yearning that came into man after eating the fruit of the Forbidden Tree in Eden. Muhammad's grandfather was known for his generosity.
- There are suggestions of real or symbolic human sacrifice in Vedic manuals. A king called Harischandra had promised to sacrifice his son Rohita to Varuna if he was cured of dropsy; later, he tried to substitute his son with Sunahshepa, the son of a poor Brahmin. Most human cultures have tales of human sacrifice in ancient times, a practice that is vehemently denied by modern descendants, as no one wants their origin to be viewed as 'savage'.
- Jewish lore focuses on the sacrifice of sheep while Islamic lore speaks of sacrifice of camel. A sheep eats grass and is fussy about food but has high fertility as compared to the camel, which eats all kinds of food, even the cactus, but has lower fertility. The sheep-rearing communities were closer to the northern part of Arabia (Levant and Mesopotamia) and more numerous along coasts of Arabia (Oman, Kuwait, Yemen), while camel-rearing was more common in the arid heart of Arabia, which was the home of the original 'Arabs'. The original meaning of the term 'arab' was the wilderness people. These were the people whose lifestyle was tough with tough, characterized by scarce access to water, and was marked by a dependence on camels with life lived in tents.

Year of the Elephant

Mecca gave shelter to many Jewish and Christian refugees.

Jewish refugees came to the city first after the Babylonians had destroyed their Temple in Jerusalem and then when the Romans had destroyed their Temple. They came here as they had seen signs that the messiah would be born in this city. Two rabbis had succeeded in stopping a king of Yemen from destroying Medina and Mecca by informing him about the prophecy. In gratitude, that king of Yemen was the first to have 'clothed' the Kabah, covering the stone structure with fabric.

The king of Yemen's son, however, was not much in favour of monotheism. He built a pit of fire and ordered all Christians to either abandon their faith or walk into the fire. Many walked into the fire. A woman with child hesitated but her infant child spoke and told his mother to hold on to faith, and the woman, thus reassured, walked into the fire.

When Abdullah's wife was pregnant with child, another king of Yemen sent his army of elephants to attack the city of Mecca from the north in order to destroy the Kabah. By doing so, the king hoped to divert pagan pilgrims to a newly built church in his city where they would be introduced to the true God of Christ, and Moses, and Abraham.

However, the elephant leading the army refused to enter Mecca. A swarm of birds appeared in the sky, carrying stones in the beaks, which they threw on the invading armies, breaking the heads and arms of the soldiers and their king, forcing them to retreat.

That year came to be known as the Year of the Elephant. It was the year that Muhammad was born. It was about 600 years after the time of Jesus.

- Clothing the Kabah with Kisbwah was an ancient practice and marked the union of the settled communities who lived in stone houses and the nomadic communities who lived in tents. These were the two communities which constituted the Arab world. The stone housing was linked to Cain who practised agriculture and the cloth/tent housing was linked to Abel who practised animal husbandry.
- At one time, there were so many cloths on the Kabah that it threatened to break the structure and so the guardians of the shrine regulated the practice. The cloth is changed regularly by kings. Initially, they were of many colours such as red, black, yellow, green and white. Eventually, it was changed to black only.
- Indians knew ancient Arabs as seamen or *nauka-pati*, and ancient Central Asians as horsemen or *ashwa-pati*. The king of peninsular India was called *nara-pati*, or the lord of people, while the king of eastern India was called *gaja-pati*, or lord of elephants. The kings who controlled the ports of Kerala were called *samudra-pati*, or lords of the sea, or simply *swami-sri*, lords of wealth, which became corrupted to *zamorin*.
- The birthday of the Prophet is known as Mawlid and is celebrated in many parts of the world, except in conservative Wahabi states like Saudi Arabia and Qatar. It was introduced by Sufi mystics and was first observed in Egypt in the eleventh century.
- It is common practice amongst Muslims to say 'Peace be Upon Him' when mentioning Muhammad's name. The abbreviation PBUH is added after writing Muhammad. It's the English translation of the Arabic phrase *'alayhi s-salam'*.

Orphan with Destiny

Muhammad's parents came from respected families whose ancestors were guardians of the House of God at Mecca. Muhammad's father was Abdullah and his mother was Aminah. On the night that Muhammad was conceived, animals could talk and all idols in Mecca turned upside down.

His father had to go on many trading expeditions when his mother was pregnant, and he died six months before his birth.

It was common practice amongst city-dwellers to let their children be nursed and raised in the desert by nomadic Arabs. Each year, women from the desert would come to the city and take a child and return them a few years later, having trained them in the ways of the desert and to speak in Arabic. The women were paid a fee for their services.

When it was Muhammad's turn, the women avoided him as his father was dead and they were not sure they would be compensated adequately. But the Bedouin lady, Halimah, accepted the child, even though her she-camel had stopped giving milk, making it difficult to feed her own children. As soon as Halimah accepted the child, prosperity came into her family. Her camels thrived and gave milk even when drought caused other camels to fall ill and die.

One night, Halimah's son, who was playing with Muhammad, ran to his mother and said that two strange men dressed in white had caught Muhammad and ripped open his chest. When Halimah rushed to her foster son, he seemed fine. Muhammad said, 'Two angels washed my heart with Zamzam water and made it pure.' Halimah knew then that Muhammad was special and she was fortunate to be his foster mother.

Muhammad was returned to Aminah when he was five. He visited his mother's relatives at Yathrib. When he was six, his mother died. He was then raised first by his paternal grandfather and then his paternal uncle.

- This story comes from the Hadith and Sira traditions.
- The idea of prosperity following those who align with God is a consistent theme in Abrahamic lore.
- Many great heroes in cultures around the world have two mothers: a biological and a foster mother. Sargon of Akkad was set adrift in a basket and left to a river's whim and raised as a foundling; Moses of the Old Testament was born in a Jewish household and raised in the Pharaoh's household; Krishna was born to Devaki and raised by Yashoda.
- Trade was an essential part of Arab life. Ships carrying spices and textiles from South and South East Asia travelled with the help of monsoon winds to Yemen via Mecca and made their way to Syria and thence to Rome. In exchange, Indian merchants sought gold, which is why the Roman exchequer called India the land of the golden bird. Hindu merchants avoided sea travel for fear of losing their caste, and so it was entirely outsourced to Arab merchants. This lucrative sea trade was eventually taken over by Europeans in the sixteenth century.
- Mecca and Yathrib (later known as Medina) play a key role in the life of Muhammad. One is the father's city and the other is the mother's city. The father's city gave him status. The mother's city gave refuge and wealth.

Black Stone

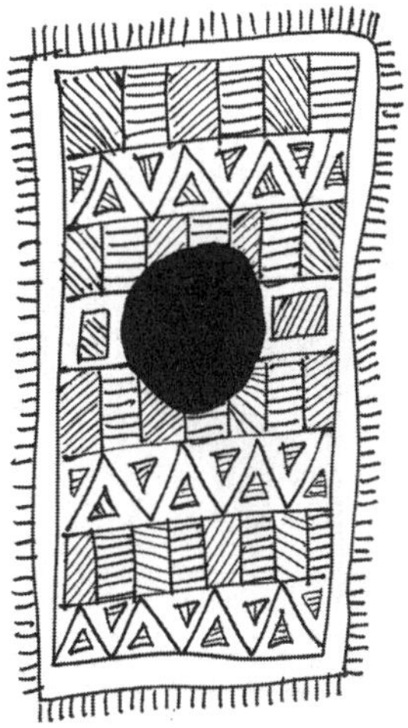

In his early youth, Muhammad travelled to Syria as part of a caravan, where a sage recognized him as the much-awaited prophet who would take people back to the true path. People spoke of how honest he was. His integrity and fairness became the talk of many caravans. The expedition to Syria sponsored by the wealthy businesswoman Khadija was a success. He brought back more than twofold profit and was given more than twofold commission.

At the heart of Mecca was the Kabah, which housed numerous pagan images. It was the centre of worship for the locals, an important pilgrim site. Muhammad's family members were caretakers of the shrine and pilgrims. On the eastern corner of the Kabah was a black stone, said to have fallen to the earth from the heavens. A flood caused the stone to slip from its niche. The various Arab tribal leaders could not agree as to who should have the honour to replace it.

Muhammad was asked to help. He placed the stone on a carpet and made all the tribal leaders hold the edge of the carpet and carry the stone as a group. This act of unifying quarrelling leaders impressed all and they gave Muhammad the honour of placing the stone in its niche.

- The Black Stone marks the point on the Kabah from where people on Hajj and Umrah begin their counterclockwise circumambulation (Tawaf). Many believe it fell on a mountain from paradise and has the power of speech. But it keeps quiet watching those who perform the Hajj, and will speak of their deeds on the Day of Judgement. Since it was kissed by Prophet Muhammad, many do the same. Those who cannot kiss, simply touch it. Those who cannot touch it, simply point to it and say 'Allahu Akbar', God is great.
- The stone, once intact, broke into many pieces when it was struck by another stone flung from a war catapult in the seventh century; it was also stolen for ransom in the tenth century. Finally, the jewellers of Mecca put the stones together with pins and put them in a silver frame, as is seen today.

Marriage to Khadija

'Will you consider marriage?' Muhammad was asked, to which he replied he had no wealth. 'Will you consider marriage to a woman who has her own wealth?' Muhammad had no problems with that. She was older than him by fifteen years. Muhammad had no problems with that. She had been married before, twice. Muhammad had no problems with that. She had children by her previous husbands. Muhammad had no problems with that. Thus did Khadija, the rich widow, propose marriage, and thus did Muhammad accept the proposal. He married the lady known for her piety and charity, wisdom as well as business acumen.

Theirs was a happy marriage of twenty-five years. The sons she bore Muhammad died. Her daughters survived. Some say only one daughter, Fatima, survived; she married Ali, and her sons were Hasan and Husain, who later led the faithful, known as the Shia.

- Muhammad's life before and after Khadija is dramatically different. After her death, he is forced to leave Mecca and seek shelter in Medina. He becomes more political and marries many women, even more than the stipulated four.
- In the Shia view, Khadija was not a widow as she never married before she married the Prophet. She bore him only one daughter, Fatima, who married Ali, the fourth Caliph, and the first of the Twelvers. The other daughters were Khadija's nieces, whom she adopted.
- In the Sunni view, Muhammad had four daughters, not just one. Two of his daughters married Uthman, the third Caliph.
- Marriage is a key idea in Judaism and Islam. Abraham and Moses and Isaac and Ishmael were all married and had children. Jesus, however, did not marry. There are those who argue that it was because he valued chastity as a discipline and a virtue. The Gospel of Matthew even makes the claim that 'eunuchs will be welcomed in the Kingdom of God' and speaks of three types of eunuchs: those who are born eunuchs; those who are made eunuchs by others; and those who choose to become eunuchs. Some believe these are metaphors for celibacy, a doctrine that became powerful in the Catholic Church. Others believe Jesus was referring to the castrati, eunuch priests of temples of the Near and Middle East.
- In Hindu mythology, ancient sages known as *rishi* had wives and children. But in the Bhakti period, more and more holy men or *sants* seem to be shying away from married life and choosing celibate ascetic lives. This is also observed amongst many Sufi mystics, who challenge gender roles too, and see themselves as married to Allah, a heresy as far as conservative Sunnis are concerned.
- Marriage of a younger man to an older woman is uncommon in most cultures, indicating the liberal nature of tribal practice in ancient Arabia. In Hindu mythology, Radha is considered to be older than Krishna and Krishna's son Pradyumna marries an older woman called Mayavati according to the Bhagavata traditions.

Angel in the Cave

Muhammad was a pious man who often left the city and retired to the caves outside Mecca to contemplate on society, on life and on God, as he was drawn to monotheism from an early age. In the fortieth year of his life, he experienced something that would change his life, and the world, forever.

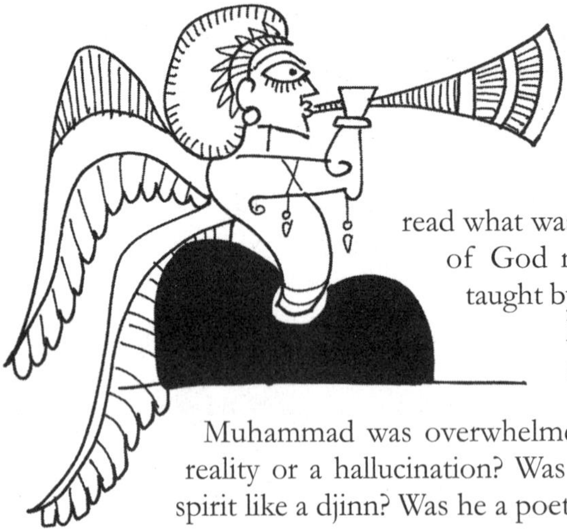

He was visited by the angel Gabriel who asked him to read. 'But I don't know how to read,' said Muhammad. The angel Gabriel grabbed him and hugged him tight and told him to read once again. And suddenly, Muhammad was able to read what was being shown and recite, 'Read, in the name of God most merciful, who created humanity, and taught by the pen what humanity does not know.' The language was refined Arabic, transcendental, melodious and hypnotic.

Muhammad was overwhelmed by this experience. Was it a dream or a reality or a hallucination? Was it God's angel or demon or a mischievous spirit like a djinn? Was he a poet, a seer or a prophet?

He returned home shaken. Who would believe what he saw? His wife did. A cousin did. A friend did. Others were not so sure.

- The Quran is the word of the one true god, God (Allah in Arabic), and was revealed directly to Muhammad. And so, it is the primary source of Islam. It is in 'high' Arabic, not the regular spoken language. There are over 6,000 verses (*ayaat*), arranged from the longest to the shortest in 114 chapters (*sura*). It was transmitted orally over twenty-three years, written in parchment, skin and bones, and was finally compiled and organized twenty years after the death of the Prophet during the reign of the third Caliph.
- The first word, *ikra*, means simultaneously to read and to recite. Muhammad is illiterate but still he is able to 'see' and 'read' the revelation. This idea of 'seeing' the 'revelation' is also found in the Vedic world, where rishis can 'see' the chant (mantra). Rishi means 'seer' or 'observer'.

- The concept of revelation by the written word is key to the Abrahamic world. Jewish lore speaks of stone and clay tablets, Christian lore speaks of parchment and Islamic lore speaks of paper (*kagaz*) and pen (*kalam*).
- The pre-Islamic world did have soothsayers and poets immersed in mysticism and occult, whose language was different from the regular spoken Arabic.
- In the eighteenth century, Umaru Pullavar, which means Omar the Poet, wrote the *Sira-Puranam* in Tamil, a Purana for Muslims, of approximately 5,000 verses about the life of the Prophet Muhammad. The word *Sira* is the Arabic word for traditional hagiographies on the life of the Prophet. Umaru Pullavar uses local Tamil/Indian/Hindu figures of speech. He speaks of four Muslim holy books mirroring the four Vedas of the Hindus: Torah given to Moses (Musa in Islamic mythology), Zabur (Psalms) given to David (Dawood), Injil (Gospel) given to Jesus and Purukan (Quran) given to Muhammad. The *shahada* or declaration of Islamic faith is called *mula-mantra* or the seed-hymn of Hindus. The influence of Tamil Hindu literature is obvious, especially in the use of figures of speech. There is a traditional description of how clouds from the sea hover over mountains of Arabia, and burst into torrential rains, giving rise to a river full of sparkling gems and fragrant sandalwood, whose water is collected in ponds to nourish all of life. The city of Mecca is described in the way that Tamil poets would describe Mithila or Madurai: full of lakes where lotus flowers bloom. Mecca is even described to be as beautiful as the gem on the hood of Adi Sesha.

More Revelations

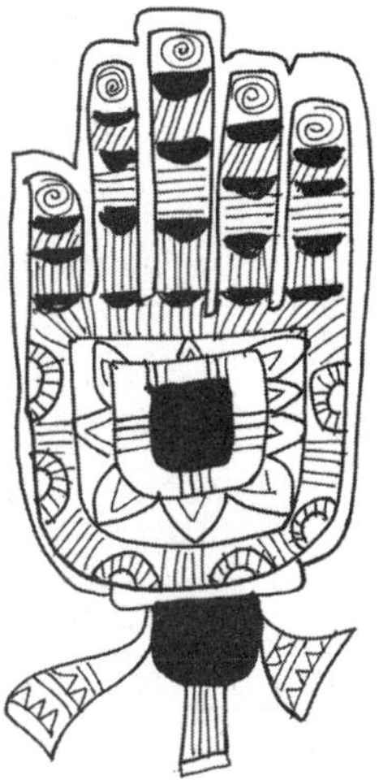

After a three-year gap, when all doubts had departed, the angel returned, and Muhammad received more of God's messages. Short and cryptic, they spoke of God's mercy, and the responsibilities of humans towards fellow humans, their generosity and kindness, and submission to the word of God. They spoke of resurrection of the dead, of the Day of Judgement, of the tortures in Hell and the joys in Heaven.

Every time there was a revelation, it seemed like the ringing of a bell. Muhammad would sweat on the coldest nights. He knew these were transmitted thoughts, not his own imagination.

He began sharing what he heard and people were drawn to what he had to say. He was seen as a believer of the one true god, whom he called Allah, an ancient name of an Arabic high god who was never represented as an idol.

There were many who believed in the idea of God, the one true god, like the Jewish refugees and the Christian refugees. But something about this was different. It was rooted to the language and the spirit of Arabia.

- The 'high' Arab language of the Quran is different from the spoken Arabic, and its melodious hypnotic quality was once used by seers of pre-Islamic Arabia. For the faithful, this 'high' Arabic is the language through which the one true god, Allah, chose to communicate not only to bring his word to the world through the Prophet, but also unite the quarrelling tribes into a single nation, to help spread his message.
- Besides the Quran, Islam values the Hadith. Hadith are records of the words and deeds of Prophet Muhammad that are meant to guide the faithful. These were compiled after the death of Prophet Muhammad, and it has been noticed that they seem to be more detailed the farther they are from the times of the Prophet, which makes many people sceptical over their authenticity. Over a million traditions have been compiled, each tradition accounting for nearly every eight minutes of the Prophet's life. So, greater value is placed on 'authentic' traditions, which account for approximately 5,000 traditions. But there is no consensus. The Sunni value the memories of the Prophet's third wife, Aisha, which the Shia reject. Shias prefer the memories of Ali, the cousin and son-in-law of the Prophet.
- Muslims believe that all scriptures—Torah, Psalms, Gospel, Quran—were revealed in the ninth month of the Islamic calendar, the Ramadan (Ramzan in Persian). Hence, during this month, people fast all day long and eat before sunrise and after sunset.
- Since the Islamic calendar is based on the moon, it is not aligned to the movement of the sun, and so the season of Ramadan keeps changing with time.

First Converts

Muhammad shared his revelations with his family and friends. Many of the revelations alluded to stories told by Jewish and Christian folk. But not all.

Muhammad said the original sin was not Adam and Eve eating the forbidden fruit; it was Iblis, the devil, disobeying Allah and not bowing to Adam, like all the other angels did. Besides Sodom and Gomorrah being destroyed by fire, he spoke of Aad and Thamud, cities destroyed by wind and earthquake, for rejecting the warnings of prophets Lut, Hud and Saleh. He spoke of how Noah's disobedient wife was swept away by the floods. He spoke of how even the mighty Pharaoh of Egypt regretted his decision to oppose Moses's march out of Egypt.

Muhammad's wife believed what Muhammad said. So did his daughters. But not all his sons-in-law.

One remained steadfast. Two divorced his daughters. One neither divorced nor converted. The steadfast son-in-law, Ali, would become the fourth Caliph of the Islamic world after Muhammad's demise. The divorced daughters eventually married Uthman, the richest merchant of the tribe, who would become the third Caliph of the Islamic world after Muhammad's demise. The daughter who was not divorced was later separated from her husband. She was taken to Medina by Muhammad, and reunited with her husband, only after he had realized the error of his ways, and converted.

- The first two Caliphs of the Islamic world, after the death of Muhammad, were his fathers-in-law, Abu Bakr and Umar, and the next two were his sons-in-law, Uthman and Ali. It was politically important for everyone to show these four were amongst the first converts, considering the violence on matters of succession following the Prophet's death.
- Sunnis insist that Abu Bakr was the first convert while Shias insist it was Ali. Sunnis insist that Uthman had married two of the Prophet's daughters while Shias insist that Ali married the only daughter of the Prophet.
- Battle between brothers is a constant theme of Abrahamic mythology (Cain

and Abel, Jacob and Esau, Isaac and Ishmael) and Abrahamic history (Jews and Christians, Christians and Muslims, Catholics and Protestants, Shias and Sunnis). It is also a theme of Hindu mythology (Vali and Sugriva, Ravana and Kubera, Pandavas and Kauravas, Devas and Asuras) and Hindu history (Vaidika and Puaranika, Tantrik and Vedic, Shaiva and Vaishnava, Brahmin and Buddhist). Fighting between brothers over inheritance is clearly a global phenomenon.

Opposition and Support

Christians believed that Isa, who they called Jesus, was born in a stable, but Muhammad said he had taken birth under a palm tree that provided nourishment to his starving mother.

Christians believed that Isa had died on the cross and that three days later he had resurrected himself. But Muhammad's revelations spoke of how Isa had never died, and was now in Heaven, and would return to earth at the time of the Apocalypse, alongside the final prophet, to fight the Devil and his false prophet.

Very few tribal elders, unlike Abu Bakr, accepted the message as well as the messenger. Most rejected the message, and ordered an economic and social sanction against Muhammad. No one was allowed to trade with him. Amr ibn Hisham went to the extent of killing his slaves who converted and attacking anyone who had anything good to say about the messenger or the message. Even a miracle performed by God, the splitting of the moon between the hills, did not convince this disbeliever, which is why this once wise man known as 'father of knowledge' was renamed 'father of ignorance'.

Some tribal elders found the message blissful but were jealous of Muhammad as he was the chosen messenger. Some, like Umar, wanted to kill the messenger, but changed their mind after relatives helped them realize the wisdom of the message. Some, like the mighty Amir Hamza, did not understand the message initially, but converted nevertheless, mainly to defend the messenger. He noticed that Muhammad was being treated unfairly by his own people. What was the use of a tribe that does not protect its members?

One old woman would throw garbage every time Muhammad passed by her house. The prophet never complained. One day, he did not find her throwing garbage on his path. He went to check on her and found that she was sick with no one to take care of her or her home. She feared Muhammad would reprimand her petty behaviour but he said not a word. Instead he took care of her and her house. The old woman was overwhelmed by gratitude and shame.

- Muhammad's humiliation by his tribal leaders in many ways resonates the humiliation of Jesus by Jewish elders. Muhammad's revelation divided his clan into those who supported him and those who opposed him. Not everyone supported his message, but they owed him family loyalty.
- Abu Lahab, who boycotted Muhammad, died of a terrible disease called black measles. His body was covered with boils and all his wealth and power and relatives could not save him. He died in isolation, alone and in pain. His body had to be cast out into the desert as it was so terribly infected. And he ended up in Hell, suffering hellfire, given little respite, that too only because he had once liberated an old slave woman who had at one time breastfed Muhammad. Abu Lahab's wife, who threw thorns in Muhammad's path, suffered a similar fate.
- Amir Hamza, Muhammad's uncle, was known for his strength, and he became an early defender of Islam. He was killed in the Battle of Ubud. He became part of Persian folklore from the eleventh century. A collection known as *Hamzanama* described his exploits with fairies and djinns and dragons and monsters and princesses. The most popular illustrated retelling of this work was created by the Mughal Emperor Akbar the Great, in the seventeenth century.
- Umar, who initially opposed Islam, later submitted to it and went on to become Muhammad's close friend, his father-in-law and eventually, the second Caliph.
- The story of the old woman who threw garbage on the Prophet's path comes from Hadith, which recounts events in the life of the Prophet.

- The role of all great heroes and sages is heightened by the presence of opponents, many of whom persecute them. In the eighth century, Adi Shankaracharya of India, who spoke of the *gyan marga* of Veda (intellectual approach) was challenged by Mandana Mishra, who followed the *karma marga* of Veda (ritual approach). In the sixteenth century, Meera, a Rajput princess, publicly acknowledged her love for Lord Krishna, who she considered her true husband, and was ostracized and hounded by her royal family. The Sikh gurus in the seventeenth century faced great persecution at the hands of Mughal emperors.

Satanic Gossip

There were many in Mecca who believed in one God. They lived alongside people who believed in many gods. Both went around Kabah. Therefore, Muhammad's words did not seem radical or revolutionary to the Quraysh, at least initially.

But as time passed, Muhammad began speaking more and more against paganism, worship of false gods and the adoration of idols. This annoyed the tribal leaders who warned Muhammad to stop. But Muhammad would not stop, he could not. He shared what was being transmitted through him fearlessly, angering and annoying more and more tribal leaders.

Fearing for their lives, one group of Muhammad's followers left Mecca and travelled across the sea to Ethiopia and sought shelter with the Christian king there. But these followers returned when they learnt that Muhammad had reconciled with the tribal elders by acknowledging that their three goddesses—

Allat, Uzza, Manat—were indeed the daughters of Allah, through whose mediation Allah could be approached. It seemed like a compromise that could bring peace between monotheists and polytheists.

But when they returned to Mecca they realized this story was false. The Prophet would never have stooped to such negotiation and compromise. These were Satanic verses never uttered by Muhammad. It was gossip spread by the Devil.

- Author Salman Rushdie's novel *The Satanic Verses* based on this incident angered the Islamic world, and led to the book being banned (first country to ban it was India). Clerics in Iran called for his death, forcing him to go underground for many years, sparking international tension on the nature of religious and secular societies, and debates on the freedom of speech.
- Islamic chronicles state that Mahmud of Ghazni attacked the Somnath temple in Gujarat, in the eleventh century, as he believed it held the last statue of the pagan goddess Manat. The name 'Somnath' was assumed to be corruption of the word *su-manat*. He plundered the temple of its gold, its sandalwood doors and granite image.
- The idea of three goddesses, and the worship of the Black Stone in Kabah, has led to wild conspiracy theories that ancient Mecca was the centre of Hindu deities.

Journey to Heaven

One night, ten years since the first revelation, when Muhammad was resting in the sanctuary of the Kabah, he was visited by a creature that was part mule, part bird and part angel. It was Buraq, who could travel through time and space like lightning.

Guided by the angel Gabriel, Muhammad mounted Buraq, who took him in a flash from Mecca to the farthest mosque in Jerusalem and from thence upwards to Heaven.

In the first heaven, he met Adam. In the second, he met Isa and Yahya. In the third, he met Yusuf. In the fourth, he met Idris. In the fifth, he saw Harun. In the sixth, he saw Musa. And in the seventh, he met Ibrahim.

Then, finally, he was in the presence of Allah, and was told that humanity must pray fifty times each day. This was too much and so, advised by Moses, Muhammad negotiated with Allah and reduced the prayers to five.

Buraq brought Muhammad back to Mecca. The entire journey from Mecca through Jerusalem to Heaven and back took place in just one night. It was thus firmly established that Muhammad was not just God's prophet, he was also the final messenger. But not everyone believed he had made this journey.

- The Quran refers to the journey of the Prophet to Heaven and back and this is known as Isra and Miraj. The event is elaborated in the Hadith. The Quran refers to the 'farthest mosque', which is believed to be in Jerusalem, often assumed to be the spot where the Dome of the Rock mosque, built after Muhammad's time, now stands. This journey is seen in both physical and mystical terms.
- Muhammad's flight to Jerusalem and then to Jannat in one night and back, where he meets earlier prophets, angels and God Himself, is a key narrative in Islamic lore, as it establishes Muhammad as the final prophet beyond all doubt. After this event, Muhammad becomes more confident in his assertions, earning the ire of the Meccan elite, which forces him to shift to Medina. This event can be compared to the Transfiguration of Jesus in the New Testament, through which Jesus is clearly connected to prophets of the Old Testament.
- Buraq is part mule, part bird and has a human face, as per artworks made in

medieval Iran. It was the holy mount of prophets. It used to carry Abraham from Sarah's tent to Hagar's tent, and back, every day.

- For Muslims, the 'Wailing Wall' of Jews is known as 'Wall of Buraq' as the celestial beast was tethered there when Muhammad halted in Jerusalem before travelling to Heaven.
- Muhammad's heart was cleaned three times—first, when he was a child in the desert being raised by Halimah; second, when he had his first revelation; and third, before he rose to Heaven.
- The idea of the flying horse is found in many mythologies. In Greek mythology, the flying horse is called Pegasus and in Hindu mythology it is known as Ucchaishrava. Middle Eastern Zoroastrian temples had the winged bull, the Lamassu, since Sumerian times, who were guardian spirits.
- Buddhist chronicles have stories of kings such as Nemi, who are taken on a journey of Heaven and Hell. Buddha himself, after his transformation, first travels to Heaven to enlighten the gods themselves. In Greek myths, heroes often travel to the underworld and the land of the dead. Such mystical and magical journeys reinforce the status of a hero and a sage in mythology.

No Refugc in Taif

Across Arabia, all fighting stopped during the pilgrimage season. Arabs would fast, and pray, and turn into pilgrims, visiting holy shrines, the holiest of which was Mecca.

In Mecca, more and more pilgrims came to see Muhammad, for his message convinced them he was the long-awaited prophet that the Jewish folk spoke of, and his integrity and wisdom made him the fairest and wisest of all judges. As his popularity grew beyond the city, the Meccan elders got increasingly uncomfortable. Some wanted him killed; others wanted him to leave Mecca.

Then, Muhammad's wife, Khadija, died. And so did his uncle, who had raised him since childhood. It was a year of sorrow. Without his rich wife and his powerful uncle, the protection of the tribe reduced. Their hostility was now in the open. Muhammad had to leave Mecca. But where could he go?

Muhammad went to the city of Taif, known for its fields and gardens, its wheat and its grapes, with his former slave and adopted son, Zayd. But the people of Taif rejected his word, and him, and told him to leave and threw stones at him.

Humiliated and wounded, Muhammad took refuge in a farm outside the city, where a slave named Addas tended to his wounds, offered him grapes, and heard his words, and converted to Islam.

- Taif was closely connected with Mecca and was the centre of worship of the goddess Allat in pre-Islamic times. Closer to the sea, it was less dry than its neighbours and famous for its grape and fruit.
- The slave Addas was a Christian from the city of Ninevah. He was sent by his masters to protect the man who claimed to be God's prophet. He saw Muhammad pray before eating. Though Addas was a salve, Muhammad treated him with love and respect. He enquired about his origins and when Addas said Ninevah, the prophet knew it was the city of Jonah (Yunus), something only a few knew. Addas was convinced this man was special. When he conveyed this to his masters, they warned him that the prophet may try to convert him, indicating that while they had felt sorry for Muhammad they did not quite believe in his words.
- Companions of the Prophet (*sahabah*) are classified as those who migrated with him out of Mecca (*mujahirun*), those who gave him shelter in Medina (*ansari*) and those who fought with him in Badr (*badriyun*). Such lists remind us of Jesus's words, 'A prophet is not without honour save in his own country'. Shias and Sunnis disagree on who should be included in the list.

Shift to Medina

Having lost his wife and uncle, having been rejected in Taif, and feeling increasingly isolated and vulnerable in Mecca, Muhammad finally decided to take refuge in Yathrib, the city of his maternal grandmother, which had long sought him to serve there as judge.

Muhammad escaped in time on the night when the Qur'aysh had sent men to kill him. They found in his bed Ali instead. Many chased him, but every time they came near Muhammad, their horses and camels would stumble and fall. Thus, Muhammad made his way to his new home. This departure from Mecca marked his rupture from his tribe, and the beginning of a new epoch, the Hijrah.

- Migration from Mecca to Medina is a historical event that happened in 622 CE and marks the beginning of the Islamic calendar. It is known as the Hijrah.
- The year when Muhammad lost his wife and uncle, 619 CE, is called the Year of Sorrow.
- Mutim's son was engaged to marry Aisha but he broke the engagement when he learnt that Aisha's father had embraced Islam. Aisha was then engaged to the Prophet and the marriage was consummated years later in Medina. The engagement gave security to Muhammad while he was in Mecca as Aisha's father, Abu Bakr, was an influential man, and would go on to become the first Caliph after Muhammad.
- Abrahamic lore draws much attention to how new revolutionary ideas need royal patronage in order to survive. Buddhism survived as it received the patronage of kings like Ajatashatru, and later of the Kushan and Pala kings of the first and tenth centuries, respectively. Christianity survived as it became the state religion of the Roman Empire in 300 CE. Zoroastrianism survived as Zarathustra received the patronage of King Vishtaspa and later it became the state religion popularized in Persia by Sassanian rulers from 200 CE. Instead of seeking royal patronage, Islam became a political force by itself. This made Islam unique.

Medinan Revelations

Yathrib was different from Mecca. It had many more date palm orchards and fewer hills. It had many Jews who had popularized monotheism and it was a city badly in need of a fair judge, a leader. Muhammad brought order to Yathrib, which soon became known as Medina, the city, of the Nabi or Prophet.

Muhammad declared Friday as the day of prayer. It was also the day when transactions in the market would not be taxed. He put together a constitution stating the rights and the duties of citizens and their relationship with other communities. This helped resolve disputes, and bring order to the city. Thus began the formal process of establishing the Umma, the brotherhood.

Revelations in Medina were different in quality from those made in Mecca earlier. The verses were now longer, the vocabulary easier; there was more talk on legal matters related to family, financial transactions, and acts of worship, more call for conquest of non-believers, and less patience with hypocrites, polytheists, and the People of the Book such as Jews and Christians who did not accept his revelations. Prayers offered in the direction of Jerusalem were now offered in the direction of Mecca.

Earlier, Muhammad and his followers were called Hanif, or monotheists, but now the preferred term was Muslim, those who have found peace by submitting to Muhammad's revelation of God's message.

- Quranic verses display a complex symmetry of words and this is considered proof by many that it was not a human creation but a divine one. It is one of the many reasons given on why the verses have to be heard, not read, in the original Arabic, and not in translation.

- *Qibla* means 'direction'. It is the direction in which people are supposed to pray. Jewish people prayed facing Jerusalem, which was the centre of monotheistic faith. Muhammad also prayed facing Jerusalem until one day, in Medina, he began to pray facing Mecca. With this shift, the Prophet asserted that Muslims were different from the Jewish people, and other People of the Book. In a mosque today there is a special niche known as *mihrab* identifying the qibla.
- The tension between the spiritual and the political is evident in Quranic verses. Such tension emerges as all religions claim to be other-worldly but they do influence the affairs of this world. In Sikhism, a clear division is made between *piri* (holy men) and *miri* (governors or amirs), similar to the division between Sufis and Sultans in the Islamic world, and rishis and rajas in the Hindu world.

Mothers of Believers

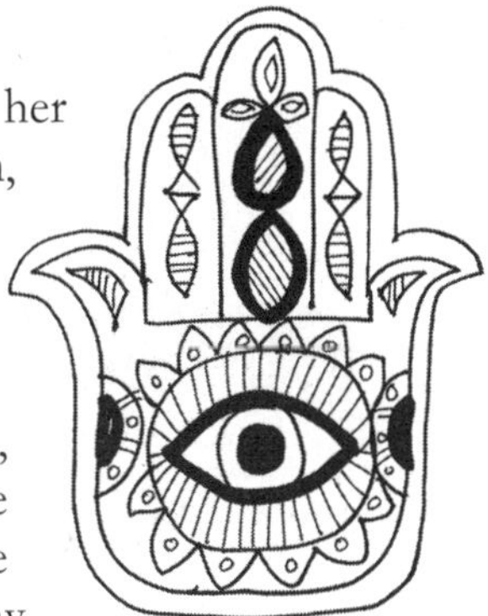

For twenty-five years, the Prophet had only one wife, Khadija. After her death, he married many women, some say eleven, some say thirteen, during his stay in Medina mostly.

Many of these unions were political—to make friends, to appease foes. These included Aisha, daughter of Abu Bakr, and Hafsah, daughter of Umar. Some were young, some old. Some widowed, some divorced. Some given as gifts by kings. Some Jewish, some Christian. Some marriages were planned but never took place. Some women declined marriage. Some died, some were divorced. Many outlived him. They were all known as the 'mother of believers'.

- Of all his wives, Aisha was the Prophet's favourite. She was an intellectual and enjoyed long conversations with him. She outlived him by over forty years. She contributed over 2,000 traditions to the Hadith, including many involving property disputes and inheritance. Since she opposed Ali, she is not well regarded amongst Shias. The Prophet died in the arms of Aisha.
- The Prophet had three sons, two by Khadija and one by Maria, his Christian consort. All died when they were young.

- There is controversy about how many daughters the Prophet had. Sunnis believe he had four. However, Shias believe he had only the one, Fatima, who married Ali, and who had two sons Hasan and Husain. Ali was the fourth Caliph. Ali, Hasan and Husain were the first three Shia Imams.
- Jesus never married and his Church valued celibacy. By contrast, Muhammad had many wives and Islam frowns on ascetic practices.
- Women played a key role in the life of Jesus. He stood up for the fallen woman. Likewise, Muhammad spoke a lot in favour of women's rights and freedom, aware of how widows and slaves had little agency or resources or power. Most people feel that patriarchy and misogyny seen in Christianity and Islam stem not from the leaders but from later organizational and institutional politics.
- Descendants of the Prophet are highly respected in many Islamic communities, especially amongst the Shias, and have surnames like Hashmi, Sayyid, Syed and Sharif.

Three Battles and a Truce

The Muslims who migrated to Medina with Muhammad had lost all their property in Mecca. They had no source of income. They had no choice but to raid the rich caravans that made their way to and from Mecca. The raids were small at first, but over time, with continued success, became bigger and bolder.

The Meccans retaliated. This led to the Battle of Badr, where the Muslims were outnumbered three to one. Still, Muslims won a decisive victory. It established Muhammad as the foremost military leader.

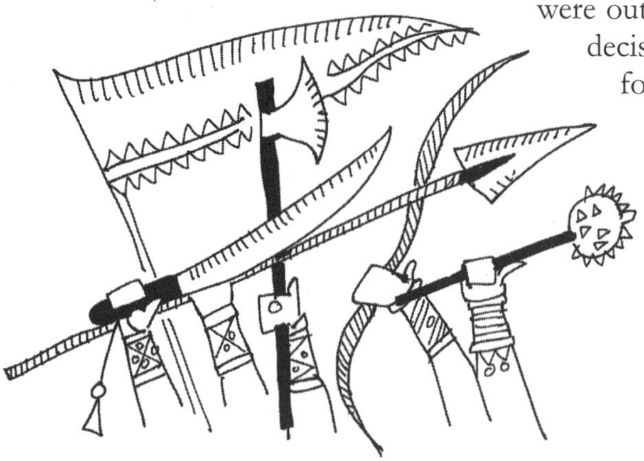

The Meccans avenged their defeat by attacking Medina. Followers of Muhammad rode out of the city to meet the Meccan army. In this battle in the valley of Uhud, Meccan women joined their men, cheering them to avenge the deaths at Badr of their fathers, brothers, husbands and sons. The Meccans overpowered the Muslims, killing many including Muhammad's uncle Hamza, and injuring Muhammad. The Meccans retreated assuming Muhammad was dead.

Muhammad revealed that the defeat of Muslims was a test to see who would be humble in victory and steadfast in misfortune. It was also a punishment for transgression and overconfidence.

Soon, the Meccans returned with a larger army and laid siege to Medina. But this time, thanks to the help of one Salman of Persia, the Muslims were prepared. Salman, raised Zoroastrian and educated in Christianity, was the first Persian to become Muslim. He taught the Muslims to dig a trench around Medina, and this caught the Meccan cavalry by surprise, leading to their defeat.

Muhammad's power and prestige were reinforced by this victory. So much so that he led many Muslims to perform their first pilgrimage at Kabah. They came purified, bearing no arms, with perfumed body, wearing two pieces of cloth, as pilgrims should. This confidence made Meccans nervous and the Quraysh made a treaty with the Muslims for peace.

As per the treaty, Muhammad would no longer be seen as fugitive, Muslims would no longer be persecuted and war would cease, provided Muhammad completed his pilgrimage the following year. Muhammad agreed.

- The battles of Badr, Uhud, and the 'trench' are key landmark events in the life of Muhammad. They establish him from gentle spiritual to an astute military leader.
- Amr ibn Hisham was killed and his army defeated in the Battle of Badr.
- Many felt the treaty was unfair and that Muhammad had conceded too much. But eventually, they saw the wisdom of the Prophet and his determination to bring peace.
- The lady Hind opposed Muhammad initially, but eventually became his greatest supporter after his triumphant entry into Mecca. Her husband suspected her of adultery. A sorceress was called to prove her innocence. The sorceress revealed that not only was she innocent, she would eventually be the mother of a king. When this was revealed, her husband decided to accept her but she divorced him instead, and married another man, a powerful man, and through him bore sons who would eventually form the Umayyad Caliphate after the first four

Caliphs, who formed the Rashidun Caliphate. Most of her family was killed in Badr and so she went out of her way to inspire Meccans to defeat Muhammad at Badr. It is said she got an Abyssinian to kill Amir Hamza with a spear. She bedecked herself with the blood and entrails of the fallen enemy. Hind regretted her actions and later in life was forgiven by Muhammad. Later, it is she who inspired the Caliphate army to defeat the powerful Byzantine Empire and spread Islam beyond Arabia. While Hind is highly regarded in Sunni narratives, in Shia narratives she is held responsible for the transfer of power from the Prophet's bloodline of Ali, Hasan and Husain to the Umayyad Caliphate.

- In 629 CE, Muhammad did the 'lesser pilgrimage' (Umrah). During this time, the pagans left the city and moved into tents on the hills outside the city. They had heard the Muslims were struck with a fever and would be weak. But the Prophet insisted that his followers demonstrate not just devotion but also strength and vigour. And so, they ran three times around the Kabah and walked the rest of the time, exuding energy and faith, impressing and humbling the Meccans.
- The ideas of the disobedience to God leading to defeat and the obedience to God leading to victory are themes we find in the Old Testament in the stories of Joshua's military defeats and victories. In many ways, the military rise of Islam mirrors the military rise of Judaism in the Promised Land. The military success is projected as a testimony of faith.

Return to Mecca

Unfortunately, the Meccans did not keep their end of the bargain, and broke the truce. And so, the Prophet marched to Mecca with 10,000 Muslims, each bearing a torch. So awesome was the sight of 10,000 torch-bearing followers of Allah's words marching into the city that the pagan residents of Mecca ran out to the hills and allowed the Prophet to enter unopposed.

Once he entered the city, Muhammad refused to move into houses that had been occupied by idol worshippers. He pitched a tent and having rested and bathed, mounted a camel and went around the Kabah smashing the idols around it with his bow, while his followers chanted, 'God is great, Allahu Akbar', filling the air with the sounds of victory and power and the message of the one true god. The final triumph over Mecca was thus achieved without bloodshed.

The Prophet, however, chose not to stay in this city and returned once again to Medina.

Muhammad proclaimed, henceforth, only the follower of the Prophet would be allowed into Mecca, and no one would go around the Kabah naked, as pagans once did, and polytheism would not be tolerated in the city.

- Non-Muslims are not allowed to enter Mecca.
- The theme of return recurs in Abrahamic lore—Return to Eden; Return to Jerusalem; and Return to Mecca.
- Unlike Jesus, who is a pacifist, Muhammad transforms into a military general, with extraordinary and unprecedented military success.
- Sufism is the mystical side of Islam that began in Iran and was based on austerity and ascetic practices. The Persian poet Rumi, under the influence of Shams, introduced the idea of love into it in the twelfth century. Sufi introduced music and dance as means to realize the divine, an idea that was rejected by orthodox Muslims, who saw the performing arts as forbidden (haram). Sufism spread to India and became influenced by Hindu ideas such as Vedanta and Yoga, where humans are seen as connected with, and fragments of, the divine, who can reconnect with and dissolve themselves (*fanah*) into God. Islamic mysticism is rejected by orthodox Muslims, especially the Sunni.

The Farewell Pilgrimage

Muhammad did his first and only Hajj pilgrimage the following year. He was accompanied by his wives and a large number of Muslims from Medina, Mecca and surrounding cities. His companions observed everything he did, for that would then become the way to observe Hajj henceforth.

The pilgrimage involved ritual cleansing and wearing of two pieces of unstitched cloth. Muhammad went around the Kabah in the counter-clockwise direction seven times. He touched the Black Stone, kissed it, and completed his prayers. He drank the waters of the Zamzam. Then he walked between Mounts Safa and Marwah seven times. He rested at Mina and climbed Mount Arafat and gave a sermon. He threw stones at the three pillars that represented the Devil, sacrificed camels, distributed the meat in charity, ate sparsely, got his head shaved, prayed again at the Kabah and returned.

The sermon at Mount Arafat marked the end of the old ways of ignorance and the birth of a new way, based on being witness to the one true god, Allah, his prophet, Muhammad, and by praying to God five times a day, by observing Friday as the day to congregate and pray, by observing fast from sunrise to sunset during the holy month of Ramadan, by sharing wealth with the less fortunate and by going on pilgrimage to Mecca to pray at the Kabah at least once in a lifetime.

Muhammad said every human is a child of Adam and Eve. Everyone is equal before the eyes of God. Humans are supposed to treat other humans kindly, and share their fortune. He told men to respect women, and children, and orphans. He told men to be fair in trade, generous in life, and bequeath wealth to family at the time of death. He told people to follow God's message, and be wary of the Devil, for they will all be judged on the Day of Judgement.

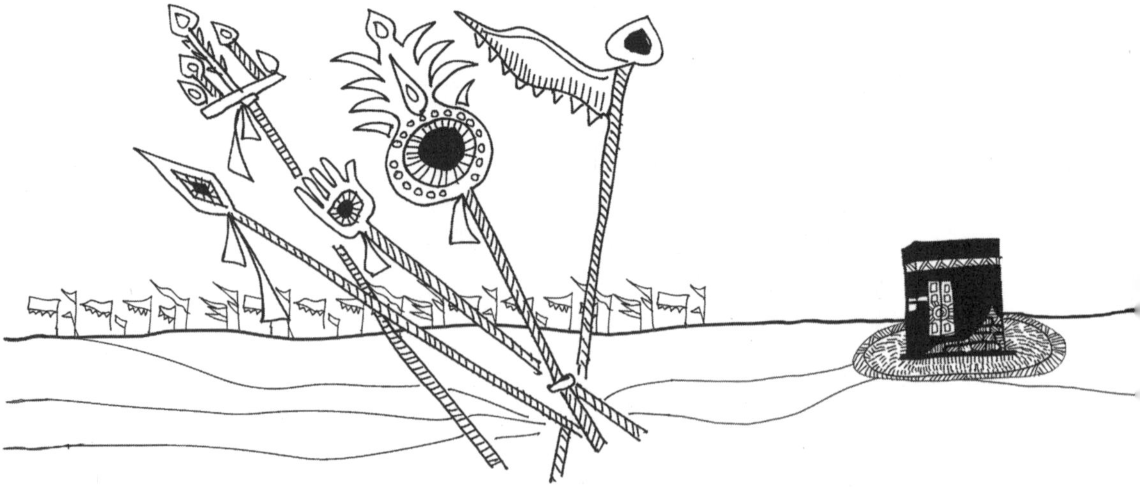

Shortly after his pilgrimage, Muhammad fell ill and died. He was buried at Medina. His mission was complete.

- The Prophet did the Hajj in 631 CE and died in Medina in 632 CE.
- Islam spread militarily from the Middle East in the seventh century to the east and the west. In the east, it destroyed much of Persia, wiping out Zoroastrianism. In the west, it challenged the Byzantine Empire, and spread to the North African coast, after which the old Mediterranean world was split into the Christian North (Europe) and the Muslim South. The war with the Christian world continued in the form of the Crusades in the tenth century, fought over Jerusalem. It ended when Constantinople was conquered by Ottoman Sultans in the fifteenth century.
- The Islamic corridor from the eighth century to fifteenth century, connecting Asia and Europe, spread many ideas around the world, including the Indian numeral system that introduced the zero, Indian medicine, cane sugar, coffee, and the water wheel for irrigation and spinning wheel for weaving. They also spread the Chinese art of making paper throughout the world.
- In Islam, drawing human forms is generally considered haram, and equated with idolatry, a stipulation that is not based on the Quran but on Hadith. However, the sixteenth-century Safavid rulers of Iran, sixteenth-century Ottoman rulers of Turkey and seventeenth-century Mughal emperors of India did promote art involving human and animal figures. We even find miniature paintings of events involving prophets, especially in Persian Art, even though the face of Prophet Muhammad is always covered with a veil.
- Islam travelled with traders to the coasts of South Asia and the islands of South East Asia. It penetrated the north of India militarily from the thirteenth century onwards.
- In India, Islam spread through sailors in South India, and with invaders and immigrants in North India. Conversion was both forced through the *jizya* tax, and voluntary, by offering careers in the courts of Muslim sultans and nawabs. Despite this, only 20 per cent of South Asia became Muslim even after 500 years of Muslim rule. Contrast this with Spain, which became Christian in the first century CE, was conquered and controlled by Muslims from eighth century to sixteenth century, and then reconquered by Christians following the Battle of Granada, following which Christians purged the land of Islam. Thus, we find deep discomfort with diversity and coexistence in Europe as compared to South Asia.

- The Bukhari Hadith claims that the Prophet had spoken of twelve men from the Banu Hashim clan who would follow him as spiritual leaders. These would be the twelve imams, respected by the Shia sect, known as the Twelvers. The first three imams were Ali, Hasan and Husain. The eleventh was killed by poisoning. His son, the twelfth imam, disappeared, and many believe he was taken to Heaven and will return as Mahdi before the Day of Judgement (qayamat) and fight Iblis, creator of evil, while Isa (Jesus) will fight the evil Dajjal.
- Muslims want to live their one and only life the right way following the rules of Allah (halal) revealed to the Prophet Muhammad as well as by following the way the Prophet conducted himself in his life (sunnah) as revealed in his many biographies.

BOOK TWELVE

Caliphs and Pirs

Hasan and Husain

Muhammad was the last messenger. He left behind the word of Allah for all mankind. His life was documented by his friends and companions, the Sahaba, and served as a model for future Muslims.

The brotherhood of Muslims needed a leader.

The first two leaders of the Muslim world were his fathers-in-law: Abu Bakr, father of Aisha, and Umar, father of Hafsah.

The next two were his sons-in-law, Uthman, who was married to two of the Prophet's daughters, Ruqayyah and Umm Kulthum, and Ali, who was married to Fatima.

These four were the Rashidun Caliphs, during whose time the Quran, the revelations of Allah, was put down in writing. The early Hadith, documenting the life of the Prophet, was also compiled at this time.

Abu Bakr died of old age and illness while the next three were assassinated, their legitimacy hotly disputed. The first three Caliphs saw the spread of Islam as a political empire, extending from Arabia in the south, towards Anatolia in the west and towards Persia in the east. The fourth Caliph oversaw a civil war.

This civil war was over who should lead the Muslims. Should he be from the bloodline of the Prophet, who had no surviving sons? Or should he be chosen as per old Arab tribal traditions?

The Persians, used to long dynastic rules, favoured bloodline, while the Arabs preferred consensus. The Persians supported the claim of Ali and his sons, Hasan and Husain. Later, those who preferred the consensus route came to be known as Sunnis and those who valued the bloodline came to be known as Shias.

After Ali was assassinated, Hasan became Caliph but was forced to abdicate and he lived the rest of his life in Medina. When he died, probably assassinated, Husain, rejected the new caliphate, especially when the leader, who argued against bloodline, appointed his own son as his heir.

Husain then decided to move to the city of Kufa in Iraq but was ambushed and killed on the way, at Karbala. This massacre became a major event in Islamic history, with Shia Muslims remembering this tragedy each year in the month of Muharram.

Shias believed that noor, the light of Allah and his final messenger, was transmitted from Muhammad through his family. The twelfth heir disappeared and would appear as the Mahdi, at the end of time, to fight the Devil.

- The first four Caliphs are known as the Rashidun Caliphs. Then came the Umayyad Caliphs, who descended from the third Caliph, Uthman. Soon after the Battle of Karbala came the Abbasid revolution, led by Muhammad's uncle, Abbas, and this led to the formation of the Abbasid Caliphate, based in Baghdad, with a strong Persian bureaucracy, that created the golden age of Islam based on learning. This thrived until the Mongol invasion led to the destruction of Baghdad in the fourteenth century, after which the expansive Islamic model was replaced by continuous power struggle with the religious leaders, the ulema, who valued religious learning over secular learning and preferred imitation of the past over innovation for the future.
- Islamic lore has many branches, the most prominent being the Sunni and the Shia, that thrived in Arabia and Persia, respectively. They strongly, even violently, disagree on many details of Islamic lore, especially on matters of bloodline and succession of the Prophet.

- In India, both Sunni and Shia faiths were patronized. Delhi tended to be more Sunni while Lucknow and Hyderabad tended to be more Shia. But there were many denominations often led by charismatic Sufi leaders, who had an ambiguous relationship with both the Shia and Sunni establishments. Also, there was an unspoken hierarchy depending on cultural moorings of the new invaders and immigrants with Arabs and Persians, Mughals (Mongols) and Afghans (Pathans) and Turks claiming relative superiority. Those who claimed descent from the Prophet (Sayyad) were seen as spiritually superior. This aligned well with India's traditional caste hierarchy. This is why caste as well as cultural roots play a key role in Indian Islam despite the fundamental egalitarianism of Islam.
- In Bengal, the divide between the upper-class immigrants and lower-class indigenous folks was also based on language. The upper classes spoke Persian and read Arabic while the lower classes spoke Bengali and so were less familiar with Islamic texts. This led to the rise of writers who retold Islamic lore in Bengali, a move that was frowned upon by puritans.
- Lucknow became a major centre for a very Indianized form of Shia Islam under the nawabs, but after the brutal suppression of the 1857 Uprising, the city was destroyed, and its unique Indo-Islamic culture started to wane.
- In 1974, Pakistan defined a Muslim as a person who believes in the finality of Prophet Muhammad, and so minority Muslim groups like Ahmadis, who follow a leader while respecting Muhammad, are declared non-Muslims.
- In the nineteenth century, Indians who migrated to Trinidad as indentured labourers participated in a ten-day ritual of mourning known as Hosay (from 'Husain') where they carried replicas of the tomb of Hasan and Husain. This was Muharram. But the British authorities saw even Hindus participating in it and so assumed this was a pagan festival of India.
- On the tenth day of Muharram, known as Ashura, Shia Muslims mourn the brutal killing of Husain and his followers at Karbala. They were denied water for days before being massacred. People carry *tazias* or replicas of the mausoleum of Imam Husain, and alams or flags in the shape of an upraised palm indicating peace. They carry replicas of Husain's two-bladed sword called Zulfikar. Also in the procession is a white horse, to remind everyone of his horse Duldul or Zuljanna who returned covered with blood and pierced with arrows, to convey the sad news.

Shaheeds and Ghazis

Across India, there are stories of holy men who came from Mecca, and brought with them the message of the one true god revealed to his final messenger, Muhammad. There are stories of how these educated and noble men arrived on flying carpets, flying hats and even on water, riding fish and tigers and floating rocks. They fought for justice and were called 'ghazi' or warriors. Those who died fighting were called shaheed or martyrs.

Shah Ismaili Ghazi, who was born in Mecca but who helped spread the faith in Assam and Odisha, was beheaded by his sultan because he suspected him of betrayal. The severed head spoke words from the Quran and the headless body continued to fight. And so, everyone, even the sultan, concluded Shah Ismaili Ghazi was a holy man. Different parts of his body were buried in different places and they all became holy shrines. Since he died in the cause of Islam, he was called Shahid, the martyr, who died as witness to the true message of the one true god.

Shah Jalal was educated in Mecca. His uncle gave him a fistful of soil and told him to spread Islam to a land where the earth smelt the same. So, Shah Jalal travelled east, collecting companions and disciples from Yemen and Persia and Central Asia and Kashmir and Punjab and Bihar, until he reached Bengal, where the smell of the earth matched the smell of the soil given to him by his uncle. But here he was opposed by the local Hindu king, who tried to block his path with rocks and prevented boatman from taking him across rivers. But Shah Jalal and his companions had occult powers—they caused the rocks to move aside and flew across the river on magic carpets and established themselves in the land known as Gaur.

- Muslims venerate the shaheed and Christians venerate martyrs. Both words mean 'those who die as they bear witness to Truth'. Muslims turned shaheeds into pirs, that is, holy men and Christians turned martyrs into saints. They play a key role in the spread of the faith. These ideas are not found in Hinduism, Buddhism or Jainism.

- In Bengali and Hindi there are many romances written speaking of the deeds of the Ghazis: of their journey from Arabia, of their miraculous powers, their love for beautiful women, which they sacrificed in order to serve Allah, and their martyrdom while fighting thieves.
- British historians translated Arabic works describing how Mahmud of Ghazni destroyed the Somnath temple in the eleventh century. They never bothered with the Indian sources of the same period, which do not refer to this allegedly monumental destruction. For local kings, this was yet another raid by barbaric marauders, but the temple survived for centuries thereafter before being abandoned in the fifteenth century.
- The survival instinct of Hindus took the rising and falling fortunes of temples in its stride as part of natural cycles. Historians see the arrival of Islam as 'changing' Hindu culture 1,000 years ago, just as the arrival of Yavanas (Greeks) and Sakas (Scythians) and Kushans (Yuezhi) had changed Hinduism 2,000 years ago. Hindutva world view insists Islam 'destroyed' Hindu culture.
- Muslim kings established their authority by building a communal mosque (Jama Masjid) where prayers were offered in the name of the king. A usurper to the throne simply replaced the king's name with his own during Friday prayers to establish his authority. This model of kingship was very different from the Hindu model. Hindu kings secured legitimacy from a deity in a temple. And so, to destroy authority of a local Hindu king, a rival Hindu king would claim the deity and grant it inferior status to his own temple complex, while a rival Muslim king would simply break the temple and replace it with a mosque and gain renown as 'idol-breaker' and 'herald of God's law'.

Sufis and Faqirs

Islam spread through military raids of Ghazis as well as ascetic practices and mystic visions of Sufis. The Sufi orders began as ascetics, who wore simple woollen robes and shunned material pleasures. Gradually, it became mystical, with talk of love, where the Sufi is the seeker, seeking union with the divine, the beloved.

Many Sufis saw themselves as led by the light (noor) of Muhammad. Besides love, the quest was also of recognition of the divine, within and without, for Sufis believed that God created the world so that he is discovered.

The Sufi orders were led by teachers who established schools of thought. They played a key role in bringing new farming and governance skills to distant frontier lands, settling local disputes, performing miracles, healing the sick, combining law with love.

Sufis sang and danced at night to connect with the divine but for many orthodox Muslims singing and dancing was haram, forbidden by God's law. Sufis were famous for their visions, their magical powers, their ability to solve disputes and offer solutions, and for their songs of ecstasy. They could cure the sick, fulfil wishes like marriage and children, help in recovery of lost cattle and property. All this made them very famous. But the orthodox frowned on all talk of magic and miracles, and insisted these were haram, forbidden by God's law.

Both Ghazis and Sufis were often called pirs and faqirs, holy mendicants. Since they had a large following of people, local warlords and sultans sought their support to legitimize their claim as rulers of people on earth, aligned to the Islamic way.

When Sufi masters died, people built tombs for them. And people prayed at these tombs, offering cloth and flowers and incense, seeking their power to solve everyday problems. The orthodox saw this practice as idolatry and condemned it. But it is through these practices, more than doctrine, that Islam spread, especially in India.

- People argue that Indian Muslims either descended from immigrants or from Hindus who converted to Islam. Reason for conversion is often seen as opportunistic for the ambitious, and resistance of those oppressed by Hindu caste system. But many who converted belonged to the fringes of Hindu society, often tribal communities, whose gods were seen as manifesting as pir-babas. In fact, in many Bengali lore, the divine spirit who took the form of Ram and Krishna, took the form of a local ghazi or pir in Kaliyuga.
- Veneration of holy men and their shrines (dargah) is considered idolatry (shirk) in Sunni Islam.
- Sufi culture in India intermingled with local *sant* and *nath-jogi* culture. And, so many Sufis had both Hindu and Muslim followers.
- Many pirs were seen as village heroes. The word pir was seen as a variation of the Hindu word for guardian-god (*bira/vira*).
- Sai Baba is a popular nineteenth-century saint who settled in Shirdi, in the state of Maharashtra. He is venerated by Hindus and Muslims, and his veneration across religions has been popularized by Bollywood films such as *Amar Akbar Anthony*. He is linked to Islam as well as nath traditions. He is considered a yogi and *siddha* by Hindus. Like wandering mystics, he was famous for his community meals, his community hearth and miracles like turning water into oil and enabling the blind to see. His doctrine was simple. Two words: faith and patience. Over time, the rituals increasingly follow Hindu norms, which is unusual as the central shrine is a burial site.
- Islam in India was concentrated in Western Punjab and Eastern Bengal. In both these places charismatic Sufi leaders played a key role in creating—the hitherto unacknowledged—new agricultural communities from people who were not part

of the mainstream. Jat herdsmen migrated from Sindh to Punjab and cultivated barren lands, having learnt new techniques like the Persian wheel from these Muslim holy men. Bengali hunter-gatherers and fishermen, who followed Buddhist–Tantrik–shamanistic practices and folk religions, were encouraged to establish farms as the river Padma shifted east, exposing new fertile lands. This was done by entrepreneurial Sufis to increase revenue of Mughal kings. They served as community leaders, warriors, judges, mystics, artists and teachers in their lodges (*khanqah*). As a result, over three centuries, from the fifteenth to eighteenth centuries the communities became 60–70 per cent Muslim, despite a Hindu elite. This was realized only in the 1872 census conducted by the British. Eventually, these areas gave birth to Pakistan and Bangladesh.

Satya-Pir and Panch-Pir

Satya-pir is a very important concept in Bengal. Some say it refers to God, some say it refers to God's greatest messenger, while others say it refers to the local deity who is now linked to Islamic theology.

One of the unique features of Islam in South Asia is the veneration of five holy men, or saints (*auliya*), known collectively as pancha-pir. They are often represented by the palm of the hand, mounted on a mound. Shrines of pancha-pir have been found in Punjab, Rajasthan, Uttar Pradesh and Bengal.

The five are sometimes identified as the five pure ones of Shia Islam: the Prophet Muhammad, his daughter Fatima, his son-in-law Ali, and his two grandsons, Hasan and Husain. Others identify them as the Prophet Muhammad and the first four Caliphs. Still others say they are five Sufi saints, often the teacher with his four students, who travel in the four directions.

In local lore, it is said they travel each day to Mecca either on a flying carpet or a flying camel, and come to the rescue of those in distress. In Bengal, they are venerated by sailors before setting out on a long journey.

This veneration of pirs in dargahs is however frowned upon by Islamic purists, who believe that veneration should be reserved for God, and none other.

- The pancha-pir of India is often equated with Hindu concepts like the five-heads of Shiva (*pancha-mukha*) or the five heroes (*pancha-vira*) or the five virgins (*pancha-kanya*).
- Illiterate Muslims were drawn to Hindu stories and so many local Muslim scholars tried to present Islam using regional languages. This was frowned upon by puritans, who insisted that Islam could be presented only in Arabic, and at best, Persian.
- Indian kings started using the phrase 'Hindu dharma' from the thirteenth century onwards as they felt their way of life was being threatened by the incoming *Turuku dharma* or the culture of the Central Asian Turkish tribes. But the threat was cultural, not religious, the replacement of the thousand-year-old Sanskrit cosmopolis by the newly emerging Persian cosmopolis. As the two cultures intermingled, Sanskrit sources referred to Turkish Amirs as Hamira, and to Hindu kings as Suratana or Sultan.

Kashuf and Meer

Hazrat Suleiman, the prophet-king of Jerusalem, came on his flying chariot and saw a beautiful lake north of India and realized there stood beneath the lake a beautiful land. He asked his djinns to drain the lake. But the djinns could not. Suleiman promised to satisfy the desire of whosoever managed to do his bidding.

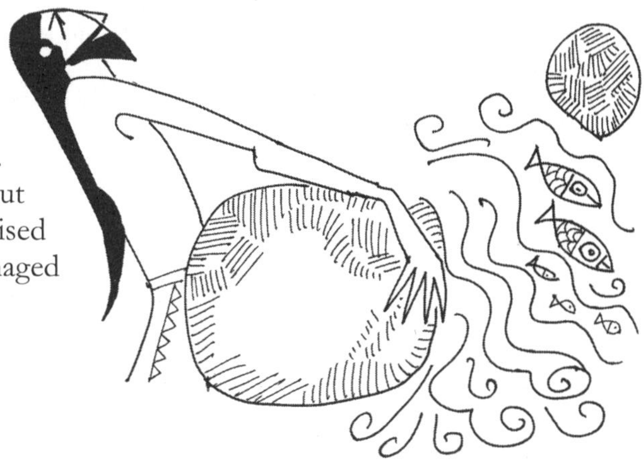

A djinn called Kashuf was able to drain the lake. His wish was to marry his beloved Meer. Thus, the land came to be known as Kashmir, the land of Kashuf and Meer, drained by djinns on the instruction of Hazrat Suleiman.

As the water was draining, Kashuf had collected the seeds that were flowing out, and threw those on the hills around, giving rise to the dense forests that one finds in Kashmir today.

- Kashmir was the centre of Buddhism and Hinduism for centuries, resisting Muslim attacks, before finally succumbing to Islamic rule in the fourteenth century.
- The Sufi saint Bulbul Shah is credited with converting Rinchan Shah and introducing Islam to Kashmir in the fourteenth century.
- For centuries, Kashmir had a unique system where the king and his subjects were Muslim but the courtiers and bureaucracy were composed of Hindu Pandits who practised Kashmiri Shaivism.
- Hindus narrate many folklores about how Kashmir came into being. The Kashmir Valley was a lake of the goddess that was drained by Vishnu, who took the form of Varaha, or the wild boar, on the request of Sage Kashyapa and the local Nagas or serpent beings. The name Kashmir comes from Kashyapa's Meru (mountain). The mountain was probably a pebble cast by the Goddess, which became a mountain that crushed demons, or it was Shiva's trident transformed.
- Kashmir's Martanda Temple of the sun god, built in the eighth century was destroyed in the fourteenth century by Sikhander 'But-shikhan', which means the idol-breaker.
- In the fifteenth century, Zain-ul-Abidin followed a policy of tolerance and reconciliation, translating the Ramayana and Mahabharata into Persian and inviting Hindus back to Kashmir.
- The word 'but' used by Muslims to indicate idols comes from the word 'Buddha'. In Northwest India, most statues encountered by invading Turks and Afghans were those of Buddha, built by Mahayana Buddhists. And so, the word 'buddha' became synonymous with 'idol' in the local tongue.

Bon-Bibi and Shah Jangali

Sundarbans, the mangrove forests of Bengal, is called the land of eighteen tides, and is often submerged by water, filled with poisonous snakes and man-eater crocodiles and tigers. The local boatmen, woodcutters and honey collectors are asked to pray to Bon Bibi and her brother Shah Jangali for protection.

They were children of a faqir, Berahim, who lived in Mecca, and his junior wife, Golbibi. They were abandoned in the wilderness on the instructions of his senior wife, Phulbibi. But Allah sent angels to protect them and feed them.

Both sister and brother grew up with an intimate knowledge of forests and of Allah. They had mystical visions and occult powers. They were given magical hats to travel to the Sunderbans to protect the local people, who were harassed by the tiger-eating Dakhin-rai, and to invite them to follow the way of the one true god, Allah.

Bon Bibi and Shah Jangali fought Dakhin-rai until a truce was announced between them. The inhabited part of the mangrove delta would be where Bon Bibi and her brother would be venerated and the wild uninhabited deep forest would be for Dakshin-rai, and his mother, Narayani.

The truce-maker between Bon Bibi and Narayani was one Ghazi-pir, who was often seen holding a venomous cobra in his hand and riding a tiger that stood on the back of a crocodile.

- In the seventeenth century, *Nabi-bansa* was composed in Bengal, seeking to integrate Hindu mythology with Islamic mythology. It tells the story of how prophets were needed as Hara (Shiva) and Hari (Vishnu, Krishna, Ram) failed to make people righteous.
- The upper-class (ashraf) Muslims of Bengal often traced their ancestry to migrants from Persia and Arabia. The lower-class (atraf) Muslims of Bengal were seen as local tribes, and hence drawn to pagan shrines that had come to be associated with pir-baba.
- The Jewish and Christian bibles have been translated since 1500 CE in various languages. Islam still resists translations and insists that God's word can only be understood in Arabic, just as in Hindutva there is the belief that Vedic truth can only be understood by those who know Sanskrit and are trained in Brahminical rituals.

The King Who Saw the Moon Split

The Chera king of Kerala saw the moon split over the hills. Seafaring merchants of Arabia told him that this was a miracle that occurred to prove that Muhammad was indeed Allah's messenger. The king decided to meet this messenger of one true god. So he deputed his son to the throne and travelled to Mecca.

He met Muhammad and was the first Indian to convert to Islam. He established the first mosque in India.

- This fascinating tale of a Kerala king meeting the Prophet was first recorded in 1510 CE by the Portuguese writer Duarte Barbosa.
- This story was common lore amongst the seafaring merchants who plied between Kerala and Arabia taking advantage of the monsoon winds.
- The name Cheraman Perumal is a title used for the kings of Kerala.
- As per legend, the oldest mosque, the Cheraman Juma Masjid, was built in Kerala in the seventh century on orders of the local Chera king, who had a dream of the splitting of the moon, and even travelled to Mecca to confirm it. It was originally built by Malik Deenar, a Persian, companion to the Prophet, who came to Kerala. It repurposed an old Buddhist shrine and so faced east instead of Kabah, and had a pond and hanging lamps. It was destroyed by the Portuguese 500 years ago and rebuilt in the Kerala style, though now, the traditional form has been replaced by a more Arabic style.
- Kerala's ports were ruled by kings who were called Samudra-pati (lord of sea) or Swami-sri (lord of resources), which became Zamorin on European tongues. One of the early visitors to Kerala is believed to have been St Thomas who travelled to India along the popular trade routes to spread the good word that Jesus had arisen to save the world. One of the Zamorins was an early convert to Islam and travelled to Mecca, and returned to build a mosque in the lifetime of the Prophet, around 1,400 years ago.
- In the sixteenth century, Vannapparimalappulavar, known also by his Muslim name Ceyku Mutali Icukakku, composed the *Ayira Macala*, the Tamil rendering of the *Book of One Thousand Questions*, a poetic adaptation of the Prophet's dialogue with Ibnu Salam, a Jewish man, who is finally convinced to convert.
- In the eighteenth century, the *Sira-Puranam* was composed in Tamil, and it uses classical Sanskrit metaphor to describe Mecca and the life of the Prophet.

Majnun

In Arabia, Qais met Laila in a classroom where they were being taught the holy message of Allah. Qais fell in love with Laila and Laila fell in love with Qais. Qais expressed his love openly, without being self-conscious, unmindful of those around him. Laila blushed but everyone around thought Qais was mad and so they called him Majnun, the crazy one. Qais asked for Laila's hand in marriage but her father did not want his daughter to marry a crazy boy and so got Laila married to a sensible man, who took her away to his house far away. Laila served as a good wife but her heart was with Qais and she pined for him each day and each night and finally died of heartbreak. Qais could not bear the separation and left home, choosing to wander in the wilderness shouting his beloved's name, writing her name on rocks and sand, composing poetry about her. His family tried to bring him home but he would always run away. He did not care for food or clothes or shelter. All he cared about was Laila.

In Sindh, there were stories of Punnu and Sassi. Punnu, the prince, fell in love with Sassi, a washerwoman. Punnu's brothers got him drunk, and while he slept, took him back to the palace across the desert. Not knowing where he lived, Sassi wandered across the desert looking for him, shouting his name, until finally she died of thirst and heartbreak. The earth opened up to accept her dead body. Punnu too wandered the desert looking for Sassi and when he learnt where she had died, he pined for her over the rock that marked her grave until he could breathe no more. The earth accepted his body too and so in death the two lovers were united.

In Punjab, was told the story of Sohni and Mahiwal. Sohni was in an unhappy marriage and would swim across the river each night to meet her beloved Mahiwal, the buffalo herdsman, who played the flute. But Sohni did not know how to swim and would use a pot to stay afloat. Her sister-in-law was so disgusted and jealous of Sohni's behaviour, that she replaced the baked pot Sohni used to swim across with an unbaked pot. This unbaked pot dissolved midstream and Sohni drowned as a result. Mahiwal, pining for his beloved, became mad, like Majnun, and wandered the countryside shouting her name till he too died of heartbreak.

The stories of two lovers, and their unfulfilled ecstatic craving and yearning for the beloved, made people realize the power of love. Songs about the lovers inspired them to find in the love between man and woman, the sweet quest for truth, for justice, for Muhammad, for Allah, in spite of all odds. It inspired many to surrender to Allah, and be not just a Muslim, surrendering to God's law, but a Majnun, lost in God's love.

- Pre-Islamic society valued the poet who sang of lost love, and of yearning for the beloved long gone. Some of these poems were even hung on the walls of the Kabah. One of these early songs was by Antar, a black slave of an Arab, who despite being a great knight was never allowed to marry the Arab princess he loved. These yearnings were sometimes seen literally as love for a woman and sometimes metaphorically as love for God. With the rise of Islam, poets and poetry were frowned upon as they glamorized wine and women. But these poems became part of high culture when puritanical forces were kept in check by Islamic kings keen to showcase the arts as indicators of their glory.
- Many historians argued that devotion in India was influenced by the arrival of

Islam, that the idea of submitting to God was not an essential feature of Vedic Hinduism. But this has been disputed. At best, the arrival of Islam amplified the idea of nirguni bhakti, devotion to the formless divine.

- The idea of 'bhakti' as submission to the divine is found in Bhagavad Gita, composed nearly 2,000 years ago. The idea of connecting with God through love is found explicitly in the Tamil poetry of Alvars and Nayamnars, which started to be composed 1,500 years ago. By the time of vernacular literature, bhakti became more about love and emotional connect. This was amplified 500 years ago in the works of Mira, Kabir, Tulsi and Surdas.
- Sufis have the concept of Fanah, or destruction of ego, 'to die before you die so you will not die when you die'. This is found even in Christian mysticism, Hindu mysticism as well as Tantrik Buddhism. The path to achieve it is through losing oneself in love, surrendering to a higher reality in complete abandon. This state is achieved through ritual meditation which involves singing and dancing. Such practices are forbidden and even considered 'haram' by more puritanical schools of Islam.

EPILOGUE

Judgement Day

The stories were intense. The lord of the sea was happy, but tired. It was time to rest as the one true god did after creating the world. 'On which day did your god rest?' asked the king.

'Friday,' said the Arab.

'Saturday,' said the Judean.

'Sunday,' said the Roman.

The king rolled his eyes. Do they ever agree on anything?

The king's sister had a question, 'What happens after we die?'

The Judean said, 'When we die, our body decomposes, our immortal soul waits listlessly in the darkness of Sheol until the annual day of judgement when God separates the righteous from the unrighteous. The unrighteous have yet another option of atonement on the final day of judgement so that their immortal soul joins God.'

The Roman said, 'When we die, our soul moves to purgatory, awaiting the Rapture, the Second Coming and the Day of Judgement, when all shall face Jesus when he returns, and the righteous will rise to Heaven and the unrighteous shall go to Hell, to eternal damnation.'

The Arab said, 'When we die, our lifeless bodies covered with shroud are buried in the ground. Our soul is questioned by two angels, Munkar and Nakir, whether we testify to Allah, the one true God, and to his Prophet, and whether we have prayed as prescribed and lived by the message. There we wait in joy or pain, for the final release, on the Day of Judgement, at the end of time. The wait is longer for the disbelievers and shorter for the believers. At the time of judgement, more opportunities are given to accept the truth of the one true god. Finally, we have to cross a bridge. At the end of the bridge is the paradise, Jannat, and below the bridge are the horrors of Jahannum. The bridge is narrower for disbelievers and wider for believers.'

'See, all three firmly believe there is only one life to live, though they disagree on the details,' said the king's sister. She then asked another question, 'You told me what happens after we die. But how does the world end eventually?'

The Judean began, 'At the end of days, everyone exiled will return home, to Israel, the Temple will be rebuilt, the House of David will rise with the messiah, non-believers will be finally judged, the bodies of the dead will be recomposed and souls will be restored, so that all can live in justice and peace forever in the Messianic Age. Residence will be granted in the seven levels of Paradise, or beyond in the seven levels of Eden itself, where God resides. Depending on one's level, one will reside forever with the penitent, the innocents, the martyrs, the keepers of the law, the patriarchs, or even the prophets.'

The Roman had a slightly different version. 'The story of the last days was revealed to John. He speaks of a Church Age where the seven churches of the world will be warned of their sins, and be given an opportunity to accept Jesus. This period will end with the Rapture, when the truly faithful will rise to Heaven with Jesus, which will be followed by seven years of Tribulation for the wicked left behind, during which there will be peace, until the peace is shattered and temple destroyed; the seven seals will be broken and seven trumpets blown, bringing in its wake natural disasters, floods and drought and war and famine and plague and suffering, leading to a terrible war called Apocalypse at a place called Armageddon, when the forces of evil led by Satan will rise and fight as a beast, a multi-headed monster, a dragon,

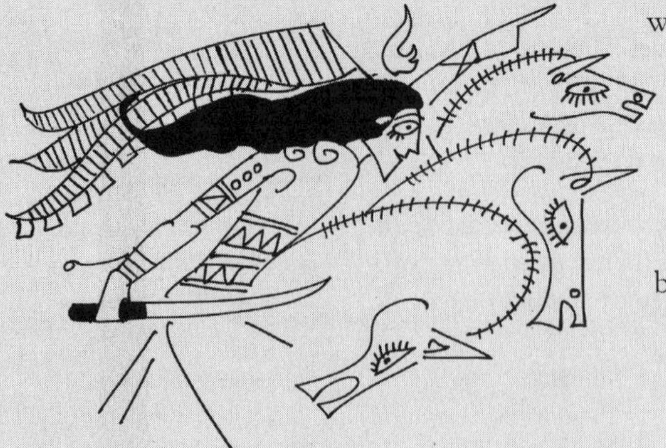

until they are overpowered by the Lion of Judah, who is the sacrificial lamb, Jesus, our saviour, who will return. Following this Second Coming, there will be a Millennium of peace, followed by the Last Judgement, followed by the establishment of a New Earth and a New Heaven for all eternity.'

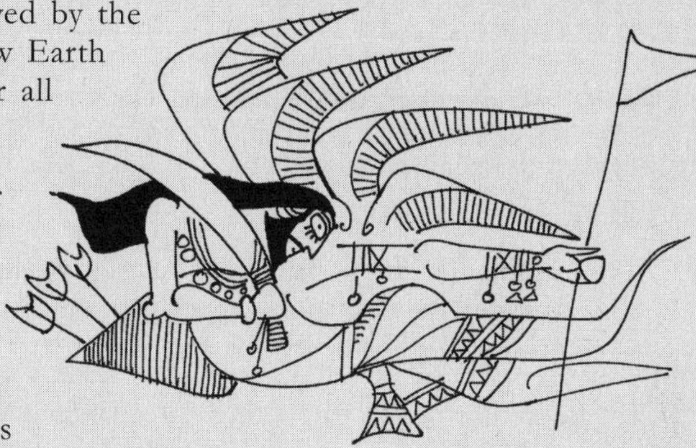

The Arab had yet another view. 'The end of time is indicated when people will go on pilgrimage for leisure, and traders will cheat on weights and wages, and brothers will fight over property, and morals will be loose and integrity lost. That is when the sun will rise in the west, smoky clouds will cover the sky and three great depressions will appear on earth. That is when a cool breeze will blow, killing the righteous so that they do not suffer the deeds of the unrighteous. That is when Gog and Magog will escape their imprisonment and attack and destroy all structures in the world until disease and worms consume them by the grace of Allah. That is when the Dajjal will rise and spread havoc and Isa will return again to defeat him. That is when the Mahdi, a descendant of Muhammad, will rise, and defeat Iblis, the foremost shaitan, the creator of evil. That is when the dead will be resurrected and asked to cross the bridge, which will widen for the faithful and the righteous and will narrow for the unfaithful and the unrighteous. And that is how the true believers, the good, will reach Jannat, abode of angels, prophets and Allah, full of joys and beauty unimaginable, and the rest will suffer in Jahannum.'

The Judean spoke of the end of the world without referring much to Devil or Hell. It was all about returning home from exile. The Roman's version was full of violence, a clash between the forces of the Devil and God. The Arab spoke of two devils, Dajjal and Iblis, and two prophets, Isa and Mahdi. It seemed almost as if each succeeding faith was competing with and building on the previous one.

The king said, 'So you are never reborn and your world is never recreated.'

'No,' said the Arab.

'No,' said the Judean.

'Not that we know of,' said the Roman.

Well, they did agreed on something, thought the king, as he retired for the night.

'Do you realize they never gaze into the eyes of a god or goddess, as we do,' he told his sister, the next morning, as they returned to the coconut grove.

'That is all right. We are all different,' she said. 'Why should they be like us? Why should they be like each other? Areca palm are not same as toddy palm are not same as coconut palm. In our land, men live with their sisters, not their wives. Elsewhere in Bharat-varsha, men live at home with wives, not with sisters and nephews as in Chera-nadu.'

The lord of the sea nodded his head. 'That does not help me. I have to make a judgement. I have to decide what is the forbidden fruit: apple, pomegranate or banana, maybe wheat?'

'Let us go to the temple of Bhagawati. There is something there that may help you,' said his sister reassuringly.

The matriarch entered the temple first, as was custom, and after lighting the lamp, she let her brother enter the inner courtyard. She pointed to a painting of a tree behind the image of the goddess. 'That is the Kalpataru, in the garden of our gods. It can bear whatever kind of fruit you want. Maybe it bore a pomegranate for the Judean, an apple for the Roman, and a banana or wheat for the Arab.'

The answer made total sense to the lord of the sea.

But not to the sailors.

'No tree can do that,' argued the Arab, softly, eyes to the ground, aware he was in royal presence.

'That is just imagination, your majesty,' said the Judean, smiling, not wanting to upset the king.

'With respect sir, that is false,' said the Roman rather bluntly, bowing his head.

'But it is an answer that will bring peace,' said the matriarch.

'We would rather be right,' said the three in unison.

The king was about to explain, but his sister touched his arm and he let it be.

The king gave each of the sailors an ivory box full of spices and cloth in return for narrating the epic of the forbidden fruit that grows in the garden called Eden. It had expanded his mind and his sister's, taken them closer to infinity. With this small gift, their debt to the storyteller was repaid.

'Shalom,' said the Judean.

'Salam,' said the Arab.

'May peace be upon you,' said the Roman, translating the traditional Hebrew and the Arabic farewell.

The royal siblings chuckled, and watched the three sailors, still arguing, return to the harbour.

- In the twelfth century, after his victory over the local Rajputs, Aibak became the first Muslim Sultan of Delhi. He belonged to the Mamluk or Slave Dynasty. He succeeded his master Mahmood of Ghuri. He was the first sultan to build a mosque in India next to his victory tower that we now know as the Qutub Minar. These were built using pillars of local Hindu and Jain temples that were destroyed by the invading army. It marked the beginning of 600 years of India's domination by Muslim rulers.
- In the twelfth century, an epigraph found in Bengal's Sujanagar, referred to the repairs of a *vihara* dedicated to a deity named Allahabhattarakasvami. The name shows how the word Allah was incorporated into the local language by local writers.
- In the thirteenth century, an Arabic Sanskrit inscription was found in Veraval, Gujarat, which refers to a mosque (*mijigiti-dharma-sthana*). The deity is referred to as Vishwanatha (lord of the universe, for Allah) who embodies nothingness (Shunya-rupa) as well as the whole world (Vishwa-rupa). Arab merchants are referred to as boat-people (*nau-jana*) and Prophet Muhammad as a wise elder (*bodhaka*).
- The *Bhavishya Purana* refers to a king called Bhoja who conquers the world, and goes beyond Sindhu to the desert lands, where he learns of Shiva being worshipped as Mahakeshwar or Makkeshwar, and is informed of a demon called Mahamada who will come in the future. Are these references to the Black Stone of Kabah and Muhammad? We can only speculate. But scholars have shown that these references are later entries, made as late as the eighteenth or nineteenth century, and not prophetic. Some writers have even tried to find reference to the Prophet and Islam in the Atharva Veda using elaborate semiotics and arguments.
- In South India, there are temples such as the one at Srirangam, in Tamil Nadu, where Hindu gods have Muslim consorts (Bibi Nachiyar) and many temples such as the Draupadi temples of Arcot, in north Tamil Nadu, where the guardian is a Muslim cavalryman (Muttul Ravuttan). These were the results of intermingling and attempts at syncretism.

Select Bibliography

For Jewish Tales

- Bandstra, Barry L. *Reading the Old Testament: An Introduction to the Hebrew Bible.* 2004. Wadsworth.
- Ginzberg, Louis. *Legend of the Jews*. Translated from German by Henrietta Szold. 1919.
- Kass, Leon R. *The Beginning of Wisdom: Reading Genesis.* 2003. New York: Free Press.
- Lim, Timothy H. *The Dead Sea Scrolls: A Very Short Introduction.* 2005. Oxford: Oxford University Press.
- Miller, John W. *Meet the Prophets: A Beginner's Guide to the Books of the Biblical Prophets.* 1987. Paulist Press.

For Christian Tales

- *The Holy Bible: King James Version*. 1991. Random House.
- Hardy, Grant. *The Book of Mormon: A Reader's Edition*. 2003. Illinois: University of Illinois Press.
- Roche, Paul. *The Bible's Greatest Stories*. 2012. USA: Penguin.
- Stott, John R.W. *Understanding the Bible.* 1982. Michigan: Zondervan.
- Nixey, Catherine. *The Darkening Age: The Christian Destruction of the Classical World.* 2017. London: Pan Macmillan.
- O'Collins, Gerald. *Christology: A Biblical, Historical, and Systematic Study of Jesus.* 2009. Oxford: Oxford University Press.

For Islamic Tales

- Brown, Jonathan A.C. *Muhammad: A Very Short Introduction*. 2011. Oxford: Oxford University Press.
- Dawood, N.J. *The Koran.* 2014. Penguin Classics.

- Fitzpatrick, C. and Walker, A. (eds). *Muhammad in History, Thought, and Culture: An Encyclopaedia of the Prophet of God* (2 vols). 2014. Santa Barbara: ABC-CLIO.
- Khan, Maulana Wahiduddin. *The Quran.* 2013. Goodword Books.
- Irani, Ayesha A. *Sacred Biography, Translation, and Conversion: The Nabivamsa of Saiyad Sultan and the Making of Bengali Islam, 1600–Present.* 2011. Publicly Accessible Penn Dissertations.
- Kathir, Hafiz Ibn. *Stories of the Prophets.* International Publishing House 2003.
- Mackintosh-Smith, Tim. *Arabs.* 2019. Yale University Press.
- Peters, F.E. *Muhammad and the Origins of Islam.*1994. Albany: State University of New York Press.
- Ronit Ricci. *Islam Translated: Literature, Conversion, and the Arabic Cosmopolis of South and Southeast Asia.* 2011. University of Chicago Press.
- Rippin, Andrew, et al. *The Blackwell Companion to the Qur'an.* 2006. Blackwell.

For Mythology and Religion

- Anderson, Albert A. *Mythos, Logos, and Telos: How to Regain the Love of Wisdom.* 2004. Rodopi.
- Armstrong, Karen. *A Short History of Myth* (Myths Series). 2010. Canada: Knopf.
- Doty, William G. *Myth: A Handbook.* 2004. Greenwood Publishing Group.
- Dundes, Alan (ed.). *Sacred Narrative: Readings in the Theory of Myth.* 1984. University of California Press.

YOU MAY ALSO LIKE

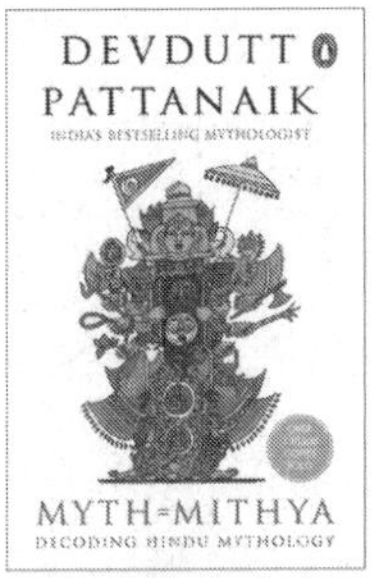

YOU MAY ALSO LIKE

Scan QR code to access the
Penguin Random House India website